Sabbatical Journey

HENRI J.M. NOUWEN

Sabbatical Journey

THE DIARY OF HIS FINAL YEAR

A Crossroad Book
The Crossroad Publishing Company
New York

*With special thanks to Sue Mosteller, Henri's literary executor,
who in her love for and dedication to Henri,
summoned great energy to complete the enormous task
of bringing Henri's Sabbatical Journey to publication.*

The Crossroad Publishing Company
370 Lexington Avenue, New York, NY 10017

Printed in the United States of America

Library of Congress Cataloging-in-Publication Data
Nouwen, Henri J. M.
    Sabbatical journey : the diary of his final year / Henri J.M.
Nouwen.
        p. cm.
    ISBN 0-8245-1708-3 (hardcover)
    1. Nouwen, Henri J. M. – Diaries. 2. Catholic Church – Clergy –
Diaries. I. Title.
BX4705.N87A3 1998
282'.092 – dc21
[B]   98-26746

1   2   3   4   5   6   7   8   9   10   03   02   01   00   99   98

To each one of my friends who offered me
the precious gift of love

Foreword

On September 2, 1995, Henri Nouwen began his sabbatical year and promised himself that he would not let a day pass without writing down the things that were happening within and around him. When, on August 30, 1996, he made his last entry in the nearly seven-hundred-page manuscript, he completed his final book, and his vocation as an author was fulfilled. He died before rereading or editing the journal and before sending it, as was his custom, to several of his friends for feedback. I know that had he edited it he would have given much attention to his initial jottings and that he would have made many changes. In trying to be faithful to his original text I have not made many changes. The result is that the book lacks his completeness and finesse but it brims with his life and with his spirit.

In September 1995, after living with Henri for nine years, we, the people of his community, L'Arche Daybreak, sent him off for his sabbatical year with a mandate to say no to all work except writing. We overlooked, however, his need and his gift for friendship and what his appropriate response to that might be. This book recounts an "odyssey" of friendship; it required the stature of a "Ulysses" to make the exhausting journey and write five books along the way.

In the original journal Henri meets, celebrates, consoles, counsels, and connects with over a thousand people, and in friendship he mentions over six hundred of them by name. On the day after Christmas he says, "My heart was full of gratitude and affection, and I wished I could embrace each of my friends and let them know how much they mean to me and how much I miss them. . . . I felt my whole being, body, mind, and spirit, yearning to give and receive love without condition, without fear, without reservation." Many of those he mentioned in the journal testify that their meeting with him was an "event" in their lives because he was so loving, so listening, and so generous with his time and his presence. For the most part Henri describes small, good encounters, but for the person in front of him, "small" was both beautiful and deep.

Henri, in his journal as in his life, is first and foremost priest and pastor. His passion for the daily celebration of the Eucharist is a thread running through the whole book. He celebrates with large groups at weddings and funerals, but personally he seems to be more nourished by small, intimate celebrations where there is a felt sense of community among the people. He comments on the Scripture texts of the day in conjunction with social issues, current events, a new book, or an artwork, and he makes amazing connections between his insights and his life experience. It is this dialogue between his mind and his heart's lived reality that characterizes his spirituality and that is a rich source of spiritual reading.

Throughout the journal Henri is plagued by fatigue. "Why am I so tired?" he asks himself. "Although I have all the time I want to sleep, I wake up with an immense feeling of fatigue. . . . Everything requires an immense effort, and after a few hours of work I collapse in utter exhaustion, often falling into a deep sleep. . . . My body aches and longs for a place to rest." He is totally spent, yet neither he nor his friends recognize the foreboding quality of his exhaustion. His self-questioning — "Am I tired simply because I want to do my thing and can't get it done, or am I tired because I am carrying something larger than myself, something given to me to alleviate the burdens of others?" — is a thought-provoking theological reflection, but it is not a consoling one in the light of his untimely death.

His friends the Flying Rodleighs appear and reappear in his journal, connecting him more consciously to a new and deeper call in his vocation and his writing. The warmth of their friendship, their skill and grace on the trapeze, and their lifestyle as a small community of artists touched something very deep within him. He saw in their performance the artistic realization of some of his deepest yearnings, and he confesses that meeting them catapulted him into a new consciousness. He and his friends hoped that he would write his "circus book" during his sabbatical, but this project was related to a passage in his life and his writing that was pregnant in his consciousness but not mature enough to be born. He writes, "It [knowing the Rodleighs] was so intense, that even today I do not dare to write about it because it requires a radical new step not only in my writing but also in my life." And, "Whenever I start to write I experience an enormous hesitation, even fear." Much of Henri's attraction to the trapeze performance had to do with the special relationship between the flyer and the catcher. The daredevil flyer swinging high above the crowd lets go of the trapeze to simply stretch out his arms and wait to feel the strong hands of the catcher pluck him out of the air. "The flyer must never catch the catcher," Rodleigh had told him. "He must wait in absolute trust." This relationship spoke to the inner aspirations of Henri's heart and to his yearning to fly in the spiritual life, but only in relationship with and yielding more and more into the loving hands of the Eternal Catcher.

Throughout the sabbatical journey Henri is engaged in an inner tug-of-war between his growing attraction to solitude, prayer, writing, and more intimate friendship, and his lifelong attraction for preaching, lecturing, traveling, celebrating, and working with others to make things happen. Each time he returns to his writing he is happy to be there, and he often comments on his desire to be there more. But his struggle to close the gap between the ideal and the reality is so real, so painful, and so human!

He always lived passionately, and in *Sabbatical Journey* Henri acknowledges his need for friendship and intimacy. Occasionally he describes his feelings of isolation and loneliness. The beauty of this is not in the sharing of his pain but in his simple revelation of his response to his pain. He did not flee into conventional escapes, innocent or dangerous, but he experienced the pain, and when it was too intense he reached out and shared his anguish, asking for support. He knew his fragility, and he chose to live it as faithfully as he could. This "thorn" beneath all his success and popularity was something that he could not control but that he gradually tried to integrate and to accept as part of the vocation that he loved. At his funeral in Holland, Jean Vanier commented on Henri's suffering by saying, "His anguish fueled his genius."

Henri is conscious that he is moving into new places in his thinking, his feelings, and his emotions. He is pushing down into new depths as a human being and also as a person committed to others and to the church. But he is hesitating too. He ponders to himself, "Without wanting to, I feel a certain pressure within me to keep living up to that reputation [as a Catholic priest, writer, spiritual director] and to do, say, and write things that fit the expectations of the Catholic Church, L'Arche, my family, my friends, my readers.... Lately I feel caught in it and I experience it as restricting.... What does it mean to fulfill my vocation? Does it require that I be consistent with my earlier way of living or thinking, or does it ask for the courage to move in new directions, even when doing so may be disappointing for some people?" These new questions, he goes on to say, refer to all levels of his life, including community, prayer, friendship, intimacy, work, church, God, life, and death. Just as the "circus book" was not yet mature inside of him, neither was the full integration of the new freedom that beckoned him. He says, "I know I am not completely free because the fear is still there." The way he lives these questions without blame or shame and pushing for a new integration of them allows the reader to witness how passionately he longed and gave himself to the insecurity of new directions. He was fearful but unashamed, searching with the wisdom of his years for new freedom beyond adolescence and beyond human limitations, and for deeper communion with people and with the unseen God in whom he trusted and with whom he communed on a daily basis.

In the late seventies, after his mother's death, Henri wrote two books about his mother and his relationship with her, but he seldom wrote about his relationship with his father because it was complicated and communication was difficult for them. *Sabbatical Journey* paints several touching pictures of a ninety-three-year-old father and his sixty-four-year-old son spending quality time together. Arriving in Holland from Canada for a visit, Henri jokes about his father's greeting, "Well, you badly need a haircut!" and "You better go to bed right away, so you can catch up with your sleep." He says, "A father is always a father!" Henri poignantly reveals some of the history of their relationship and his recognition of the profound reconciliation between them. He says, "A long time ago when we had a conflict, [my father] said, 'As a psychologist you know everything about authoritarian fathers. Try to be happy that you have one, but don't try to change him!'...When I was thirty-two and my father was sixty-one, we belonged to different generations and we were far apart. But as we both grew older and a little less defensive, I came to see how similar we are. As I look in the mirror today, I see my father when he was sixty-four....I quickly see that the main difference between us is age, not character....Thirty years ago the closeness that now exists between us was unthinkable...[Now we are] two old men sitting close to the fireplace warming our hands....Maybe he had to be ninety-three and I had to be sixty-four to make this possible! Today it seems that we have become part of the same generation and grown very close, close to death and close to each other. I thank God for my father." Not only did they have to be ninety-three and sixty-four, but also they both had to remain faithful to each other during the difficult years when it might have been easier to break free and end the pain of misunderstanding. Each of them brought a distinct vulnerability to the relationship, and the warm feelings of intimacy that they finally enjoyed were fruits of a long and painful passage that each one chose to live over the long years of ambiguity.

Sabbatical Journey is utterly simple, outlining Henri's thoughts and activities on the final lap of his journey home. His beliefs about the journey and the home are scattered throughout, witnessing to his life-long desire and struggle to live his vocation by his ever-growing, ever-changing faith in God. This testimony alone renders this a precious record. The book begs to be read slowly, the reader paying attention to, and reflecting with Henri on, the meaning of a particular encounter, of the event in Scripture or in the news, of the insights from a new book, or of the background shaping the concert or artifact. There is so much quiet, hidden depth and beauty here that the rapid, curious reader risks disappointment.

Unbeknown to Henri, *Sabbatical Journey* was his immediate preparation for his death, which occurred only three weeks after his return to L'Arche Daybreak. This book is the living embodiment of words he penned a few years earlier in his book *Our Greatest Gift* about his changing attitude toward death:

> Somehow, I believe that this lonely task of befriending my death is not simply a task that serves me, but also a task that may serve others. I have lived my whole life with the desire to help others in their journey, but I have always realized that I had little else to offer than my own, the journey I am making myself. How can I announce joy, peace, forgiveness, and reconciliation unless they are part of my own flesh and blood? I have always wanted to be a good shepherd for others, but I have always known, too, that good shepherds lay down their own lives — their pains and joys, their doubts and hopes, their fears and their love — for their friends.

May the gift of Henri's word and example shepherd us and lead us to find each other in friendship, welcome the questions arising from our search, share our joys and pains, and befriend death by trusting the One Who waits to catch and reunite us in everlasting joy.

SUE MOSTELLER, C.S.J.
Literary Executrix
Henry Nouwen Literary Centre
L'Arche Daybreak
May 1998

Acknowledgments

Henri would have wanted to acknowledge how the publication of this book would not have been possible apart from the generous love of some of his friends.

Henri's community, L'Arche Daybreak, supported him in planning and living his sabbatical time.

In Watertown, Massachusetts, Sarah Doering made her apartment in the home of Margaret and Robert Bullitt-Jonas and their son, Sam, available to Henri during the first four months of his writing sabbatical. Peggy McDonnell in Peapack, New Jersey, welcomed him to her guesthouse during the last seven months. Hans and Margaret Kruitwagon and Wendy and Jay Greer also offered him a home away from his home during this sabbatical journey.

Ginny Hall and Kathy Christie typed the original manuscript from Henri's impeccable handwriting.

Susan Brown did the initial editing, reducing the text by half. She also copy edited the final manuscript.

Henri's brother Laurent Nouwen gave much time to critically reading the original manuscript and the edited text. He gave advice and encouragement regarding decisions to make small changes and to delete some details.

Wendy Greer read the complete text and made suggestions for wider and deeper understanding of Henri's written word.

Kathy Christie was the backbone of the preparation with her untiring attention to details and her enlivening hope in the final product!

Sabbatical Journey

September 1995

Oakville, Ontario, Saturday, September 2, 1995

This is the first day of my sabbatical. I am excited and anxious, hopeful and fearful, tired, and full of desire to do a thousand things. The coming year stretches out in front of me as a long, open field full of flowers and full of weeds. How will I cross that field? What will I have learned when I finally reach the other end?

During this weekend nine years ago, I arrived at Daybreak. I had just finished the journal in which I wrote down the many thoughts, emotions, passions, and feelings that led me to leave Harvard Divinity School and join "the Ark." It had taken me a year to make that transition. It was in fact my first sabbatical, during which my heart was gradually opened to a new life, a life with people with mental handicaps. *The Road to Daybreak* was the record of that sabbatical.

Now, exactly nine years later, I am sitting in my little apartment in the house of Hans and Margaret in Oakville, near Toronto. Hans and Margaret invited me to spend the first two weeks of my "empty year" with them, "just to relax." Hans said, "Just sleep, eat, and do what you want to do."

I feel strange! Very happy and very scared at the same time. I have always dreamt about a whole year without appointments, meetings, lectures, travels, letters, and phone calls, a year completely open to let something radically new happen. But can I do it? Can I let go of all the things that make me feel useful and significant? I realize that I am quite addicted to being busy and experience a bit of withdrawal anxiety. I have to nail myself to my chair and control these wild impulses to get up again and become busy with whatever draws my attention.

But underneath all these anxieties, there is an immense joy. Free at last! Free to think critically, to feel deeply, and to pray as never before. Free to write about the many experiences that I have stored up in my heart and mind during the last nine years. Free to deepen friendships and explore new ways of loving. Free most of all to fight with the Angel of God and ask for a new blessing. The past three months seemed like a steeplechase full of complex hurdles. I often thought, "How will I ever make it to September?" But now I am here. I have made it, and I rejoice.

One thing that helps me immensely is that the Daybreak community has sent me on this sabbatical. It is a mission! I am not allowed to feel guilty for taking a whole year off. To the contrary, I am supported to feel guilty when I am getting busy again. Although many of my Daybreak friends Carrie and Geoff said, "We will miss you," they also said, "It is good for you and for us that you go." They affirm my vocation to be alone, read, write, and pray, and thus to live something new that can bear fruit not only in my own life but also in the life of our community. It is such a support for me that I can live my time away not only as a way of doing my will but also as a way of doing the will of the community. I can even think of it as an act of obedience!

Last night, Hans and his daughter Maja came to Daybreak to participate in the Friday night Eucharist and to pick me up. As we drove to Oakville, Hans said, "I came to be sure that you had no excuse to stay another day."

Right now I have no excuses for anything but to embark on a new journey and to trust that all will be well. It is clear to me that I have to keep a journal again, just as I did during the year before coming to Daybreak. I have promised myself not to let a day pass without writing down, as honestly and directly as possible, what is happening within and around me. It won't be easy, since I don't know the field I am entering. But I am ready to take a few risks.

I am starting this year with the prayer of Charles de Foucauld, the prayer I say every day with much trepidation:

> Father, I abandon myself into your hands.
> Do with me whatever you will.
> Whatever you may do, I thank you.
> I am ready for all, I accept all.
> Let only your will be done in me,
> and in all your creatures.
>
> Into your hands I commend my spirit.
> I offer it to you with all the love that is in my heart.
> For I love you, Lord, and so want to give myself,
> to surrender myself into your hands,
> without reserve and with boundless confidence,
> for you are my Father.
>
> Amen.

Sunday, September 3

My unconscious certainly has not gone on sabbatical yet! Last night was full of the wildest and most chaotic dreams. Dreams about not making it on time for a meeting, not being able to keep up with all my obligations, and not finishing anything that I was supposed to finish. My dreams were full of people who were angry with me for not doing what they asked me to do, and full of letters and faxes that urgently needed responses. Every time I woke up between my dreams and found myself in the quiet, peaceful, guest room of my friends, without any plans for today, I laughed. The only thing I could say was that simple prayer, "Lord Jesus Christ, have mercy on me."

Prayer is the bridge between my unconscious and conscious life. Prayer connects my mind with my heart, my will with my passions, my brain with my belly. Prayer is the way to let the life-giving Spirit of God penetrate all the corners of my being. Prayer is the divine instrument of my wholeness, unity, and inner peace.

So, what about my life of prayer? Do I like to pray? Do I want to pray? Do I spend time praying? Frankly, the answer is no to all three questions. After sixty-three years of life and thirty-eight years of priesthood, my prayer seems as dead as a rock. I remember fondly my teenage years, when I could hardly stay away from the church. For hours I would stay on my knees filled with a deep sense of Jesus' presence. I couldn't believe that not everyone wanted to pray. Prayer was so intimate and so satisfying. It was during these prayer-filled years that my vocation to the priesthood was shaped. During the years that followed I have paid much attention to prayer, reading about it, writing about it, visiting monasteries and houses of prayer, and guiding many people on their spiritual journeys. By now I should be full of spiritual fire, consumed by prayer. Many people think I am and speak to me as if prayer is my greatest gift and deepest desire.

The truth is that I do not feel much, if anything, when I pray. There are no warm emotions, bodily sensations, or mental visions. None of my five senses is being touched — no special smells, no special sounds, no special sights, no special tastes, and no special movements. Whereas for a long time the Spirit acted so clearly through my flesh, now I feel nothing. I have lived with the expectation that prayer would become easier as I grow older and closer to death. But the opposite seems to be happening. The words *darkness* and *dryness* seem to best describe my prayer today.

Maybe part of this darkness and dryness is the result of my overactivity. As I grow older I become busier and spend less and less time in prayer.

But I probably should not blame myself in that way. The real questions are, "What are the darkness and the dryness about? What do they call me to?" Responding to these questions might well be the main task of my sabbatical. I know that Jesus, at the end of his life, felt abandoned by God. "My God, my God," he cried out on the cross, "why have you forsaken me?" (Mt 27:46). His body had been destroyed by his torturers, his mind was no longer able to grasp the meaning of his existence, and his soul was void of any consolation. Still, it was from his broken heart that water and blood, signs of new life, came out.

Are the darkness and dryness of my prayer signs of God's absence, or are they signs of a presence deeper and wider than my senses can contain? Is the death of my prayer the end of my intimacy with God or the beginning of a new communion, beyond words, emotions, and bodily sensations?

As I sit down for half an hour to be in the presence of God and to pray, not much is happening to talk about to my friends. Still, maybe this time is a way of dying with Jesus.

The year ahead of me must be a year of prayer, even though I say that my prayer is as dead as a rock. My prayer surely is, but not necessarily the Spirit's prayer in me. Maybe the time has come to let go of *my* prayer, *my* effort to be close to God, *my* way of being in communion with the Divine, and to allow the Spirit of God to blow freely in me. Paul writes, "What you received was not the spirit of slavery to bring you back into fear; you received the spirit of adoption, enabling us to cry out, 'Abba, Father!' The living Spirit joins with our spirit to bear witness that we are children of God" (Rom 8:14–16).

My wild, unruly dreams will probably keep reminding me of the great spiritual work ahead of me. But I trust that it is not just I who have to do the work. The Spirit of God joins my spirit and will guide me as I move into this blessed time.

Monday, September 4

Last night I drove to downtown Toronto to have dinner with Nathan and Sue. Nathan is the director of Daybreak, and Sue its pastor, replacing me during my sabbatical. We came together just to affirm the friendship between us that has grown during the past nine years. Nathan and I came to Daybreak on the same day, and Sue, who has lived at Daybreak during most of its twenty-five years of existence, was one of the main voices calling me to Canada to become member and pastor of the community. The three of us not only live in the same community and work together in many ways but also have become close friends. Last night was a night to celebrate that friendship.

As I reflect on the year ahead, I realize that friendship will be as important a concern as prayer. Maybe even more important. My need for friendship is great, greater than seems "normal." When I think about the pains and joys of my life, they have little to do with success, money, career, country, or church, but everything to do with friendships. My friendship with Nathan and Sue proves that clearly. The moments of ecstasy and agony connected with both of them mark my nine years at Daybreak.

I have felt rejected as well as supported, abandoned as well as embraced, hated as well as loved. All through it I have come to discover that friendship is a real discipline. Nothing can be taken for granted, nothing happens automatically, nothing comes without concentrated effort. Friendship requires trust, patience, attentiveness, courage, repentance, forgiveness, celebration, and most of all faithfulness. It is amazing for me to realize how often I thought that it was all over, that both Nathan and Sue had betrayed me or dropped me, and how easily feelings of jealousy, resentment, anger, and depression came over me. It is even more amazing to see that we are still friends, yes, the best of friends. But it certainly has been hard work for all three of us.

My question as I leave Daybreak for a year is, "How can I live my friendships during this time?" Am I going to feel that out of sight means out of mind and give in to despair? Or can I move to a new inner place where I can trust that both presence and absence can deepen the bond of friendship? Most likely I will experience both ends of the spectrum of human relationship. I had better be prepared for it. But whatever I will "feel," it is important that I keep making inner choices of faithfulness.

In this respect, my struggle with prayer is not so different from my struggle with friendship. Both prayer and friendship need purification. They need to become less dependent on fleeting emotions and more rooted in lasting commitments. As I write this, it sounds very wise! But I know already that my body and soul might need an immense amount of discipline to catch up with this wisdom.

After our dinner together, Sue, Nathan, and I saw the movie Apollo 13, about an aborted moon flight and the successful attempt to bring the three astronauts safely back to earth. Underneath all the spectacular technology there is the story of human relationships and the discipline required to make them lifesaving. As the three of us watched it, I realized that somehow we too are astronauts in a spaceship trying to make it home safely. I guess that is true of all people who take the risk of friendship.

Wednesday, September 6

From the bay windows of Hans and Margaret's house I have a splendid view of Lake Ontario. My eyes are continually drawn to the mysterious line where water and sky touch each other. It is blue touching gray, or gray touching blue, or blue touching blue, or gray touching gray. Endless shades of blue and endless shades of gray. It is like an abstract painting in which everything is reduced to one line, but a line that connects heaven and earth, soul and body, life and death.

Just focusing on that line is meditating. It quiets my heart and mind and brings me a sense of belonging that transcends the limitations of my daily existence. Most often the water and sky are empty, but once in a while a sailboat or a plane passes by in the distance, neither of them ever crossing the line. Crossing the line means death.

Last Sunday during the Canadian National Exhibition Air Show, a Royal Air Force Nimrod with seven airmen onboard plunged into Lake Ontario. None of the crew survived. The blue sky became a treacherous vault, and the peaceful, glistening water a devouring monster. And that line became a tightrope from which you cannot fall without losing everything.

I must keep looking at that line. It forces me to face life and death, goodness and evil, gentleness and force, and cracks open my heart to experience the depth of being.

Now the darkness gradually covers it all. The line vanishes from sight, and everything falls silent.

Thursday, September 7

Last night I called Cardinal Joseph Bernardin, the archbishop of Chicago, to ask him about his health. He said, "Henri, I'm so glad to hear from you. Yesterday I went back to work, half days. I am doing really well." His voice was strong and energetic. I said, "Ever since I visited you in July I've been thinking of you a lot and praying for you, and I'm so glad that you feel so well and are ready to go to work again." Then he said, "I can't tell you, Henri, how much it meant to me that you came to see me, prayed with me, and gave me some of your books. Thanks again. This truly is a time of special graces for me."

I vividly remember my visit to the cardinal in July. At that time I was at the National Catholic HIV/AIDS Ministries Conference in Chicago. The newspapers had widely reported that Cardinal Bernardin was suffering from pancreatic cancer and had undergone intensive surgery and follow-up radiation treatments. Soon after I arrived in Chicago my priest friend Bob called to say that the cardinal would like me to visit him.

I spent half an hour talking and praying with him. I was deeply moved by our conversation. He told me about Steven, who had falsely accused him of sexual abuse and had later withdrawn his accusation. It had been major news and had caused great suffering for the cardinal. After it was all over he decided to visit Steven in Philadelphia and offer him his forgiveness, pray with him, and celebrate the Eucharist. Steven, who lives with AIDS and had very hostile feelings toward the church, was deeply touched by this gesture of reconciliation. For Joseph Bernardin as well as for Steven this had been a most important moment of life, a moment of true healing.

"Now both Steven and I are severely ill, Steven with AIDS and I with cancer," the cardinal said. "We both have to prepare ourselves for death. Steven calls me nearly once a month to ask me how I am doing. That means a lot to me. We are now able to support each other."

As the cardinal was telling me this, I started to feel very close to him. He really is a brother to me, a fellow human being, struggling as I do. I found myself calling him Joseph and dropping the words "Cardinal" and "Your Eminence."

"This is a very graced time," Joseph said. "As I go to the hospital for treatment I do not want to go through the side door directly to the doctor's office. No, I want to visit the other patients who have cancer and are afraid to die and I want to be with them as a brother and friend who can offer some consolation and comfort. I have a whole new ministry since I became ill, and I am deeply grateful for that."

We spoke about death. My mother had died after surgery for pancreatic cancer, so I knew how dangerous Joseph's illness was. Although he was very optimistic and expected to survive and be able to return to his work, he was not afraid to talk about his death. As I sat with him I became deeply convinced that his illness and possible death might be the greatest gift he has to offer to the church today. So many people are dying of AIDS and cancer, so many people are dying through starvation, war, and violence. Could Joseph's illness and death become a true compassionate ministry to all these people? Could he live it as Jesus did, for others? I was so grateful that he didn't go through the back door to the hospital but through the front door, visiting the patients. I was so grateful that Steven, living with AIDS, is there to encourage him. I am so grateful that he is willing to drink the cup of sorrow and to trust that this is his finest hour.

Obviously I hope that Joseph will completely recover from his cancer, and I am very glad to know that he has returned to his work. In my view Cardinal Joseph Bernardin is one of the most significant leaders in the Catholic Church today, and I know how much his people in Chicago hope that he will be able to continue his leadership.

Still, Joseph will die someday. His illness has confronted him with the closeness of death. I pray that what he has lived this year with Steven and his own cancer will make the time ahead of him, whether short or long, the most compassionate time of his life, a time that can bear fruit far beyond the boundary of his death.

Friday, September 8

Last night the Toronto International Film Festival started. It will last until September 16 and bring hundreds of new films from different countries and cultures to the city. Hans bought the richly illustrated catalog in which all the films are described and gave it to me to "study."

Going through the pages of the catalog, it strikes me that this is a contemporary storybook. Each film tells a story about how people live, suffer, and die. Most stories are about human relationships, gentle and caring, violent and abusive. All of them offer glimpses of what our world is like today, in Africa, Asia, Latin America, Australia, and North America.

Although the catalog is subtitled *Nourishment for a Modern Age* much of the food tastes quite bitter. Ours is certainly an age of immense confusion, radical upheavals, and emotional and moral bewilderment. But in the midst of it all there is heroism, kindness, sacrifice, and a deep yearning for belonging. I can hardly think of a better way to learn about the human aspirations at the end of the twentieth century than through this festival. The stories that it tells are the stories of men, women, and children of our day and age. One might object by saying that most of these stories are abnormal or exceptional, but it does not take much to realize that they are touching the most sensitive nerves of our society.

It is very hard, if not impossible, to get tickets for any of these films at this late date. They were sold out long before the beginning of the festival. People want to see and hear stories and experience their own stories in the context of larger, maybe more dramatic, more explicit, or more intense ones. I have written many essays, reflections, and meditations during the last twenty-five years. But I have seldom written a good story. Why not? Maybe my moralistic nature made me focus more on the uplifting message that I felt compelled to proclaim than on the often ambiguous realities of daily life, from where any uplifting message has to emerge spontaneously. Maybe I have been afraid to touch the wet soil from which new life comes forth and anxious about the outcome of an open-ended story. Maybe. But I am sure that we all want to hear stories, from the moment we are born to the moment we die. Stories connect our little lives with the world around us and help us discover who we are. The Bible is a storybook, and the Gospels are four stories about the birth, death, and resurrection of Jesus, who himself was one of the greatest storytellers.

As I begin this sabbatical year I realize that as a priest I must become a storyteller. I have many stories to tell. The first question is, "How can I tell them well?" It is not easy to tell a story, certainly not when you have an inclination to run quickly toward a happy ending. The second question is, "How can I find the courage to write stories that don't fit a prefabricated frame?"

Whatever is ahead of me, the Toronto International Film Festival is a clarion call to write stories and not be afraid.

Saturday, September 9

Today it is a week since I started my sabbatical year. But I have not started to write yet. Yes, I have written every day in this journal and jotted down "thoughts for the day" in my little notebook, but I have hesitated to start with my first project: a small book about Jesus' question to his followers John and James: "Can you drink the cup?"

I wonder where my hesitation comes from. I know what I want to say, but I do not know how to say it. I dream about a new style of writing, more direct, personal, and narrative, but when I am awake I don't think I can do it. Delaying longer won't help. So today I had better start, without worrying about "a new style."

Frankly, Jesus' question "Can you drink the cup?" is a very personal question for me. There are so many things in my cup I do not want to drink but must drink if I ever want to fulfill my vocation. During the last month "drinking the cup" has become for me the best expression for living my life. As I reflected more on it I realized that the cup is a cup of sorrow as well as a cup of joy.

Last night and this morning I looked up all the texts in the Bible where the word *cup* is used. All together there are sixty-eight texts from Genesis to Revelation. What is most remarkable is that sometimes *cup* is used as a word of condemnation and sometimes as a word of salvation. It is a cup of wrath and a cup of blessings, a cup for the wicked and a cup for the chosen. Thus the question "Can you drink the cup?" becomes very rich in meaning. Life is full of sorrow and full of joy. Do they belong together?

How can we live them both to the full, and trust that condemnation can become salvation?

Well, I better jump into the writing. There is no excuse to wait longer.

Sunday, September 10

Each evening before dinner I celebrate the Eucharist in the dining room with Hans and Margaret and their guests.

I am always grateful for the opportunity to bring friends together for prayer before we share a meal. Listening to the readings from the Bible, reflecting on their significance for our lives today, praying for the many people of whose needs we are aware, and receiving the Body and Blood of Jesus unite us in a way that no good conversation or good meal can accomplish. The Eucharist indeed makes us church — *ecclesia* — which means people called away from slavery to freedom. Yes, we are family, we are friends, we are business associates. But more than that we are people of God journeying together to our home, the place where Jesus went to prepare a place for us.

There is much to enjoy in life, but unless it can be enjoyed as a fore-taste of what we will see and hear in the house of God, our mortality will easily make all pleasure vain, transitory, and even empty.

The second reading today (Phlm 10, 12–17) is a part of the remarkable letter that Paul wrote to Philemon to plead for Onesimus, a runaway slave who Paul had converted to Christ while in prison.

This letter is a masterpiece. There is affection for Philemon and his slave Onesimus, there is persuasive arguing asking Philemon to take his fugitive slave back not as a slave but as a brother. There is even some subtle cunning, suggesting that Philemon owes Paul a favor. Paul is "pru-dent as a snake and gentle as a dove." His deep love for Onesimus is obvious. Indeed he would have liked Onesimus to remain where he was. But Philemon, most likely a landowner in Colossae and a convert of Paul, is a powerful man, and Paul doesn't want to alienate him. So he sends Onesimus back to his owner, but not without loading some hot coals on his head. He writes, "If he has wronged you in any way, or owes you any-thing, charge that to my account. I, Paul, am writing this with my own hand: I will repay it" (Phlm 18–19).

But then he adds in a nearly mischievous way, showing that he does not expect to pay anything, "I say nothing about your owing me even your own self." In Paul's opinion, Philemon's conversion is worth a lot more than whatever Onesimus might owe him, and if he takes his conversion — and his personal relationship with Paul — seriously, he had better treat Onesimus in the way Paul wants him to!

To be in the world without being of the world, to use the tactics of the world in the service of the Kingdom, to respond to people with wealth in a fearless way, convinced that you have more to offer than to receive, to plead for the poor in ways that the rich can understand, to carry the Gospel in one hand, a stick in the other...all of that is part of Paul's militant servanthood. It is also part of our common journey home.

We might think about ourselves as converted slaves who continue to live in this world and ask our many "bosses" to treat us as brothers and sisters. Not every Philemon in our lives will respond favorably to our request. It might not hurt to have with us a letter such as Paul wrote. Sometimes we might even have to write such a letter to our converted friends!

Monday, September 11

Why am I so tired? Although I have all the time I want to sleep, I wake up with an immense feeling of fatigue and get up only because I want to do some work. But I feel extremely frustrated. I want to write, read, and respond to some people's requests, but everything requires an immense effort, and after a few hours of work I collapse in utter exhaustion, often falling into a deep sleep. I expected that I would be tired after the intense and busy summer, but now, after ten quiet days, it feels that the more I rest the more tired I become. There seems no end to it.

Fatigue is a strange thing. I can push it away for a long time, I can go on automatic, especially when there are many routine things to do. But when finally the space and time are there to do something new and creative, all the repressed fatigue comes back like a flood and paralyzes me.

I am quite possessive about my time. I want to use it well and realize some of my long-cherished plans. I can't tolerate wasting time, even though I want to write about wasting time with God, with friends, or with the poor! There are so many contradictions within me.

Hans keeps laughing at me. "You are here to relax, to turn off your busyness, but you are living your vacation as a big job!" He is right, but the distance between insight and practice is huge.

The real question for me is how to live my fatigue as an experience that can deepen my soul. How can I live it patiently and fully experience its pains and aches?

But I am not the only one who is tired. When I walk in downtown

Toronto, I can see fatigue on the faces of the men and women moving quickly from one place to another. They look preoccupied, thinking about family, work, and the many things they have to do before the night falls. And when I look at the faces that appear on the television newscasts from Bosnia, Rwanda, and many other war-torn places, it feels like all of humanity is tired, more than tired, exhausted.

Somewhere I have to connect my little fatigue with the great fatigue of the human race. We are a tired race, carrying a burden that weighs us down. Jesus says, "Come to me, you who are tired and feel the burden of life. Take on my burden — which is the burden of the whole world — and you will discover that it is a light burden." It moves me deeply that Jesus says not "I will take your burden away" but "Take on God's burden."

So what is God's burden? Am I tired simply because I want to do my thing and can't get it done, or am I tired because I am carrying something larger than myself, something given to me to alleviate the burdens of others?

Wednesday, September 13

Since I have been with Hans and Margaret, I have driven several times to downtown Toronto. The ride on the QEW (Queen Elizabeth Way) and the Gardiner Expressway gives me an experience of the city no other highway gives. On the QEW, I see the CN Tower with the SkyDome and its surrounding high-rise buildings gradually appearing before my eyes. Then when the QEW ends and I drive up on the elevated Gardiner Expressway, all these tall buildings become like a huge theater set where a great show is going to be performed.

For the first time I have the feeling that I love Toronto! I do not think that I have ever loved a city. I lived in South Bend, Indiana, in New Haven, Connecticut, and in Cambridge, Massachusetts, but I have never felt any attachment to these places. Nor do I feel much affinity to the several Dutch towns and cities where I lived before coming to North America. But after nine years in Toronto, I am starting to feel that this is my city, and that I belong here.

I was deeply moved when, arriving by ship from Holland, I first saw the New York skyline. I was overwhelmed by the view of the Chicago skyline when a friend drove me for the first time on Lake Shore Drive. And the skylines of San Francisco, Dallas, and Houston have imprinted themselves on my mind as pictures I will never forget. But when I saw the Toronto skyline several times this week, I heard myself saying, "This is my city, this is my home, and I am excited about it. It is beautiful. I am proud to live here." It is a wonderful sensation. It is the sensation of belonging.

Last night I invited two Daybreak friends, Carrie and Geoff, for dinner at the revolving restaurant on the top of the CN Tower. From the large restaurant windows we saw the city turning beneath us. Within seventy minutes we saw the Toronto Islands, the Harbourfront, Ontario Place, the Music Hall, City Hall, the Convention Centre, the Royal York Hotel, and the railroad station, with its many tracks going west and east. We saw planes coming and going, boats moving on the lake, and thousands of cars crawling on the expressway. Overseeing the city in this way I felt the desire to come to know it better and to make it truly *my* city, a city I can love.

Thursday, September 14

This is the end of my time here. I will return to Daybreak for the weekend and then drive to Boston, where I plan to stay until Christmas.

The weekend at Daybreak will be important for me. Six friends will visit the community from Friday until Sunday. The community decided that this would also be a good occasion to "officially" send me on my sabbatical. That will happen during the Eucharist tomorrow evening.

So it looks like the coming days will be extremely busy. While I am looking forward to all these events, I still am nervous about it all, wondering if things will go well and if everyone will be satisfied after such a busy weekend!

Friday, September 15

This has been a very emotional day. At 5:00 p.m. Joan, Phil, Joanne, Amanda, and Scott arrived. Regrettably, Fred couldn't come. A small accident with his foot during his vacation forced him to stay home.

At supper we were a mixed group. Our guests told us a little about themselves and about their interest in coming to Daybreak to get to know us better. Then Bill, Linda, and other core members and assistants talked about Daybreak and answered their questions. There was a wonderful spirit among us.

At 8:00 p.m. the whole community gathered for the Eucharist, the farewell celebration for me. I was quite overwhelmed by the affection, friendship, and care that came my way. There were good words, colorful cards, and funny skits, all to let me know that I was loved by my community and was being sent on my sabbatical with many prayers and much encouragement.

At the end of the celebration I was blessed by all the members of the community. Then Nathan, in the name of the community, handed me a letter written by him and Sue, containing my sabbatical mandate. It reassures me of the support of all the members of Daybreak, commissions me to say *no* to all work except writing, and offers me all the help I need to be faithful to my "mission." It is a beautiful letter that expresses tough love and calls me to true obedience.

The more I let the events of this day sink in, the more I know how crucial it is for me to belong to this community. My restless mind, anxious heart, and tired body easily lead me to experiences of loneliness and uselessness and tempt me to faithlessness. Tonight's mandate is a clear and unambiguous declaration that I am neither alone nor useless and empowers me to be faithful to my vocation as a writer.

Saturday, September 16

A very full and happy day! In the morning Sue and I gave a miniretreat to our guests about communion with God, community with people, and compassion for the poor. At 12:30 we celebrated the Eucharist together, and after a short lunch we visited the little Daybreak bookstore and two of the Daybreak homes. Joan was moved to meet Adam, about whom she had read. Amanda and Scott met and talked with some of the younger assistants, while Phil and Joanne asked many questions and seemed happy to come to know us better.

In the evening I went out for supper with my guests, and we enjoyed very open and uninhibited conversations about Daybreak and what they had seen and heard, about our relationships with one another, and about ways to support one another in the coming months and years. I was especially happy and grateful to hear how deeply my friends had been touched by their short but quite intense visit to our community.

Utica, New York, Sunday, September 17

At noon Nathan picked me up to drive with me to Boston, where I will be with my friend Robert Jonas and his family until Christmas. I had worried about doing the twelve-hour drive from Toronto to Boston alone, and I am deeply grateful that Nathan was willing to drive me there and take a plane back to Toronto so that I could have my car in Boston. We made it as far as Utica, New York.

Watertown, Massachusetts, Monday, September 18

A beautiful, sunny day. We left Utica at 9:00 a.m. and arrived at Jonas and Margaret's home at 2:00 p.m. The long drive gave us the opportunity to talk about many things, including my community send-off and the visit of our guests over the weekend. We also spoke about illness and death. Nathan said, "Tell me what you want if you should get in a serious accident or become terminally ill." It was good to talk about this, since I had just made a "living will" and given Nathan the authority to act in my name. I told him about my gratitude for the life I have lived so far and my desire not to be kept alive artificially, or to have any organ transplant or extraordinary surgery. I said, "I do not feel any desire to die soon, but in case of an accident or serious illness I am ready to die, and I want you to feel empowered to discontinue life support when there is no real hope of recovery." "And when you die? What do you want to happen?" Nathan asked.

I thought a little and said, "I do not want to control my own funeral or burial. That's a worry I do not need! But if you want to hear my preference, then I can say this: Keep me away from a funeral home, make a simple wooden coffin in our woodery, let people say good-bye in the Dayspring chapel, and bury me in a plot at Elgin Mills Cemetery, where other members of Daybreak can also be buried. And ... keep it very simple, very prayerful, and very joyful."

We also talked a little about my unpublished writing: letters, notebooks, and so on. I told Nathan that I had given Sue the authority to use her own judgment about what should be published. The idea of people posthumously exploring the details of my personal life frightens me, but I am reassured by the knowledge of having friends who know me intimately and will guard me not only in life but also in memory.

Jonas, Margaret, and their five-year-old son, Samuel, live in a beautiful home in Watertown, outside of Boston. Margaret's mother, Sarah, has a lovely apartment on the third floor and has offered it to me for the next three months while she is on retreat at the Insight Meditation Center in Barre, Massachusetts. I am very excited about this arrangement. There is solitude and community, distance from Toronto but closeness too, a very quiet home but near a city with all the bookstores and libraries anyone could want, and, most of all, time to write and time to be with very good friends.

Jonas, Margaret, and Sam welcomed us warmly. Sarah joined us for dinner. We talked about Margaret's and Jonas's plans for the fall, Sarah's upcoming retreat, Sam's first piano lesson, and Nathan's and my own dreams for the future.

After dinner I showed Jonas, Margaret, and Sarah the mandate I had received last Friday. Jonas laughed and said, "Well, we are going to make you stick to it. When people come to the door to see you, we will have them read this first, so they know why you are here!"

It feels very good to be here, and I can hardly believe that I finally have reached the place I have dreamt about for so long.

Tuesday, September 19

At 6:30 a.m. Jonas and I drove Nathan to Logan Airport. I give thanks to God for the gift of his friendship.

Jonas and I met during the early eighties while I was teaching at Harvard Divinity School. He came to a lecture I gave at St. Paul's Church in Cambridge and asked whether I could offer him some spiritual guidance. Soon it became clear that I could use his guidance as much as he could use mine, and a friendship started to grow. Today I marvel at the many ways our lives became connected. When I left Harvard to go to Europe for a year, Jonas came to see me twice, and after I joined L'Arche Daybreak in Toronto, he also came to visit. He became a friend of the community and developed warm relationships with Nathan, Sue, Carl, and many other Daybreak members. After Jonas married Margaret in 1986 I became a friend of the new family. In the years that followed Margaret and Jonas strengthened and deepened their professional as well as personal lives. Jonas, a psychotherapist, acquired a master of theological studies degree, while Margaret was ordained to the Episcopal priesthood by Bishop Barbara Harris. On December 6, 1989, their son, Samuel, was born, and on July 29, 1992, their daughter, Rebecca, was born. She lived only a few hours, and died in Jonas's arms.

One of the special joys of the last ten years has been occasionally to give retreats and workshops with Jonas, who is a wonderful musician. The amelodic music he plays on the shakuhachi, a Japanese bamboo flute, allows people to experience God's spirit in ways that words cannot express. Over the years we have complemented each other quite well and enjoyed letting our friendship become fruitful in the lives of others.

While at Harvard, before I even knew Jonas or Margaret, I met Sarah. I remember how impressed I was by her peaceful and gentle spirit. I am filled with awe that I will now be living with Jonas, Margaret, and Sam, and using Sarah's apartment as my hermitage.

Wednesday, September 20

This morning, while Margaret took Sam to kindergarten, Jonas and I cele-brated the Eucharist in the Empty Bell, a small, very beautiful meditation center behind Jonas and Margaret's house. Originally it was a large two-car garage. The Empty Bell is the realization of Jonas's longtime dream to integrate his psychotherapeutic formation with his skills as a spiri-tual guide, and to create a place where people from different religious traditions can meet and pray.

What better place could there be for me to live my sabbatical? A place where psychology and spirituality meet, a place of prayer and contempla-tion, a place of family life and interreligious dialogue, a place of solitude and a place of friendship, a place for children and adults. This is not a big center or gathering place. It is very simple, small, and intimate.

The Empty Bell has a little vestibule where people can take off their shoes and prepare themselves to go to the prayer room on the second floor. The prayer room is an empty space — not barren, cold, or forbid-ding but quiet, spacious, and inviting. The ceiling is white with wooden crossbeams and indirect lights. On the wooden floor, cushions are placed in a circle. A large, saucer-shaped bell, which gives a beautiful, reso-nant sound when struck at the rim, closes the circle. On the windowsills different Oriental flutes are placed.

For Jonas the Empty Bell is a place where body, mind, and spirit can find healing and integration. I am deeply convinced that the Empty Bell will also become a place to renew and strengthen my own spiritual life.

Thursday, September 21

At 8:30 this morning I joined a group of nine people who come every other Thursday morning to the Empty Bell for a time of meditation and reflection. After playing the shakuhachi for a few minutes to help us quiet down, Jonas gave a short instruction about "staying with your breathing." Then we meditated for twenty minutes and listened to the Gospel story in which Jesus calls Matthew, the tax collector, with the words "Follow me." This story became the focus of a time in which each one of us sitting in the circle offered some personal reflections. Finally we all prayed.

It was a simple but very beautiful time. Although I knew only two people in the circle, there was a spiritual intimacy among us that could only be understood as a sign of God's presence.

In the afternoon, Sarah showed me her apartment and told me how to use it during her absence. A few hours later she left on her three-month retreat. Before she stepped into her car, Margaret, Sam, Sarah, and I embraced while I prayed. I asked God that Sarah's time in solitude would bear fruit not only in her own heart but in the hearts of many people.

Sarah looked gratefully at me and said, "Yes, my time away is a time for others." Then she drove off.

I feel very connected with Sarah. I am sure that her solitude at the Insight Meditation Center and my solitude in her apartment will greet each other and support each other. I think about it as a Buddhist-Christian dialogue of the heart.

Tonight I will move from my room into Sarah's apartment on the third floor of Jonas and Margaret's home. It is another beginning!

Friday, September 22

Jonas is a member of a nearby health club. Both Nathan and Jonas urged me to join. So I did. Today was the second time that Jonas and I did our exercises.

There is little if anything in me that likes to work out at a health club. Sports never played a role in my life, and except for a little swimming here and there, I have done nothing to stay fit. But my increasing physical fatigue and the simple fact that I have ample time made me give in to my friends' pleas.

The world of a health club is quite overwhelming for an outsider. It looks like a torture room where men and women are moaning and groaning as they run the treadmill, lift weights, and get boiled in the hot tub. Nobody says a word. Everyone is completely preoccupied with his or her own heart, lungs, and muscles.

Jonas and I ran the treadmill or "trotter" for twenty minutes. It is a machine with a running belt that makes you walk, trot, or run, depending on the speed you program in. As you run, you get all the information you want, or don't want, to know: your time, your distance, and your inclines. In front of you is a panel that describes your regularity in colored dotted lines.

On our way to the health club I had bought a Walkman to listen to an audiotape with a talk by Matthew Fox called "Creation, Spirituality, and the Seven Chakras." So, while working up a sweat on the trotter, I tried to make my time useful listening to Matthew Fox. It didn't work! Matthew's invitation to let my first chakra, at the place where animals have their tails, receive divine messages from all of creation and my simultaneous eagerness to make it to the end of my twenty minutes with some sort of dignity didn't go together. All I could do was run and watch the clock!

The swimming pool, hot tub, and steam room were a lot more humane. It felt as if water and steam were once our natural surroundings. I said to Jonas, "Maybe once, long ago, we were fish."

When we came home I felt so mellow that I had to sleep for a few hours to be able to do anything human again, like thinking and writing.

I still don't know if the health club is where I want to be. But I have no choice. I paid my fee, and Jonas goes three times a week and expects me to join him. Well, next time I will leave Matthew Fox home and try to talk with Jonas while running without going anywhere.

Saturday, September 23

It's a little game, but it works. I bought a little notebook with a hard cover portraying the Angel from the Pérussis Altarpiece at the Metropolitan Museum of Art. The book is called "Museum Notes" and contains 160 blank pages of acid-free paper.

Tom and John of HarperSanFrancisco have asked me to make a yearbook with a thought a day. I wondered how I could do that considering the fact that a year has 365 days. I don't think I have that many new thoughts, or, for that matter, that many old ones!

But my Museum Notes book helps me a lot. I write a few thoughts each day and have decided not to use more than one page for each thought and to leave the opposite page free for corrections.

It is indeed becoming a game. I sit at my desk and say to myself, "Do you have a thought for your Angel?" Usually something emerges in my mind when I bring my ballpoint to the paper. Today I even surprised myself with eight thoughts. When I have filled my book with eighty thoughts, I will send it to Toronto and ask my secretary, Kathy, to put them on the computer. Then I can read them all and see how often I repeated myself. Right now I am not looking backwards! It does worry me a bit that I have to fill nearly five of these notebooks before Tom and John are going to be content. However, it is only September; there are many days to write in my Angel Book.

Sunday, September 24

Last night I saw the film *Apollo 13* for the second time at a small theater in Watertown with Jonas and Margaret. When we came home, Margaret

showed me the photo book *The Home Planet*, conceived and edited by
Kevin W. Kelley for the Association of Space Explorers.

Looking at the magnificent photographs of planet Earth taken from
outer space, and reading the comments of the astronauts and cosmonauts,
I had a sense of being introduced to a new mysticism. The observations
made from outer space seem very similar to those made from inner space.
They both reveal the precariousness of life, the unity of the human family,
the responsibility of the "seer," the power of love, and the mystery of God.
James Irwin, who flew on *Apollo 15* in July 1971, writes:

> The Earth reminded us of a Christmas tree ornament hanging in the
> blackness of space. As we got farther and farther away it diminished
> in size. Finally it shrank to the size of a marble, the most beautiful
> marble you can imagine. That beautiful, warm, living object looked
> so fragile, so delicate, that if you touched it with a finger it would
> crumble and fall apart. Seeing this has to change a man, has to
> make a man appreciate the creation of God and the love of God.

All the astronauts and cosmonauts were overwhelmed by the unspeak-
able beauty of their own home, the planet Earth, and in some way or
another raised the question "How can we care better for our own home?"
Seeing your home planet as a precious little gem that needs care and pro-
tection is a deeply mystical experience that can only be captured by words
such as *grace* and *responsibility*. Russell Schweickart, who flew on *Apollo 9*
in 1969, writes:

> You think about what you are experiencing and why. Do you de-
> serve this, this fantastic experience? Have you earned this in some
> way? Are you separated out to be touched by God, to have some
> special experience that others cannot have? And you know that the
> answer to that is no. There's nothing you've done to deserve this,
> to earn this; it's not a special thing for you. You know very well
> at that moment, and it comes through to you so powerfully, that
> you're the sensing element for man. You look down and see the sur-
> face of that globe that you've lived on all this time, and you know
> all those people down there, and they are like you, they are you,
> and somehow you represent them. You're up here as the sensing el-
> ement, that point out on the end, and that's a humbling feeling.
> It's a feeling that says you have a responsibility. It's not for yourself.
> The eye that doesn't see doesn't do justice to the body. That's why
> it's there; that's why you are out there. And somehow you recognize
> that you are a piece of this total life. And you're out there on that

forefront and you have to bring it back somehow. And that becomes a rather special responsibility, and it tells you something about your relationship with this thing we call life. So that's a change. That's something new. And when you come back there's a difference in that world now. There's a difference in that relationship between you and that planet and you and all those other forms of life on that planet, because you've had that kind of experience. It's a difference and it's so precious.

It is a mystic, a seer, who speaks here. Isaiah could have said this or Joan of Arc or John of the Cross. What they saw evoked deep humility and great responsibility. They experienced their vision as a grace and as a call, as a gift not just for themselves but for all of humanity. What is experienced as most intimate is lived out as most universal. The human heart unites with the heart of the universe, and this unity becomes the source of a new mission.

The "seers" are like "holy men" who have a special radiance because of what they have seen. Robert Cenker, who flew on *Columbia 7* in January 1986, writes:

> Of all the people I've spoken to about the experience of space, only those closest to me can begin to understand. My wife knows what I mean by the tone of my voice. My children know what I mean by the look in my eye. My parents know what I mean because they watched me grow up with it. Unless you actually go and experience it yourself you will never really know.

That's the loneliness of the mystic. Having seen and experienced what cannot be expressed in words and still must be communicated. The astronauts and cosmonauts gave words to my own experience of priesthood. It is a grace, it allows me to see a vision, and it is a call to let others know what I have seen; it is a long loneliness and an inexpressible joy.

Monday, September 25

The days go too fast! After the Eucharist with Jonas and Margaret at the Empty Bell, I worked on an outline for my little book about the cup. At noon Jonas and I went to the health club. When we returned I was so tired from "dry walking" on the "trotter" and climbing on the StairMaster that I fell into a deep sleep for more than two hours.

Now I feel guilty for not having done enough today. There is so much I want to think about, read about, and write about that I get very frustrated when I see it getting dark again. But I am very grateful to be here. I can't think of a better place, or a better time, or better friends. I just have to be patient and trust that my body will gradually gain some strength and be able to do with less sleep.

In the Gospel today, Jesus says, "For there is nothing hidden, except to be disclosed; nor is anything secret, except to come to light" (Mk 4:22). These words encourage me to live my "hidden and secret life" well. I have to trust that the more faithful I am to my solitude, the more fruitful it will be in my community. I realize now how important it is to live this time with a pure heart. My most intimate thoughts and feelings will somehow, somewhere come to light. I pray that, placed in the light, they will delight those who see them.

Tuesday, September 26

Last Sunday at 7:00 a.m., Secretary of State Warren Christopher got a telephone call from Yasir Arafat and Shimon Peres announcing that they had reached an agreement on Palestinian self-rule. This major accomplishment in international politics wouldn't have been possible without the quiet, self-effacing Dennis B. Ross, the U.S. Mideast negotiator.

I have always had a deep admiration for this forty-five-year-old gentleman, who avoids publicity and fame but is truly committed to peace. Mr. Ross's successful mediation all took place by telephone from his home in Bethesda, Maryland. When Yasir Arafat and Shimon Peres announced to Warren Christopher that they had reached an agreement, they praised Dennis Ross for conducting "the first shuttle diplomacy by telephone." Dennis Ross is not only a very competent but also a very humble man, who allows other people to be in the limelight and is himself content to keep a very low profile. I would love to meet this true peacemaker. Strong and humble, competent and self-effacing, fearless and very gentle. "Blessed are the peacemakers: they shall be recognized as children of God" (Mt 5:9).

Wednesday, September 27

The feeling of being abandoned is always around the corner. I keep being surprised at how quickly it rears its ugly head. Yesterday I experienced that nasty feeling in my innermost being. Just raw anxiety, seemingly disconnected from anything. I kept asking myself, "Why are you so restless, why are you so anxious, why are you so ill at ease, why do you feel so lonely and abandoned?"

I called and put a message on Nathan's voice mail. Soon he called back and said that he would call again in the evening so that we could have ample time to talk.

Talking lessened my anxiety and I felt peaceful again. No one can ever heal this wound, but when I can talk about it with a good friend I feel better.

What to do with this inner wound that is so easily touched and starts bleeding again? It is such a familiar wound. It has been with me for many years. I don't think this wound — this immense need for affection, and this immense fear of rejection — will ever go away. It is there to stay, but maybe for a good reason. Perhaps it is a gateway to my salvation, a door to glory, and a passage to freedom!

I am aware that this wound of mine is a gift in disguise. These many short but intense experiences of abandonment lead me to the place where I'm learning to let go of fear and surrender my spirit into the hands of the One whose acceptance has no limits. I am deeply grateful to Nathan and to my other friends who know me and are willing to bind my wounds so that, instead of bleeding to death, I can walk on to the full life.

Thursday, September 28

Last night I visited my friend Bobby. Our friendship dates from the time we spent together at Yale Divinity School, where Bobby was a student while I was on the faculty. During the twenty years of our friendship, much has happened to both of us. But Bobby's life has been a lot more tumultuous than mine. After his ordination as an Episcopal priest and his marriage to Dana, he studied at Harvard Business School and acquired a doctoral degree in business policy. He developed a great interest in the South African divestment movement and signed a contract with Doubleday to write a major book on the subject. Besides significant pastoral responsibilities in several Episcopal parishes, he was a lecturer at Harvard Divinity School. During that time his two sons, Sam and John, were born.

This sounds like a success story, but Bobby is a hemophiliac. He has to give himself intravenous infusions every day, suffers from arthritis, and is in and out of a wheelchair depending on his health. More than ten years ago it was found that he was HIV positive. Ever since I have known Bobby I have been deeply impressed by his will power, intelligence, and unwavering optimism. In no way did he allow his hemophilia or his HIV status to discourage him in his marriage or his career.

Bobby always loved politics. Two years ago, after returning from six months in South Africa, where he had been greatly inspired by that country's commitment to democracy, he began a campaign to be elected the lieutenant governor of Massachusetts. With enormous energy he went to work and was able to win the Democratic primary in September 1994. Though he sparked considerable public enthusiasm, partially as a result of his great honesty about his hemophilia and HIV status, he and the Democratic candidate for governor lost the battle against the Republican incumbents in November. He returned to Harvard Divinity School but soon found that the job that had been promised to him would not be available.

Following the loss of the lieutenant governor's race and the Harvard job, Bobby's marriage broke down from years of anxiety about HIV, and he suffered the loss of his family as well. So he had lost the campaign, his job, his family, his home, and his financial security. All his many successes had turned into failure. His immense gifts seemed to have come to nothing.

When we were talking last night Bobby said, "I didn't know if I would survive it all, but I did. I just found a house to live in and welcomed my boys. I have a good friend who cares for me. I have an attractive job offer, and in some unexpected way I again feel new joy and new hope."

What struck me the most was that in the midst of all his losses and humiliations, Bobby had come to enjoy the small gifts of life. "I love to be with the boys," he said. "Whenever they come to my home, I give them all my attention, and we have wonderful times together." He spoke about the many graces: a good meal, good friends, coaching Sam and John's soccer games, walking in the park, making a little prayer room in his house, reading a good book and finishing his own.

As I returned from my visit I marveled at Bobby's resiliency. It reminded me of Paul's experience: "We are afflicted in every way, but not crushed; perplexed, but not driven to despair; persecuted, but not forsaken; struck down, but not destroyed; always carrying in the body the death of Jesus, so that the life of Jesus may also be made visible in our bodies" (2 Cor 4:8).

Bobby's story, painful and sad as it is, evoked in me deep hope and a strong desire to be a faithful friend. Who would ever have imagined the many things that would come? It is good we can't. With a hopeful heart I wonder what we will be talking about twenty years from now!

Friday, September 29

Andrew Sullivan's new book, *Virtually Normal: An Argument about Homo-sexuality*, is one of the most intelligent and convincing pleas for complete social acceptance of homosexuality I have ever read.

Andrew Sullivan is a Catholic. He is just as open about being a Catholic as about being a homosexual. From his writing it becomes clear that he is not only a Catholic but also a deeply committed Catholic who takes his church's teachings quite seriously. That makes his discussion of the church's attitude toward homosexuality very compelling.

My own thoughts and emotions around this subject are very conflicted. Years of Catholic education and seminary training have caused me to internalize the Catholic Church's position. Still, my emotional development and my friendships with many homosexual people, as well as the recent literature on the subject, have raised many questions for me. There is a huge gap between my internalized homophobia and my increasing conviction that homosexuality is not a curse but a blessing for our society. Andrew Sullivan is starting to help me bridge this gap.

Saturday, September 30

Jonas invited me to join his Buddhist-Christian dialogue group for lunch. There was a Zen Buddhist monk, a Tibetan Buddhist nun, a Catholic priest, a Catholic nun, a Catholic married woman, Jonas, and myself. The discussion was animated and cordial.

What struck me most were the different wavelengths on which Catholics and Buddhists think. It seems that Catholics, independent of any particular subject, are mostly concerned about authority and doctrine. Somehow there is an "in or out" kind of thinking, even when the boundaries might be quite movable. "What is the truth and who has it?" is a question not explicitly stated but seeming always to be there unconsciously. The Catholic Church has a very explicit set of teachings and a very visible hierarchy among those who announce, protect, and defend these teachings.

Buddhists don't think that way. For them explicit doctrines prevent inner freedom, and true authority is rooted in the degree to which one has acquired that inner freedom. Buddhists don't divide their world between those who are "in" and those who are "out." Their spiritual goal is to find the place of limitless compassion, where all is nothing and nothing is all.

Is there a place for a Buddhist-Christian dialogue when the word itself is a questionable instrument of communication? I think it is of great importance that Buddhists and Christians meet. There is so much they have to give to each other. But maybe instead of *dialogue* the word *encounter* should be used. This word might also show the direction in which to find the most creative ways of being together.

October 1995

Sunday, October 1

During my farewell celebration at the Dayspring, two large blue candles were presented to me, one for me to take on my journey, and one to go from house to house in the community. They are prayer candles and are meant to remind me and those who sent me of our commitment to each other.

I realize how often my candle is burning! When I write my candle is lit to help make my writing a way of praying, and when I pray the candle is lit to connect me with my friends at home.

Community is so much more than living and working together. It is a bond of the heart that has no physical limitations. Indeed it is candles burning in different places of the world, all praying the same silent prayer of friendship and love.

Wednesday, October 4

At 3:00 p.m. this afternoon Pope John Paul II arrived at Newark Airport to begin his five-day visit to the United States. I watched his arrival on television and listened to the speeches by President Clinton and the Pope.

From all the words spoken, one sentence by Pope John Paul stuck in my mind: "Nobody is so poor that he has nothing to give, and nobody is so rich that he has nothing to receive." That is a powerful idea to undergird all peacemaking. As long as we keep dividing people or nations between those who give and those who receive, there will always be oppression and manipulation, even with the best intentions. The United States is a powerful nation that has much to give. But only if it is also willing to receive can its giving be a true contribution to peace.

Among the many dignitaries I saw Cardinal Bernardin. I was glad to see that he had been able to make the trip from Chicago to welcome John Paul II. His pancreatic cancer must be under control and his energy sufficient to participate in this tiring event.

I am looking forward to watching tomorrow morning's broadcast of the Pope's address to the United Nations on its fiftieth anniversary. I still have vivid memories of watching — while on vacation in Mexico

City with my parents — Pope Paul VI's visit to the UN, where he spoke these memorable words: "No more war, never war again." That was in 1965. Now, thirty years later, after many more wars, another Pope comes to the same place, with the same message. Will it ever happen: a world without wars?

Thursday, October 5

Pope John Paul's address to the United Nations struck me by its great spiritual vision. He spoke about the accelerated quest for freedom all around the world, freedom not only for individuals but for nations as well. He discussed this quest for freedom as an essential element of the inner structure of the human person. Reminding his listeners of the year 1989, when freedom was brought about in Eastern Europe without violence, he stressed the fact that in many places in our world this freedom is still a faraway goal. At the end of his address he unfolded a vision for the recuperation of the Transcendent as needed to attain the full freedom that people and nations are hungry for.

For me it was a very moving address. It was offered by a man who truly has lived much, seen much, and still has the courage to offer a spiritual vision that will allow all the people of this world to live together as brothers and sisters. In a society so full of cynicism and realpolitik, there are few leaders who can give the way John Paul II can. It is no surprise that millions of people from the most divergent social and economic backgrounds want to catch a glimpse of or, better, a blessing from this holy peacemaker.

Friday, October 6

A wonderful day for Boston, for Harvard, and for Dublin. Seamus Heaney, the Irish poet who teaches at Harvard during the spring, won the Nobel Prize in literature.

What moves me most is that this poet was chosen for "works of lyrical beauty and ethical depth which exalt everyday miracles and the living past." His person and his work express kindness, love for the land, deep bonds with family, and hope for reconciliation among people. Although Heaney is not rushing to the barricades, he feels passionately about the violence in his homeland. But instead of expressing his opinions about the politics of Northern Ireland, he writes about the suffering of the people involved and the ways the great conflict affects small lives. The citation from Stockholm explicitly mentions his contribution toward resolution of the conflict. It is no surprise that a Boston friend says about Heaney, "The Peace Prize would have been equally fitting."

As the Pope speaks of peace and offers a vision of a world in which both pluriformity and unity are celebrated, it is a grace to see this peace poet being honored. After all the ugliness of the O. J. Simpson trial dominating the TV over the past eight months, these are new signs of beauty and hope.

Sunday, October 8

This morning, I drove to the home of my longtime friend Jutta. After an hour's drive on the nearly empty highways, I arrived at Jutta's home at 9:00 a.m. Together we celebrated the Eucharist in her living room, reflecting on the readings and sharing the divine gifts of life.

Before and after the Eucharist we spoke about May Sarton, a poet, novelist, and journal writer who died a few months ago. Although I knew her name, I had never read any of her writings until recently. I bought her *Journal of a Solitude* and became increasingly interested in her life and work.

Jutta showed me her book A *Plant Dreaming Deep*, in which she speaks about her European past and the struggle to find a true home in America. Her feelings of homelessness struck a deep chord in me. May Sarton wrote the book in the 1940s, while her parents were still living. Later, she was able to cut her bonds with Europe more radically and claim the United States, especially New Hampshire, as her true home.

Both Jutta and I came to America from Europe, Jutta in 1960 and I in 1971. Reflecting on my twenty-four years in the United States and Canada, I realize how seldom, if ever, I have experienced a desire to live in Europe again. I love my country, my family, and all the good friends there, but from the moment I decided to make America my new home I felt an enormous inner freedom that has remained with me until now.

Maybe in response to May Sarton's poem, I called my father in Holland from Jutta's home. He was glad to hear from me and asked me if I had received his new book, My *Last Confession*. I hadn't yet. He said, "Be sure to read it and let me know what you think." From a little folder announcing the book, I knew that one of the chapters was called "Where Is the Good God, Where Is He?" So I said, "I certainly will read it and respond to it, especially what you have to say about the 'good God.'" He said, "Yes, yes, I am a little shocking there! I would love to get your reaction." Then he asked, "When are you coming?" I said, "I am planning to come at Christmas, celebrate your birthday, and take you on a vacation to Freiburg." He showed great enthusiasm. "I would love to go to Freiburg with you. I need to get out of this house once in a while," he said, "and a trip to Freiburg will do me a lot of good."

May Sarton was eighty-three years old when she died. My father will be ninety-three on January 3. He is still writing! I so much hope that we can be together on that day, whether in his Limburg home or in Freiburg. I pray for him today.

It has been good to spend time with Jutta in her home. Her welcome is always warm and special. I'm grateful for her faithful friendship.

Monday, October 9

I watched the Pope's departure from the Baltimore-Washington Airport on television and was more deeply moved than I expected to be. I sometimes find it hard to feel connected with all the fanfare, choreographed ceremonies, mass rallies, and overall hype that characterize a papal visit. When I see the cardinals, bishops, and civil dignitaries crowding around the Pope, and the thousands of people trying to shake his hand, touch his white cassock, or just catch a glimpse of him, I create some inner distance from it all, as if it is a spectacle that has little to do with my life and my concerns.

But as I watched several of the events and listened carefully to what John Paul II was saying, there gradually emerged for me a spiritual vision greater, wiser, and more encompassing than any other vision I have seen in our contemporary world. The Pope's vision includes the human quest for freedom, the rights of individuals and nations, the religious importance of ecumenism and interreligious dialogue, the importance of the family, the sacredness of life from conception to natural death, and the true meaning of democracy. I saw that vision unfold as the Pope spoke to the civil and religious leaders; to men and women of the most diverse cultural and economic backgrounds; to the elderly, the young people, and to the children; to policemen, security guards, airplane pilots, and stewards.

Watching him during his five-day visit, I gradually got in touch with his vision, a vision that is universal, all-inclusive, rooted in a deep knowledge of God's love, inspired by the Gospel of Jesus, and rich in concrete implications for our daily lives. I was moved that this septuagenarian leader had a language that could speak to the most secular as well as to the most religious person, that this vision has no sectarian narrowness while it is fully based on the teachings of Jesus. It is a vision for all people, and embraces all of creation. It is a demanding vision, yet full of compassion; it is a comforting vision, yet full of gentleness; it is a critical vision, yet full of understanding. It is a vision, as *The New York Times* says, that defies political labeling. It opposes abortion and euthanasia while stressing the urgency to care for the poor, to show compassion to the sick and the dying, especially those with AIDS, and to welcome immigrants generously. The words *conservative* and *liberal* do not fit such a vision.

Reflecting on this vision, I realize that the Pope was doing much more than offering his opinions on things. He spoke not for himself but in the Name of God, as revealed through Jesus. His words, although influenced by particular philosophies and theologies, are embedded in a tradition of Christian faith that is twenty centuries old.

It is very hard to know where time-bound opinions and a timeless vision need to be distinguished. Who can even fully know where personal opinions are presented as eternal truth and where eternal truth is truly eternal? As the centuries have rolled by, much that once seemed eternal has proven very temporal, and much that seemed very temporal has been revealed as having eternal significance. We have to trust that in the midst of the many ideas and statements there is a vision undergirding them all.

John Paul II has strong opinions with which many people disagree. The many controversies in the church concerning the role of women, sexual ethics, and the exercise of authority show clearly that there is a lot to discuss and to reflect on. I guess that many of John Paul II's ideas will be rethought and reformulated during the decades to come. But beyond all opinions he proclaims a vision that is more than personal, a vision that is divinely inspired and transcends human speculation and debate. It is this vision that I saw emerging during the papal visit. It is a true catholic — that is, universal — vision, a vision this world so much needs as we enter the next millennium.

Wednesday, October 11

I have always greatly admired the work of the American painter Edward Hopper. But I have equally disliked it. As much as I would desire to have a real van Gogh in my room, I would fear having a real Hopper. The light in Hopper's paintings is brilliant, but that light has no warmth. Everything in his work, it seems to me, speaks of alienation, separation, and distance. There is no intimacy, only immense loneliness.

In *Edward Hopper: An Intimate Biography* by Gail Levin, it becomes dramatically clear that Hopper lived what he painted. His relationship with his wife, Josephine, was cruel and abusive. Jo's elaborate diaries, which form one of the main sources of this biography, reflect the tragedy of their forty years of marriage.

It is amazing to see, notwithstanding, all the assertions that art should be evaluated independent of the artist's personality, how close the connections are between the artistic work and the life and personality of the artist. This certainly is the case with all the artists I have paid attention to: Rembrandt, van Gogh, and Chagall. Edward Hopper's chilling life, frightfully reflected in his chilling art, affirms this connection.

Vincent van Gogh's relationships were not any more satisfying than Hopper's. But there is a huge difference between the two. Vincent's fervent desire to be close to somebody, his dream of forming a colony of artists, and, most of all, his affectionate although turbulent love for his brother, Theo, is visible in all his works. In contrast to that of Hopper, Vincent's light is not only brilliant but full of warmth. All the people he paints are radiant like saints, and his orchids, cypresses, and wheat fields are burning with the fire of his intense feelings. His many hot yellows are radically different from the cold yellows of Edward Hopper.

The soul of the artist cannot remain hidden. The bitter, isolated, and mean soul of Hopper and the restless but love-hungry soul of van Gogh are both revealed in their works. Vincent van Gogh was and remained a minister, always trying to bring people together, even though he failed miserably. Edward Hopper was and remained a man who was only interested in himself, and he lived and died in splendid isolation.

Watertown, Friday, October 13

Last night Jonas left for a day of quiet in a nearby Carmelite monastery. Margaret chose some silence and solitude for herself, and little Sam was gone most of the time in school or at a friend's home.

I spent the day making an audiotape for friends, wrote a few cards to friends, talked with publishers in the United States and Germany on the phone, and wrote a new chapter for the book on the cup.

Outside the sun was bright, the colors of the trees magnificent, and the air soft and gentle. It was one of those days without great events but full of love and beauty.

Tomorrow I am leaving for six days. On Sunday and Monday I am going to be with my friends Wendy and Jay, and with Fred and Robin in New York. On Tuesday I plan to take the train to Philadelphia to visit another friend, Steve, and on Wednesday I will return to New York and spend some time with my publishers there. I am looking forward to this little trip. I will take my journal and my little notebook for daily reflections with me. I hope that after these weeks of relative solitude, this trip to friends will give me new inspiration and new energy.

New York, Saturday, October 14

It is 6:00 p.m., and I am sitting behind the little antique desk in the guest room of my friends Wendy and Jay in Manhattan.

I vividly remember when I arrived for the first time in New York. I came from Holland on the *Maardam*, one of the passenger ships of the Holland-America line. It was a "free" trip because I had been given the position of Catholic chaplain for the Dutch emigrants. It was in the early sixties. I can still recall the feeling I had when at 7:00 in the morning we passed the Statue of Liberty and approached the imposing skyline of Manhattan Island. With me, looking at the view, was Zita, the exiled empress of Austria, one of the many passengers I had met during the trip. I took her picture with the skyscrapers in the background. I was all excited about New York, about Zita, and about coming to the New World for the first time.

Now, thirty-four years later, I have come to know New York, its beauty and its ugliness, its wealth and its poverty, its open parks and little alleys, its splendor and its squalor. But I am no longer a tourist here. For many years New York remained for me a place with incredible sights to see: the Empire State Building, the United Nations buildings, Rockefeller Center, St. Patrick's Cathedral, the Metropolitan Museum, Times Square, Broadway, Fifth Avenue... I saw them all and took photographs of them all.

But then I came to know New Yorkers, people who had lived in New York all their lives, worked there, went to church there, and had their circles of friends there. Gradually New York City became smaller, friendlier, more intimate, and much safer for me.

Tonight I am just full of gratitude for being invited into this city by good friends, Wendy and Jay, and by other loving and generous people. Through them and many others, the United States has become my country. And although I now have my home in Canada, I still feel very much at home in this country and especially in this city.

Sunday, October 15

This afternoon at three o'clock Wendy and I went to a Gustav Mahler concert at Carnegie Hall. The program consisted of the "Kindertotenlieder" and the Sixth Symphony. The orchestra was the Metropolitan Opera Orchestra, the conductor, James Levine, and the soloist, the bass-baritone Bryn Terfel, a native of North Wales.

Many weeks ago Wendy had invited me to go with her to this unique event. It was an unforgettable experience. Just being at Carnegie Hall for the first time was a real treat.

I had never heard Mahler's "Kindertotenlieder." They are based on poems by the German poet Friedrich Rückert (1788–1866), written as an expression of grief at the death, from scarlet fever, of his children Louise and Ernst in January 1833. Gustav Mahler, who had grieved deeply over the loss of his fourteen-year-old brother, Ernst, set to music five of Rückert's "Songs on the Death of Children."

I was deeply moved by the performance and wished that Margaret and Jonas could have been there. Their grief over the loss of their daughter, Rebecca, who died only a few hours after her birth, found such a powerful expression in Mahler's music. They would have cried many tears.

After the intermission Levine directed the Sixth Symphony. It is considered one of Mahler's greatest works and expresses a great range of emotion — exuberant joy, intense anguish, pastoral serenity, great pain, sadness, fear, hope, and despair. Everything is intense, elaborate, and majestic. The orchestra was the largest I had ever seen. During the eighty-one-minute performance, I mostly looked — with Wendy's binoculars — at the percussion section. There were seven men moving from one instrument to the other, trying to keep up with the various sounds they had to produce. For certain periods, I became so fascinated by their actions and interactions that I forgot to listen to the music. These men in gray suits and ties looked dead serious, in stark contrast to the joyful noises they were making. Especially one man with a strikingly beautiful, deeply carved face and long black hair, handling the large brass cymbals, went about his business without the slightest change of expression. While looking at these figures I started to wonder what their lives looked like outside of Carnegie Hall or Lincoln Center.

When it was over the applause was long and enthusiastic. New Yorkers are spoiled and seldom applaud for very long. But this was an exception.

As Wendy and I walked back to the apartment, I realized how hard it was for me to find words for this unusual musical event. Compared with all the instruments, my language seemed quite poor. Words such as "fantastic," "fabulous," "overwhelming," "rich," "moving," "spectacular" didn't seem to express much. The only thing I was clear about was that I had to write about it in my journal. So I did!

Monday, October 16

Most of this day I spent reading my father's newest book, *My Last Confession*. He gives it the subtitle *Critical Reflections of an Old Man at the End of His Career as an Author and Tax Expert.* The first copy will be presented to the governor of the province of Limburg this coming Friday in Venlo, the city where my father was born in 1903.

It was a moving experience for me to read *My Last Confession.* It is well written, full of wit, very interesting, always with a touch of irony, and rich in surprising viewpoints. Although it is quite personal, it reflects also on many issues that concerned my father during his life as a lawyer, tax specialist, and professional in fiscal law. Although it expresses my father's own opinions about the current tax problems in Dutch society, and about his own adult life, aging, and dying, it also refers to Cicero, Cato, Montesquieu, Georges Simenon, Kafka, and many other well-known literary and political figures from past centuries and the present time. And although it touches on a great variety of subjects, such as the meaning of writing, becoming old, and faith in God, the book is primarily a critical evaluation of my father's own life. He writes not without sarcasm, but his book is in essence mild and gentle.

I immensely enjoyed reading my father's last confession, and I recognized clearly his fighting spirit, his intelligence, his sense of humor, and most of all his wisdom. He emerges in this book as a man with enormous vitality and great integrity. In the first chapter he writes that he does not want to die "playing bridge." He certainly is not doing that, and this book proves it.

In the final chapter, "The Curtain Falls," he speaks about his faith in God. There he affirms the words of a Dutch spiritual writer who says, "God infinitely transcends us but also deeply corresponds with our heart, limited and temporary as this harmony might be. Whether it sounds good, true, and beautiful depends on my own ortho-praxis (rightful action)."

My father is truly a man of "ortho-praxis." What finally counts for him is what people do more than what they say or believe. To me he always said, "People finally will remember you not for your words, ideas, statements, or books, but for what you have done for others, and for the spirit in which you did it."

I will miss not being there on Friday, when *My Last Confession* is officially launched, but, having read the book, I can truthfully say that I am proud of my father.

Today Fred and I had a delightful walk in Central Park and lunch. At 6:00 p.m. I went to Fred's home to spend some time with Robin, his wife, and their two children, the three-and-a-half-year-old Jacob and their newborn baby, Emma. A real joy. During dinner we talked about books, mutual work, friends, and future plans. A good and peaceful evening!

Philadelphia, Tuesday, October 17

Today I spent the day in Philadelphia with my friend Steve. For seventeen years Steve was an assistant bank manager in the City of Brotherly Love, and then he decided to go to seminary. He had saved up enough money to dedicate himself to the study of theology and to discern his call to the ministry.

This is not an easy time for Steve. The change from bank life to seminary life is very demanding on him. Although he enjoys his studies very much, he regrets that he has so little time left for personal reading, art, and mostly friendship.

Moreover he has to go through many hoops: psychological testing, psychotherapy, and endless interviews to qualify as a candidate for ministry. Listening to him I realized that I would never have made it to my ordination if I had been subjected, in my time, to the battery of tests they are subjecting Steve to today.

We talked long hours about vocation, competency, church work, future possibilities, and so on. Most important to me was that Steve is very glad to have left his bank job and loves his studies. What will come from it is hard to say. I kept saying, "Be sure that you love the life you're living now, your studies, your prayers, your friendships.... Then you can trust that God will reveal to you the direction to go when the time comes. But don't try to know now what you only have to know a few years from now."

I hope and pray that I can be of support to Steve in the years ahead. Steve took a risk by embarking on a road he doesn't know much about. But I feel that it is a beautifully inspired risk, worth taking. I am grateful that Steve put his trust in God, and not in a secure but basically unsatisfying job. I am convinced that one day his decision will bear many fruits.

New York, Wednesday, October 18

After returning by train to New York City, I went to see my editor Bill at Doubleday to discuss the publication of the Winnipeg journal. It is the journal that I wrote during my depression in the winter and spring of 1988 while receiving spiritual therapy in Winnipeg. Bill had shown great interest in the journal right after I returned to Daybreak in the summer of '88, but I still felt too emotionally fragile and wasn't ready to share those experiences with my readers. Things have changed, though, and now I think that the journal can be of help to people who experience pain similar to what I went through seven years ago.

Bill's office, on the fourteenth floor of the Bertelsmann Building, over-looks Times Square, with its huge advertisements and neon signs. Talking about my journal on depression while looking at the world's center of entertainment gave me a weird feeling in my stomach. "It's quite gaudy," Bill said, "especially after dark with all the gold, blue, green, purple, and yellow lights twisting and turning.... But it is the heart of New York all right." Exciting and sickening at the same time, I thought. Maybe I should write a book about depression behind these windows!

When I returned to Wendy and Jay's apartment, Wendy said, "I bought two tickets for Carmen, tonight at the Metropolitan Opera. Jay and Jon are both out tonight, and I thought we could see Carmen together." I was delighted since I had never seen Carmen, and going to the Met was certainly the best possible introduction to this famous piece of music, song, and drama.

Although I went with the prejudice that operas are most often a combination of good music and a bad story, I became completely absorbed by the drama of Carmen. Carmen was sung and acted by Denyce Graves. Her portrayal of the sensual, seductive, self-confident, fatalistic gypsy woman opened up in me the real tension between faith and fate, the obedient life and the "wild" life, agape and eros, and Christianity and paganism.

In Carmen, José, the Spanish soldier in Seville who has to obey his military superiors and cannot let "love" distract him, stands for many of us dutiful men and women who feel that life kills our vitality. Carmen's irresistible energy enlarges José's life but finally, destroying them both, represents us as people who want to break away from the constraints of normalcy but hesitate to pay the price.

Can the tension be resolved in an integrated life? Can the "wild person" in us be tamed without the cost of losing our vitality and creativity? Many forms of meditation, Buddhist as well as Christian, strive for this integration. I do not believe that we have to repress our erotic energies in order to live ordered lives. Nor do I believe that we have to give up order and discipline in order to get in touch with the wild energies of existence. But it certainly requires concentrated effort to find our own unique ways to become whole people. The literature and art of the West show that few have accomplished this wholeness. I certainly have not. I don't know what would happen if a Carmen barged into my life and swept me off my feet.

Watertown, Thursday, October 19

An in-between day! I am between the exciting time in New York and a promising weekend in Boston.

It feels good to be back in my cozy apartment. There was mail and many telephone messages, but after a few hours of responding to it all I was back behind my table writing in my journal and my museum notebook.

Tomorrow Nathan and Sue will come for the weekend. They are coming as friends but also as accompaniers, helping me to live my sabbatical well. I am looking forward to their visit. I'd better get everything ready! I have to buy food, get the apartment in shape, and plan with Jonas and Margaret the details of their stay.

A great and happy surprise is that Borys, with whom Nathan, Sue, and I spent several weeks in Ukraine, happens to be in Boston and will join us all tomorrow morning. There will be a lot to talk about.

Friday, October 20

This afternoon at 4:00 Jonas, Margaret, Sam, Jonas's brother Steve, Steve's six-year-old, Luke, and I went to the circus.

I was very happy for the opportunity to see the Ringling Brothers, Barnum & Bailey "Greatest Show on Earth," since my more than four-year-old friendship with the trapeze group the Flying Rodleighs has made me a great circus fan.

For me the three-ring circus of Ringling Brothers, Barnum & Bailey, where so much is going on at the same time, prevents any kind of personal relationship with the performers. They are reduced from very talented people to spectacular movements and colorful forms. I missed the intimacy of the one-ring tent circus of Simoneit-Barum in Germany. When I saw the Flying Rodleighs there, I was moved not only by their aerial act but also by their spirits. I wanted to know them personally and become more intimately connected with their lives. This afternoon I was impressed, overwhelmed, awestruck, et cetera, but never really moved. I was forced to forget that these people in front of me were human beings like I am. They had become parts of a huge magic machine called the circus.

I wondered how Sam and Luke would respond to it. They sat with glazed eyes looking at it all, but they never laughed or got excited. Sam crawled onto Margaret's lap and said that he was tired. I don't blame him!

There was one moment when I got "caught." It was when one man performed a one-armed handstand on the head of his partner, who kept two freestanding stilts in balance on a platform thirty feet above the arena floor. I could see them so well because our seats were right in front of their act. I could see the first man's open, smiling face and his straining, muscular body, which radiated so much vitality and energy. I felt a connection. But then they vanished in the large anonymity of the show. It was an important moment for me though, short as it was, because I recognized within me the same emotion that caught me when I first saw the Flying Rodleighs. It was the emotion that made me take the risk of introducing myself to them and that has led to a long and rich friendship. This act and the men performing it were like a flash of light in the darkness, a recognition, a memory, and an inner connection full of melancholy.

Saturday, October 21

Sue and Nathan are here. We are having a very good and peaceful day together, talking about my little life here, about Daybreak, and about the things that are ahead of us. Their friendship and support are a real gift to me.

At lunchtime Borys arrived. It was a joyful reunion. Borys was full of stories about his year of studies in Rome, his work as a vice rector of the new theological academy in L'viv, the editing of his book on the Union of Brest, and his personal joys and pains. Jonas also joined us for lunch. Borys and Jonas had heard a lot about each other through me but had never met. I was glad to finally see them together.

Sunday, October 22

At 2:00 p.m. Jonas and I dropped Sue and Nathan off at Logan Airport. It was a very good visit. My many plans to show them the Boston Common, take them to Harvard Divinity School, where I spent three years, go with them to a concert of the Boston Symphony, and offer them a nice dinner in a special restaurant all came to nothing! We just stayed home, enjoyed the apartment, talked, and talked and talked! Nathan went out shopping and cooked a wonderful dinner for us all.

I am glad that we didn't do much. It was a blessing just to be together and enjoy our friendship. This morning we celebrated the Sunday Eucharist in the Empty Bell, with Jonas and nine visitors. A prayerful and peaceful time. After breakfast we read a little, talked a little, and prayed a little. Then we left for the airport.

Nothing very unexpected, nothing spectacular, nothing very emotional. Just solid, good, lasting friendship lived well.

Monday, October 23

This was not a very good day for me. After my trip to New York and Philadelphia and after Nathan and Sue's visit, I have only one desire — to go back to my writing. For more than a week I had not worked on my book on the cup, and much of the quiet rhythm of my life here has been lost.

Borys asked if he could stay with me for a few days, since the place he was staying is noisy and restless. And he wanted to talk a little more about his life and work and get some feedback. He also just enjoys our friendship and wants to deepen it. Jonas reminded me of my not having been at the health club for a while and expected me to go with him. Meanwhile the galleys of his book about Rebecca have arrived, and Robert Heller, his editor, wants me to have a foreword ready in a week. George Strohmeyer, the priest from L'Arche Erie, called to discuss a plan for a conference for all pastoral ministers in L'Arche North America. The mail was heavy with invitations and requests for foreign translations.

It all was good but too much! Everything, even the best of things, became a distraction. I just couldn't get to my table to work on the cup book and became quite irritated and depressed. Poor Borys got the brunt of it! I nearly made him feel guilty for being here, while I couldn't think of anyone I would rather be with than him.

A moment of joy was the arrival of the first copy of the new hardcover edition of *The Return of the Prodigal Son*. It is good to see this book again in its original beauty. Werner Linz of Continuum was able to buy the hardcover rights from Doubleday and republished the book. Doubleday continues to sell the paperback. When I opened the book I read the dedication: "To my father, Laurent Jean Marie Nouwen, for his ninetieth birthday." I wrote that dedication more than half a year before my father's actual birthday, which was on January 3, 1993. At that time I wondered if I wasn't taking a risk. Yesterday when I spoke to him by phone he was full of enthusiasm about my visit at Christmastime and our plan to make a trip to Freiburg together. He said, "We can go between Christmas and my ninety-third birthday. You can go ahead and make the reservations for the train and the hotel."

Well, many reasons for gratitude, even on a frustrating day!

Wednesday, October 25

The fiftieth anniversary of the United Nations is bringing many of the political leaders of the world to the United States. The sensitivities are complex, protocol nearly unmanageable, security a nightmare, transportation causing long delays, and accommodations overbooked. The overall mood seems quite pessimistic. The UN, after fifty years, has become a huge bureaucracy without much vision, bogged down in endless diplomatic problems. Still, it is one of the few organizations that has the potential for creating peace on our planet and preventing it from being destroyed by human greed and revenge.

Compared with all the diplomatic maneuvering this week, Pope John Paul II's visit a few weeks ago seems like an unusually prophetic event.

I pray for world peace tonight.

Thursday, October 26

A full day of writing: five short reflections about being a wounded healer, a chapter in the cup book on lifting up your life for others, and a five-page meditation on unconditional love for my friend Joan, in San Diego. At 6:00 p.m. Borys appeared for dinner and talked about his busy time in Cambridge trying to finish his book and meet several people before returning to Europe.

Friday, October 27

Most of this day I spent working on the foreword to Jonas's book, *Rebecca: A Father's Journey from Grief to Gratitude*. Yesterday I had a short "interview" with Jonas, and this morning I wrote the text. I was very glad to make this little contribution to Jonas's first book, especially since I feel so connected with Jonas and with his grief for Rebecca, who was born prematurely on July 29, 1992. She lived three hours and forty-four minutes and then died in Jonas's arms. At that time I was in France. I still remember Jonas telling me by phone about Rebecca's birth and death. His grief was immense, but his willingness to let his pain lead him to gratitude was there also from the very beginning.

Later I suggested to Jonas that he write about Rebecca. He had always hoped to be a writer. Rebecca's short life, I said, could make him one. It is such a joy to see the fruit of deep grief and the product of hard work.

What struck me most was that this book can be read in two ways. It can be read as the senseless attempt of a father trying at all costs to give meaning to a meaningless event. But it can also be read as a glorious witness to the mystery that we are citizens of heaven, from where we expect our Savior, the Lord Jesus Christ, to transform the body of our humiliation into the body of his glory (see Phil 3:20–21). When one chooses, with Jonas, to see God's glory in the midst of the immense human grief, this book can truly give great hope.

Rebecca lived only three hours and forty-four minutes. She was too fragile, too little to open her eyes. But Jonas's great spiritual vision allowed him to see that the value of life is not dependent on the hours, days, or years it is lived, nor on the number of people it was connected to, nor on the impact it had on human history. Jonas "saw" that the value of life is life itself and that the few hours of Rebecca's life were as worthy to be lived as the many hours of the lives of Beethoven, Chagall, Gandhi, yes, even Jesus.

I feel privileged to be part of this remarkable and hope-giving book, in which sorrow leads to joy and grief to gratitude.

Saturday, October 28

Will Quebec break away from Canada? That's the question that will find an answer next Monday, when Quebecers will vote on a referendum deciding whether to remain part of the Federation of Provinces or go its own way.

Until a few days ago the U.S. papers showed little interest in the referendum. I guess the reason is that nobody seriously expected a separation. But recently the polls have suggested otherwise. A breakaway by Quebec is a real possibility.

I spoke to Nathan by phone this afternoon, and I was surprised to hear him say that a yes vote for separation might not be such a drama as many people think. It might, he said, wake up the several parties and provincial governments and lead to a better Canada. He supports unity but is not so afraid of separation.

I have no strong opinion, although I spontaneously think that maintaining Canadian unity is better than a divided Canada. On the other hand, a separation might lead to a situation not dissimilar to that in Belgium, where the French- and Dutch-speaking populations have separate governments while remaining one country.

I wonder if at the last moment the majority will not vote for the status quo, simply out of fear about an uncertain future. We will know soon.

Sunday, October 29

A year ago today, my friend Ted lost his wife, Nancy, and yesterday afternoon another friend, Fred, lost his dearest childhood friend, Jim. During my time at Yale Divinity School I had come to know Nancy as a gracious, warm, energetic, and very loving woman, and during the last few weeks I heard a lot about Jim's spiritual courage and faithfulness.

This morning we celebrated the Eucharist at the Empty Bell in memory of these two special people. Ted was there. Also Michael, my friend and former assistant at Harvard Divinity School, came with his wife, Marta, and their six-year-old-twins, Andrés and Nicolás.

It was a very peaceful celebration. The readings spoke about praying with humility and confidence. The sentence that most touched me was from the Book of Sirach: "The prayer of the humble pierces the clouds, and it will not rest until it reaches its goal; it will not desist until the Most High responds and does justice for the righteous" (Si 35:21). I experienced our prayers in communion with Nancy and Jim as prayers piercing the clouds, and my spirit was convinced that God was taking notice of us.

After the Eucharist Ted, Michael, Marta, Andrés, and Nicolás came to the apartment for coffee and cake. During the Eucharist the boys generously helped me with giving the cup to everyone present, and afterwards Nicolás made several drawings for me with Jesus on the cross, candles, angels, and stars. It was a time rich with memories. Nancy and Jim had died, but the two boys reminded us of the exuberance and resilience of life. What gentle and affectionate children they are!

At 6:00 p.m. I called Fred in Pittsburgh to tell him about our prayers for Jim. He told me that he had just played on his piano all the songs he and Jim used to sing together. It was his way of mourning. He was truly grateful for my call.

On a day like this I marvel over the great gift of friendship.

Tuesday, October 31

With 50.6 percent no and 49.4 percent yes, Quebec will stay in the Canadian Federation. This is a victory for those who wanted to preserve Canadian unity, but a very fragile victory. Much suffering is becoming visible. The great division in Quebec between those who want to separate from Canada and those who don't will need to be addressed in the coming years in a creative and healing way. Jean Chrétien, the prime minister of the federal government, will have to work hard to ease the tension. If nothing changes in the relationship between Quebec and the federal government, there will soon be another referendum, in which the percentages might be reversed.

November 1995

Cancún, Mexico, Wednesday, November 1

I am on my way to Cancún, Mexico. At 6:30 this morning, I left from Logan Airport in Boston to fly to Dallas. In Dallas I will meet Joe and Nathan from Daybreak, who are flying to Dallas from Toronto, as well as Malcolm, a friend from Fort Worth, Texas, who encouraged me to accept the invitation to come to Cancún.

What's going on in Cancún? A three-day meeting of The Gathering, an evangelical support network for philanthropists, who come together once a year to support and encourage one another in their philanthropic work and to discuss how to give in the spirit of the Gospel. In order to be "eligible" for The Gathering, each member must be a major donor to a charitable organization.

When I was first invited to speak to this meeting, I hesitated, since it was during my sabbatical and I also wasn't sure if I had anything special to say to philanthropists. I asked Nathan and Joe to come with me so that we could speak together from our experience in community. Now that I am flying to Dallas, I feel quite excited about this adventure.

Jesus' words "You cannot serve God and wealth" are the guideline of those we will meet in Cancún. I wonder what our contribution to this wisdom can be. Most important for me is that I can speak as a member of a community where the poor form the center. I am so glad that Nathan and Joe will be there with me.

Thursday, November 2

Here we are at the very luxurious Ritz-Carlton Hotel, with three restaurants, two large outdoor swimming pools, a large reception area, huge ballrooms, wide, curving staircases, great glittering chandeliers, and many little shops with very expensive items. All of it looks out on the blue, sun-washed Caribbean Sea.

The Mexican personnel are extremely friendly. They all are English-speaking young men and women, obviously very well trained in their jobs. Their most used expression is "my pleasure." They say it so often and with such a sympathetic Mexican accent that it starts sounding like a sacred mantra.

Last night at 6:30 Nathan, Joe, Malcolm, and I celebrated the All Saints Eucharist. It was a very intimate, prayerful celebration. We prayed for many people, living and dead. Then at 11:00 a.m. today we celebrated the All Souls liturgy and prayed for all family and friends who had died and for all the victims of violence, war, cancer, and AIDS.

After dinner The Gathering began with an opening address entitled "A Call for Hilarious Generosity." It was a very funny and entertaining talk about the joy of living and the joy of giving, with many anecdotes and some good biblical reflections.

Tomorrow morning I will give my first Bible study. I plan to speak about the story of the multiplication of bread. Against my expectation, I am quite nervous about it. I pray that I can be focused on Jesus and not too concerned about what everyone thinks or says.

I am very, very tired, which is hard to explain in such a beautiful setting. But I feel a certain homesickness for my quiet writing table in the home of Jonas and Margaret.

Friday, November 3

My morning reflections on the story of the multiplication of bread seemed to be well received. I spoke about compassion, scarcity, gifts, abundance, and solitude, following the different moments in the story, and I tried to show what it means to also give ourselves to others. The main idea was that our gifts, small as they may seem, become great by being recognized as God's gifts for God's people. When we refrain from giving, with a scarcity mentality, the little we have will become less. When we give generously, with an abundance mentality, what we give away will multiply. But as that happens people want to make us kings or queens! Then we have to go back into solitude to listen there to the voice of God, who calls us the beloved.

The rest of the day was quiet. I worked on my reflection for tomorrow. Nathan, Joe, Malcolm, and I celebrated the Eucharist in my room and discussed the outline for the talk.

Saturday, November 4

A very full day. I was mostly preoccupied with my own presentation. This morning my talk was about the text of John 21:15–19: "Do you love me? . . . Feed my sheep. . . . Somebody else will . . . take you where you would rather not go." Malcolm read the text, Nathan sang some songs in between the sections of the talk, and Joe told us the story of Zenia and Rose. People appeared to be very moved, and they responded from their hearts. Since the main speaker of the morning had to cancel, we had a longer time, and there was more opportunity to share together and to take time to absorb the message.

The rest of the day I spent preparing for the evening presentation: "Can You Drink the Cup?" Since I have been writing about this question during the last month, my problem was not ideas or materials but simplification. I had quite a struggle to keep it simple, direct, and penetrating, and not get lost in interesting but irrelevant details.

The talk went well, although I was less happy with it than with the two Bible studies. Too long, and maybe too much material. I hadn't simplified enough. But Joe's and Nathan's songs were very uplifting and the short period of responses from the audience very affirming.

We have enjoyed meeting and getting to know the participants of the conference. Our conversations have been lively, with much mutual questioning. It is clear that each of us is searching for spiritual insight and meaning. Joe, Nathan, and I have learned a lot about The Gathering and about foundation work, but mostly we have met and befriended some very wonderful and beautiful people.

During the afternoon Jonas called to tell me that the prime minister of Israel, Yitzhak Rabin, had been assassinated after a peace rally in Tel Aviv, by a right-wing law student. I felt a deep inner pain when I heard this tragic news. A peacemaker murdered. A brave man, brave in war as well as in peace, brutally shot by a fellow Jew. A leader who had the courage to risk his popularity by signing a peace agreement with Yasir Arafat, suddenly cut down by a man who thinks that God has commanded him to stop the peace process between Israelis and Palestinians. I pray tonight for Yitzhak and his family, for the people of Israel who are mourning, and for peace.

Sunday, November 5

This morning our host, Bob, suggested that the three of us stay at the hotel until we returned to Boston and Toronto on Wednesday. We had planned to go to the small town Playa del Carmen to relax a bit after the conference and to see a little of Mexican life outside the Ritz-Carlton. But Bob wanted to offer this to us as a gift, and he said that it would save us a lot of time and energy if we did not have to travel and move. I sensed that Bob and his wife, Linda, wanted to get to know us better and deepen the friendship that had grown between us during the past few days. We made the decision to listen to our friend's advice and to accept his gift.

Later, Nathan, Joe, and I took a bus to downtown Cancún. We soon realized that it is primarily one long shopping center for tourists. We did find a nice little restaurant and ate our first real Mexican food. It was a very pleasant evening.

Monday, November 6

At 7:00 a.m. I watched the funeral of Premier Rabin on CNN. A deeply moving sight. Political leaders from all over the world were present. I pray that Yitzhak Rabin's violent death will bring a new unity to Israel and give a new momentum to peace in the Middle East. I think about Jesus' words "Unless a grain of wheat falls into the earth and dies, it remains just a single grain; but if it dies, it bears much fruit" (Jn 12:24). As I saw the deep grief of Rabin's wife, Leah, and his children and granddaughter, I was hoping that their tears will become like rain on the barren desert, making it bloom with new life.

At 9:00 a.m. Bob and Linda took Nathan, Joe, and me on a day trip to see the Mayan Ceremonial Center in Tulum and to snorkel at the natural aquarium Xel-Há.

It was a wonderful day. I was deeply moved by the Mayan ruins. The Mayan culture was very sophisticated. I left the place quite overwhelmed by the thought that such a rich culture could have been so completely destroyed by intertribal wars and finally by the Spanish conquerors. The rest of the day was pleasant and playful. Nathan, Joe, and I snorkeled at the natural aquarium and saw beautiful fish crossing our path and moving around the rock formations under the water's surface.

I am grateful for the care and generosity of Linda and Bob and for the wonderful day we had together.

Tuesday, November 7

Our last day in Cancún! At 12:30 we said farewell to Bob and Linda, thanking them for their generosity and friendship.

After their departure we celebrated the Eucharist together and had lunch on the terrace of the hotel. Nathan suggested I ride in one of the parachutes that are pulled by little motorboats, taking you high up above the hotels and giving you a grand view of the Cancún area. I said that I would go if we could go together. Three Mexican boys running the off-shore operation strapped us in our "seats," put on our swimming vests, made us bend our knees while holding tight to our straps, and waved to the motorboat to pull us up. A few seconds later we were hanging in the sky! Nice breeze, nice view, nice sensation. The boat pulled us above the beach and the water for about fifteen minutes. As we returned we missed our landing spot, and we saw the boys waving and telling us to pull our red flag to steer the parachute to the beach. But we didn't make it and ended up in the rolling waves. The boys ran out to disentangle us from all the ropes, vests, and straps and lead us back to the beach.

We had a big laugh about our wet landing. The boys wanted some extra money for helping us with the safe landing, but Nathan and Joe felt we had paid them enough.

At 6:00 p.m. we went to downtown Cancún to buy some gifts and have another Mexican dinner to conclude our Mexican stay.

Watertown, Wednesday, November 8

On the plane to Dallas, we spoke a little about my future role in Day-break. I raised the question of whether it might be better for me not to return to Daybreak as its pastor but to come back without any specific obligations to the community, so that I would be free to write and to do formation work for different L'Arche communities. It was just the beginning of a conversation that probably will continue in the months ahead.

At the Dallas-Fort Worth Airport we said good-bye. Joe and Nathan flew on to Toronto and I to Boston.

I look back on this trip with great gratitude. It was an exciting and, I hope, also a fruitful experience. We received much and we gave something too! But most of all it was a truly shared experience. Going together made it something we will often bring back to mind and think of with pleasure.

By 11:00 p.m. I was back at my cozy apartment. It feels good to be "home" again.

Friday, November 10

As I started to write again today, I realized that The Gathering had raised new questions in my mind about mission, evangelization, conversion, witness, and so on. Many of the people I met in Cancún believe that without an explicit personal profession of faith in Jesus as our Lord and Savior, we cannot make it to heaven. They are convinced that God has called us to convert every human being to Jesus.

This vision inspires much generosity, commitment, and a great world-wide project. Not a few of the men and women we met had traveled far and wide, put their lives and health in danger, given large parts of their personal income, and taken many financial risks. Their love for Jesus is deep, intense, and radical. They spoke about Jesus fearlessly and were pre-pared for rejection and ridicule. They are very committed disciples, not hesitant to pay the cost of their discipleship.

Still...I felt somewhat uncomfortable, even though this belief was present in my own upbringing. My conviction as a young man was that there is no salvation outside the Catholic Church and that it was my task to bring all "nonbelievers" into the one true church.

But much has happened to me over the years. My own psycholog-ical training, my exposure to people from the most different religious backgrounds, the Second Vatican Council, the new theology of mis-sion, and my life in L'Arche have all deepened and broadened my views on Jesus' saving work. Today I personally believe that while Jesus came to open the door to God's house, all human beings can walk through that door, whether they know about Jesus or not. Today I see it as my call to help every person claim his or her own way to God. I feel deeply called to witness for Jesus as the one who is the source of my own spiritual journey and thus create the possibility for other people to know Jesus and commit themselves to him. I am so truly convinced that the Spirit of God is present in our midst and that each person can be touched by God's Spirit in ways far beyond my own comprehension and intention.

I am using my little daily reflections to articulate my own theology of evangelization, mission, salvation, and redemption. I am very grateful for my time at The Gathering. It forces me to think through my own religious convictions.

Sunday, November 19

The Eucharist this morning with Jonas and his prayer group at the Empty Bell was very vibrant and alive.

In the Gospel Jesus says, "Beware that you are not led astray; for many will come in my name and say, 'I am he!' and 'The time is near!' Do not go after them.... Nation will rise against nation, and kingdom against kingdom ... there will be dreadful portents. ... They will arrest you and persecute you. ... This will give you an opportunity to testify. So make up your minds not to prepare your defense in advance; for I will give you words and a wisdom that none of your opponents will be able to withstand or contradict. ... You will be hated by all because of my name. But not a hair of your head will perish. By your endurance you will gain your souls" (Lk 21:8–19).

What a powerful and hopeful word! Life with all its turmoil is an opportunity to witness to God's love! And our witness will be irresistible when we realize that God keeps us completely safe.

The many events of life so easily pull us in all directions and make us lose our souls. But when we remain anchored in the heart of God, rooted in God's love, we have nothing to fear, not even death, and everything joyful and everything painful will give us a chance to proclaim the Kingdom of Jesus.

Different people in the circle spoke and shared their faith and their hope. Then we prayed together and received the Body and Blood of Jesus. We are called to be fearless people in a fearful world.

Monday, November 20

A very quiet, peaceful day. Writing, reading, going to the health club with Jonas, sleeping, and making some phone calls.

One of the calls was to a longtime friend, Timothy, who is married to Phyllis and who has three young children. He is a religion teacher at a Catholic high school and an accomplished guitarist and singer, and he has written many liturgical songs with his friend Paul. He loves Jesus, Mary, and the saints, and he is a man filled with the Spirit of God.

About a year ago Timothy was told that he had liver cancer, and so he started chemotherapy. Now he is quite weak and wonders how long he has to live. Recently he made a pilgrimage to Lourdes with Phyllis. He found much hope and courage there to live this illness as part of his spiritual journey.

It was so good to talk to Tim again. He is such a man of faith. In the midst of all his suffering he speaks about his illness as a "privilege," a grace from God, a blessing calling him closer to the heart of Jesus. No sentimentality, no sweet piety, but deep, strong faith. When he speaks about Jesus and Mary, his voice brims over with love and gratitude.

What a saintly man! What a joy to have him as a friend!

Tuesday, November 21

Tired, tired, tired. I really do not know why. I got up at 6:00 a.m., prayed, celebrated the Eucharist, and wrote until noon. But all the time I felt listless, distracted, and slightly depressed.

Timothy's sickness, perhaps? The intense week in Cancún? Or just a lack of vitamins (which I forgot to take for two weeks!)? I don't know.

I went to bed at two after a luncheon with Jonas in Belmont and slept for three hours.

After writing six cards, reading *The New York Times Book Review*, and praying for all my friends who are in pain, especially Timothy, I called it a day.

Wednesday, November 22

This morning the local florist brought a beautiful flower arrangement. It was a Thanksgiving greeting from my friend, Joan. Besides some large sunflowers, there were some shining apples in the piece. I feel happy to be remembered and grateful for friendship.

A little card was added by the florist saying, "Do not eat the fruit!" Was this a reminder of paradise? It made me think of Adam and Eve in the Garden of Eden.

Later I went shopping at the nearby market. After I had paid, I wanted to fill out a form to get one of their "advantage" cards. When I finally came to the exit and looked at my shopping cart, I noticed some articles that I didn't remember buying. Then I realized that in my absentmindedness I had taken someone else's cart. Just then a store attendant and a lady came running up to me. For a moment I felt like a big thief. Luckily the rightful owner saw the humor of the situation and was just happy to have her own turkeys back!

When I came home there were more flowers . . . from Kathy and Margaret at the office in Toronto. No apples this time! I found a large vase and made a splendid bouquet. Quite a day.

Tonight Jutta is coming, and she, Jonas, my friend Vincent, and I are going to listen to Bernard Haitink conduct the Boston Symphony in Mozart and Ravel. I am very much looking forward to it. Tomorrow is Thanksgiving Day.

Thursday, November 23

Today I am staying home to write, pray, and rest. I wondered whether I should join a friend for Thanksgiving dinner, but I finally realized that the best thing for me to do would be to be quietly at home. Jonas, Margaret, and Sam left for a few days in Vermont, so I am alone in the big house. I enjoy the immense quiet, no lawn mowers, shouting kids, or garbage trucks, just complete silence.

In the silence I keep hearing the splendid music of Mozart and Ravel that was played last night. Seldom have I attended such a deeply satisfying concert. Jutta, Vincent, Jonas, and I enjoyed every minute of it. Bernard Haitink conducted the Thirty-third Symphony and the Twenty-second Piano Concerto of Mozart as well as Ravel's *Mother Goose Suite* and his *Rapsodie Espagnole.*

Although all the music captivated me, the piano concerto with Robert Levin at the piano will remain with me the longest time. The Andante and the Finale brought tears to my eyes.

When I came home I read for nearly an hour in Maynard Solomon's new book, *Mozart: A Life*. Music so harmonious, enchanting, and exhilarating, a life so painful, melancholy, and deeply tragic!

Today on Thanksgiving, I thank God for Wolfgang Amadeus Mozart.

But I also thank God for the Bosnian peace accord that was reached in Dayton, Ohio, two days ago.

Is peace going to hold? There may be more chance than ever since all the parties are exhausted from the war, since a cold winter is approaching and people are starving, since there is an enormous need for foreign aid to rebuild a depleted, devastated country, and since no one has much chance to win a better deal. But underneath all the peace talks there is much hatred and resentment, and many hard-to-forget cruelties. Will the leaders who signed the agreements bring their commanders, armies, and people to implement their peace plans?

I am also thinking of my friend Frank, who has volunteered to go to Bosnia with the peacekeeping troops. I hope he will be called to go. He wants to support the peace there and feels more needed in Bosnia than at home. I pray for him tonight.

Friday, November 24

Jean Vanier often told me that I should write about the church, but I never have, at least not directly. I always have experienced a deep inner resistance to writing about the church because it seemed like a field full of thorn bushes. I guess I fear that I will become entrapped, and for that reason I have been avoiding it until today.

After writing several reflections about baptism and the Eucharist, I spontaneously started to write about the church as the community of people fashioned by these two sacraments. Once I entered the subject that way, I discovered there was a lot to think about and reflect upon.

I love the church. I do not want to write about the church as a problem, a source of conflict, a place of controversies, but as the Body of Christ for us here and now.

It has been a very quiet day. No distractions. In the afternoon I fell asleep for three hours. I still do not understand why I keep being so exhausted after six hours of praying, reading, and writing. But I guess I have to do what the Beatles say, "Let It Be."

Tonight I will let my curiosity get the better of me and watch Barbara Walters's interview with Princess Diana about her failed marriage to Prince Charles.

Saturday, November 25

I have been watching on TV *The Beatles Anthology* and Barbara Walters's interview with Princess Diana. Both were fascinating programs because both showed in a very convincing way how the human heart craves love and acceptance even in the midst of great wealth and popularity.

In *The Beatles Anthology* I was most struck by the self-doubts of the drummer, Ringo Starr. When he was temporarily replaced because of an illness, he wondered whether he would be welcome again. Later, when he thought he was no longer good enough to belong to the band and told John, Paul, and George that he was leaving, they had to fill his house with flowers to convince him that he was deeply loved and respected and the best drummer around!

Princess Diana's too is the story of a person in search of love and acceptance. The main struggle of this most photographed woman in the world is with self-esteem. She suffered from depression, bulimia, and self-afflicted wounds, and she gave in to an adulterous relationship — all of this while trying to come to a sense of being loved for who she is.

The interview with Diana shows a woman who has grown strong through all these pains and has become a mature, self-confident person willing to put her many painful experiences in the service of others. I was very impressed by Diana's inner strength, strong conviction, clear purpose, and relative freedom from bitterness after her separation from Prince Charles.

Both the story of the Beatles and the story of Diana make it overwhelmingly clear that human happiness has little to do with money, success, or popularity but everything to do with friendship, love, and a purpose in life.

Sunday, November 26

The Feast of Christ the King. On the last Sunday of the liturgical year, Christ is presented to us as the mocked King on the cross as well as the King of the universe. The greatest humiliation and the greatest victory are both shown to us in today's liturgy.

It is important to look at this humiliated and victorious Christ before we start the new liturgical year with the celebration of Advent. All through the year we have to stay close to the humiliation as well as to the victory of Christ, because we are called to live both in our own daily lives. We are small *and* big, specks in the universe *and* the glory of God, little fearful people *and* sons and daughters of the Lord of all creation.

The great surprise of this day was the visit of Kevin, a friend I got to know in California, who had come to celebrate Thanksgiving and his birthday with his parents in Boston. It was wonderful to see him and spend some time with him. Our conversation was personal and intimate and — I trust — life-giving for both of us.

After Kevin left I found the energy to write ten short meditations on the communion of saints. I know that Kevin's visit had a lot to do with that.

Tuesday, November 28

Last night I got stuck in my writing. I was trying to reflect on the resurrection of Jesus and on our resurrection. I reflected myself into a corner, not knowing how to articulate that, on the one hand, our bodies will return to "dust" while, on the other hand, nothing we have lived in the body will go to waste.

When I sat down to write again this morning, I didn't know where to go with my thoughts. Then I saw that Paul raises my very question when he asks rhetorically, "How are dead people raised, and what sort of body do they have?" He answers with unwavering conviction, "How foolish!

What you sow must die before it is given new life, and what you sow is not the body that is to be, but only a bare grain, of wheat I dare say, or some other kind; it is God who gives it the sort of body that he has chosen for it" (1 Cor 15:35–38).

This answer really woke me up! It was as if I heard it for the very first time. Our life is a seed that has to die to be dressed with immortality! Things suddenly came together and started to make sense, spiritual sense. From then on my pen could hardly stop moving.

When I called Kathy this morning, she told me that Carrie and Geoff, members of Daybreak and dear friends, had their baby, David Friend; he was born last night at 7:00. A healthy boy, a brother for Janet and Monica, a new joy for everyone in the community.

At 3:30 p.m. Kathy called to tell me that Robin, former director of Daybreak, married to Joan and father of Emily, Laura, and Elaine, had been hospitalized with a serious heart problem. I immediately tried to reach Joan, which wasn't possible. Then I called Joe to get some more information. Joe said that Robin's condition is serious and told me he would call when he knew more.

How fragile is life. I pray for David Friend and Robin. May God embrace them both in tender love.

Wednesday, November 29

When I started to write my reflections for every day of the year, I had no outline or plan. I simply wrote what came to mind on the day I was writing. In the beginning I wrote about things I have written about often before. But as I continued I found myself choosing subjects that I never thought I would write about, such as baptism, the Eucharist, the church, the resurrection, heaven and hell. Very basic themes. Today I wrote about hell! After having written so much about God's love, God's mercy, God's all-embracing kindness, I found myself faced with strong words about hell. When I read the beautiful words about the New Heaven and the New Earth in the Book of Revelation, I also came across the words "the legacy for cowards, for those who break their word, or worship obscenities, for murderers and the sexually immoral, and for sorcerers, worshippers of false gods or any other sort of liars, is the second death in the burning lake of sulphur" (Rev 21:8).

Just as there is an eternal life, there is an eternal death, the second death. Hell is eternal death. Is this a possibility for me, for us? I felt a real resistance in me to saying yes to that question, but Jesus and his apostles give me no way out here. Eternal death is as possible as eternal life! God offers us a choice. To say yes or no to love. To offer me a choice is to respect me as a free human person. I am no robot or automaton who has no choice. God, who loves me in freedom, wants my love in freedom. That means that no is a possibility. Eternal life is not a predetermined fact. It is the fruit of our human response.

Jonas and I went to the health club again today. I have really started to enjoy my little routine there: twenty minutes on the trotter, a few laps in the swimming pool, and a steam bath. I come home from it refreshed, and we always have good conversations. I also read a little bit on the edge of the swimming pool. Today I read some of Christopher de Vinck's lovely stories in his latest book, *Simple Wonders: A Book of Meditations*. His words are good for my heart.

Thursday, November 30

This morning I had a very good meeting with Susan, a friend of Jonas who works as a freelance book editor. I had met Susan several times at the Sunday morning Eucharist, and Jonas had encouraged me to ask her whether she would be interested in doing some editing work for me.

As we talked I became excited about the prospect of working with Susan. She has much experience in editing, a great interest in spirituality, and she has time! She told me that she had no major editing commitments for January. By that time I will have two manuscripts ready for her to work with. I am so glad that this is all coming together so nicely.

When I called Kathy at 1:30 p.m. she told me that Conrad, my former editor in Toronto, had died this morning. Conrad had had several strokes during the last year and had become increasingly weak. Recently he had lost his ability to communicate.

Although I knew that Conrad was dying, his death still came as a shock to me. We worked together on many manuscripts, and his name is on the acknowledgment pages of all the books I have written since 1987. He was a former priest who lived a very simple life in a home for recovering alcoholics. He was a saintly man with a great love for the poor, a true faithfulness to friends, a wonderful sense of humor, a great gift for language, and a solid commitment to the spiritual life. I feel deeply grateful for all he did for me, with so much love and dedication.

I am sad that I cannot be at his funeral on Monday, but I am very glad that Kathy is going. Both Kathy and Connie, my former secretary, had very friendly relationships with him.

Tonight I pray for him and thank God for his life and our friendship. I guess I should also thank God for giving me a new editor on the same day that he called Conrad home.

December 1995

Friday, December 1

The most important event of this day was finishing my reflections for every day of the year. I filled my last museum notebook today with number 387. Although even in a leap year there are only 366 days, I wrote some extra meditations that can be used in place of those that are repetitive or poorly written.

I was quite relieved when the Federal Express man came to pick up this last notebook to send it to Kathy in Toronto. I feel pleased with what I wrote, especially over the last few months. Writing these reflections has definitely strengthened my love for Jesus and renewed my commitment to proclaim the unfathomable mystery of God's saving work.

The rest of the day I spent writing letters and reading a little. Tomorrow I will start editing and correcting the cup book.

Saturday, December 2

Today's *New York Times* had an article about Sen. Mark Hatfield's retirement. At yesterday's hospital dedication in Silverton, Oregon, Hatfield, age seventy-three, announced that he would not seek reelection when his fifth term as senator comes to an end next year.

In 1983, when I was doing some lobbying of the U.S. Senate in support of Nicaragua during the Sandinista regime, I came to know Senator Hatfield and developed a warm friendship with him. He was not very impressed with my lobbying activities but encouraged me to stay in touch with him and some of his fellow senators. I still remember him saying, "We do not need another lobbyist, but we do need a priest, so stick around and talk to us about the spiritual life." Several times he invited me with some of his staff for lunch in the dining room of the Senate Appropriations Committee and asked me to talk about prayer and the contemplative life.

I was deeply impressed when he pulled out of his billfold a little list of people he prayed for. "Father, you are on it," he said. "I pray for you every day." Although we have not met for several years, I think often about this honest, courageous, and deeply spiritual politician. More than anyone else he gave me a sense of true *politeia*, care for the people.

I hope to be able to visit him before he leaves Washington.

Sunday, December 3

This morning we celebrated the first Sunday of Advent at the Empty Bell. All together we were twenty-two people. It was a peaceful and joyful celebration. There was a feeling of friendship, mutual care, and spiritual unity. Jonas creates a truly safe and holy place for the people who come. I hope they will keep coming after my departure. This was my last Eucharist at the Empty Bell. I am grateful that I could be such an intimate part of Jonas's ministry.

Monday, December 4

This afternoon Kathy called and told me about Conrad's funeral. She said, "There were nearly as many priests on the altar as there were people in the church. It was an intimate and beautiful service."

I wish I could have been there. Often during the weekend I thought about Conrad. Life is so short! Carrie and Geoff just had their baby. Kathy, another Daybreak friend, is expecting a baby, and so are Alan and Judy. Conrad dies, Tim is dying.

How much longer will I live? Quite a few of my classmates have died already. But my father is nearly ninety-three and in good spirits. I could live another thirty years! Do I want to live that long? Or do I hope to be united with Christ sooner?

Only one thing seems clear to me. Every day should be well lived. What a simple truth! Still, it is worth my attention. Did I offer peace today? Did I bring a smile to someone's face? Did I say words of healing? Did I let go of my anger and resentments? Did I forgive? Did I love? These are the real questions! I must trust that the little bit of love that I sow now will bear many fruits, here in this world and in the life to come.

Conrad did so many good things for me. I pray that God dresses his mortal deeds with immortality. May he now experience the joy and peace of God's Kingdom, which were so elusive during his stay in this valley of tears.

Tuesday, December 5

I just finished reading one of the most riveting books I have read in a long time, Alan Helms's *Young Man from the Provinces*. The subtitle is *A Gay Life Before Stonewall*. Few people have seen so much, met so many, and "played" so hard. Everything is here: abuse, sex, drugs, fame, money, travel, books, films, theater, and a long, long list of famous men and women. And what is the conclusion?

In his epilogue Helms writes, "I learned a few things... I learned that being envied is the loneliest pleasure on earth, that self-absorption guarantees unhappiness, that the worst motive for action is groundless fear. And I wouldn't cross the street these days to meet someone who's merely celebrated or rich. I've seen so many of those people up close that I know how little such things count for in the effort to make a good life."

If ever I got a gut sense of the journey from entrapment to freedom, it was from this book.

I will send Alan Helms a copy of *The Return of the Prodigal Son*. He might never read it, but it makes me feel good to send it in gratitude for his "confession."

Wednesday, December 6

The Feast of St. Nicholas. Last night, St. Nicholas's Eve, my Dutch friends from Daybreak called and sang a Dutch St. Nicholas's song to me. Later in the evening I put a little gift "from the Saint" in Sam's boot outside the door of the house.

I vividly remember the St. Nicholas's celebrations in Holland. They were evenings of gifts, surprises, rhymes, and jokes, and, of course, the visit of the Holy Man himself, accompanied by the "black Peter"! No gifts at Christmas, but countless gifts on St. Nicholas's Eve! I have many childhood memories connected with this beautiful event. All are gentle, good, and rich with affection.

Peapack, New Jersey, Thursday, December 7

A lovely day. Peggy welcomed me at Newark Airport and took me to her beautiful home in Peapack.

She had invited four guests for dinner. Also Andrew, Peggy's youngest son, came from New York to join us. We had an animated discussion about the Catholic Church, being a Christian, and family values. Peggy made sure to keep the conversation from moving to small talk. She wanted us to have a real discussion about significant things. What a great friend she is, full of humor, vitality, and love. I asked her whether I could stay with her in February, after I return from Holland. She was excited about the idea and offered me her "barn house," which stands separate from her large home. It is an ideal place to have solitude and to write. I am really looking forward to making Peapack my residence for the winter, spring, and summer.

New York, Friday, December 8

At 10:30 I left to have lunch in New York with Jim and Margaret and talk about their marriage tomorrow. Jim is Jutta's son. Since I had never met Margaret and only saw Jim at his sister's wedding a few years ago, I wanted to know them a little better before preaching at their wedding. We had a very open and honest conversation.

It's been a very busy and somewhat restless day. I realize on these trips how much I miss solitude and time to write. But then everybody is so kind, so hospitable, so generous.

Saturday, December 9

What can I write about Jim and Margaret's wedding? It was beautiful, solemn, colorful, and consciously medieval. There was the Cathedral of St. John the Divine, one of the largest churches in the world, majestic, high, deep, in many ways overwhelming. The ceremony took place in front of the main altar, with the guests sitting in the choir stalls. There were the ushers and the bridesmaids, young, exquisitely dressed, good looking, self-assured New York businessmen and women. There was the choir of St. John the Divine, boys and girls with red cassocks and white surplices. There were many candles and flowers. There was a splendid organ filling the space with Bach's music. John, the Episcopal priest presiding, led us with grace.

In the homily I told Jim and Margaret, their families and friends, that I had gone this morning to the Metropolitan Museum to see Arnold Böcklin's painting Island of the Dead because it was this painting that Margaret and Jim saw and admired on their first date. It speaks of darkness and light, death and life, and "unglamorous glamour." I simply asked them, "How are you going to live your mutual love in a world of unglamorous glamour?" My answer was this: "Your love for each other comes from God's first love. Keep claiming that love. Your love for each other is a forgiving love. Keep talking to each other, pardoning each other's shortcomings, and praising each other's gifts. Your love for each other is for others, your children, your guests, the poor. Keep your attention focused on those who need to be nurtured by your love." At the conclusion I gave them a framed reproduction of Rembrandt's etching *Three Trees*, saying that they are two, but there is always a Third who is with them, guiding them through the valley of death whether they see it and know it or not.

The reception and the dinner were splendid. The dance was accompanied by a vibrant rock band, and everyone kept saying how wonderful everything was.

When it was over Jutta escorted me out. It had been good to be with Jutta during this special moment in her life. I feel good that I decided to come. My presence probably meant the most to Jutta, for whom an event like this undoubtedly creates a few extra heartbeats, as it did for me!

Watertown, Sunday, December 10

After a simple Eucharist with Wendy, Jay, and Jutta, I flew back to Boston.

Michael and his twins, Nicolás and Andrés, picked me up at Logan Airport and drove me to their home, where Marta, Michael's wife, welcomed me warmly. A little later Peter and Kate and their son, Paul, arrived. We had a wonderful time together around the dinner table and the Christmas tree, eating, praying, and singing. It was so good to be with close friends and just experience the beauty of the season, the stimulation of good conversation, the joy of children, and the presence of God in the midst of it all. Peter and Kate drove me back to Jonas's house.

I feel tired but deeply grateful.

Twenty-seven years ago today, Thomas Merton and Karl Barth died. I pray for them and thank God for their immense contributions to Christian spirituality and theology.

Tuesday, December 12

My time with Jonas, Margaret, and Sam is coming to an end. In one week's time I will be on my way to Holland. Tomorrow is my last day in the apartment, because Sarah returns on Friday. It is such a wonderful space to live in. I will miss it a lot.

Today is the feast of Our Lady of Guadalupe. May Mary bring unity to the Americas and the world. There is so much division! There is so much need for reconciliation and healing. Mary, pray for us.

Wednesday, December 13

A day full of little things. Sending Christmas gifts to friends, going to the health club with Jonas, correcting the last set of reflections, cleaning the apartment, and making phone calls to publishers.

Tomorrow I will go to San Diego to be guest for the weekend at the estate of my friend Joan. Sue is coming from Daybreak to Boston to meet me and travel with me. Joan will welcome other guests from other cities.

There are many things planned for the weekend, including a dinner tomorrow night, a lecture at the San Diego Hospice and a Christmas party on Friday, a Eucharist and a boat trip before the flight back on Sunday. I look forward to having this visit with Joan. It will be a busy time, though, so I have to live it from hour to hour so as to enjoy every part of it.

San Diego, Thursday, December 14

This morning Jonas drove me to the airport. It was snowing, and I was nervous because Sue's plane was a half hour late. When she arrived, shortly before 10:00 a.m., Jonas said hello and good-bye to Sue, our plane was deiced, and just before the snowstorm clouded over the airport, we were on our way.

At the San Diego Airport we were met, and forty minutes later we arrived at Joan's estate. It was a wonderful beginning because Joan's welcome was so warm and she wanted us to feel right at home. While showing us to our rooms, she took us through her gorgeous, elegant home. Wherever we walked we saw the most precious artifacts, vases with fresh flowers, and elegant tapestries.

There was much activity around the swimming pool on the patio, where a large tent had been set up. A crew of men were at work making everything ready for tomorrow night's Christmas party. As it became dark the whole garden lit up with what seemed myriads of little lights. In the trees large shining stars were hung, and the entrance road and the hedges surrounding the estate were all decorated with countless white and red Christmas lights.

Other guests had arrived, and at 6:00 p.m. Joan took us all out to dinner at a French restaurant. The conversation was animated, and we spoke about many things. I was asked about my writing, and we had a good discussion about *Can You Drink the Cup?* This led to a sharing of our beliefs, and our questions.

Shortly before 9:00 p.m. we were home, and I quickly retired to my room. As I processed all I had seen, heard, and felt during the past fourteen hours, my heart was filled with gratitude.

Friday, December 15

After an elegant breakfast we all drove to the San Diego Hospice, where Sue and I had been asked to speak about "a spirituality of care." About a hundred people were gathered.

For many years Joan had dreamed about a freestanding hospice in San Diego. After a complex struggle to get the necessary permissions, the wonderful building with twenty-four rooms was constructed on a cliff overlooking the city. The staff is very gentle and friendly, and the atmosphere is homey and quite intimate.

Both Sue and I spoke about preparing ourselves and others for "dying well." We sang some Taizé songs and had a lively exchange with the audience. We also met with the pastoral ministers of the hospice. It was a very good morning, and we all felt quite uplifted.

At 6:00 p.m. Joan's Christmas party began. About ninety people arrived. A small choir sang some Christmas carols, and a large group of servers offered a great variety of drinks and snacks. The surroundings were spectacular, the food delicious, the conversations friendly, the music pleasant, and everything very, very elegant. Joan is a perfect hostess, and she moved among her many guests with ease. She has a gift for making people feel special. Everyone enjoyed the warm and friendly atmosphere. By 10:00 p.m. most of the guests had left. I went to bed somewhat dazzled, puzzled, and intrigued by the life I had been part of today.

Saturday, December 16

At 8:30 a.m. Phil drove us to downtown San Diego to visit the homeless shelter founded and led by Father Joe. I had met him at the Christmas party and expressed to him my desire to see his place.

Father Joe, a stocky man with open eyes, a big laugh, and a very self-assured demeanor, welcomed us with "Don't leave your money in the car, because I can use it." He was dressed in blue shorts and a pale shirt and didn't look any different from the homeless people who were wandering around.

Father Joe did most of the talking. He showed us the building for permanent residents, the buildings for women and men who can stay only at night but are on the streets during the day, a new medical center with dental and eye clinics, and the daily food center. As we walked across the patio, a long line of women and men were waiting for their meal. Many volunteers from Christian, Buddhist, and Mormon groups were busy preparing and serving the meals, clearing the tables, and doing the dishes.

Father Joe has a vision about the way the homeless can gradually be motivated to move from coming to the food line, to spending nights at the shelter, to becoming permanent residents, to getting job training, to finding employment, to reclaiming their full human dignity. For fourteen years he has been building and running this multimillion-dollar operation with a strong authoritarian hand.

I ask myself who else would be able to do what Father Joe is doing? The work he does is incredible. But I also sometimes wonder about ministering to others. L'Arche has taught me some things about the importance of mutuality between givers and receivers. I should have liked more time to listen to Father Joe and the caregivers. I'm sure they would be able to witness how the homeless people's gifts were offered and received there.

When we returned to Joan's estate, we celebrated the Eucharist together in the garden in front of the Mexican crèche. It was a very peaceful liturgy. We sat around the little table, read the readings, shared our reflections, prayed, and received the sacred gifts of the Body and Blood of Christ.

Joan's granddaughter and her boyfriend then joined our little party, and we drove to the harbor, where we saw from a distance Joan's magnificent yacht decorated with Christmas lights. The seven-man crew were standing on the dock to greet us. As soon as we were onboard we started our harbor cruise. Phil gave us a tour of the boat. We admired the spacious lounge with separate dining space, beautiful bedrooms, a very well-equipped kitchen, the exercise room, and the large sundeck. On the bridge the captain and his crew explained some of the high-tech navigational equipment.

After the tour we were invited to a splendidly decorated table for dinner. As we ate we slowly "sailed" past the impressive San Diego skyline, went under the high Coronado Bridge, and had a view of the navy aircraft carriers. Christmas lights were all over, decorating the skyscrapers, the big hotels, and the ships in the harbor.

Joan is such a warm and gracious hostess. She was attentive to each one of us, and her deep desire was to ensure that we felt welcomed and that each one of us would have a wonderful time. At dinner we exchanged feelings about the afternoon liturgy, about "church," the meaning of life, the state of the world, and preparing for death.

There was so much to take in — conversations about life's meaning, new friendships, marvelous sights, and tasty food — that I sometimes found myself speaking in one superlative after the other: fantastic, gorgeous, unbelievable, spectacular, magnificent, delicious, fabulous.

By 9:00 p.m. we were back at the dock. We thanked the crew and the cooks and returned to Joan's home. I went to bed early. There was so much to dream about!

Watertown, Sunday, December 17

This was our traveling day. It was also a day to say good-bye to Joan, who had treated us to such a beautiful weekend with new and old friends. Some of us traveled together and had extended time to visit. By 7:00 p.m. I was back in Boston.

Jonas picked me up at the airport and drove me home. "How was it?" he asked. I replied, "Joan is an incredible person. Her guests, too, were wonderful people. I realize more and more how much we need each other. My heart is full of gratitude for this precious experience."

Then I told Jonas many of the details of our time together. There was so much to share, and I realized that my words could hardly convey the scenes that accompanied these things in my head. I tried to describe the people I had met and our conversations, my feelings about our visit to the San Diego Hospice and the shelter for the homeless. I wanted to share with him the warmth of Joan's welcome, the beauty of her home, and the way she had decorated for Christmas, and I wanted to describe the paintings and sculptures that moved me so deeply. I shared about the memorable boat ride. I talked for some time. Finally I asked, "Well, and how was your weekend?" and I was happy to listen to Jonas.

Sue's famous question "What *does* it all mean?" is mine after this moving trip, on which I experienced, met, and spoke with wonderful people who came from a world of abundance, and with beautiful people who were radically poor, close to death, and in dire need. I ponder my experience, and I recognize once more that the way for us to be in this world is to focus on the spiritual life — our own as well as the spiritual life of each one of the people that we meet. I feel convinced that it was important for us on this trip to deepen our friendships one with the other, to talk at the hospice, to celebrate the Eucharist together, and to converse and share about the spiritual life. All the rest pales before these "spiritual events," which will become part of our enduring search for the truth of life and the love of God.

Today, in my prayer I return and give thanks for my "call" to the Daybreak community. I know that it is from there that I desire to live my vocation, which is to announce God's love for all people. I am deeply grateful as I become more and more convinced of my destination in God's eternal embrace. This clarity increasingly allows me to be with each person who is with me and to receive that person's goodness, beauty, and love. My challenge, as always, is to remain at home with this marvelous and mysterious God Who sent me into the world to speak and act in Jesus' Name.

Monday, December 18

This is a day of unpacking and packing, Christmas shopping, writing letters, sending gifts, making phone calls, and planning to get ready for my departure to Holland tomorrow night.

Jonas and I had a lovely lunch at Harvard Square with Laurent, and we talked about Laurent's forthcoming book on commitment and worldwide compassion, which he is writing with his wife, Sharon, and several others. It is an impressive study based on many interviews and much research. One finding is that all people committed to large humanitarian causes had at some point had a significant encounter with someone outside their own circles who was able to widen the boundaries of their lives and show them larger perspectives. Laurent said, "Underneath all the great commitments, you always find a significant relationship with someone who is truly 'other.'" I found that very insightful. And it confirmed my own experience. Without meeting Jean Vanier I would never have moved from Harvard to L'Arche. My commitment to live and work with handicapped people is indeed based on a relationship with someone who broke through my boundaries and radically enlarged my perspective.

Tuesday, December 19

A big snowstorm prevents me from leaving for Amsterdam. Just when I was all packed and ready to go, my Northwest flight was canceled. Happily I found this out by phone, so I didn't have to go to the airport.

I made endless phone calls to reschedule my flight. If all goes well I will be able to fly to Toronto tomorrow and from there to Amsterdam. But a blizzard is predicted, and my plane from Boston to Toronto might not be able to take off. Well, I hope I can live it patiently. I am most worried about making it to my father before Saturday, since we are planning to go on vacation to Germany that day. I just have to wait, see, and use my time well!

Toronto, Wednesday, December 20

A lot of snow but no blizzard yet! At 11:00 a.m. Jonas drove me to the airport. Although the plane was not supposed to leave until 2:00 p.m., I wanted to be sure to get there on time, get my tickets changed, and let Jonas go home before the weather got worse.

The snow got heavier, but the plane did come and was able to leave just before the airport was closed again. I arrived in Toronto at 5:30 and was quite nervous about making it to the KLM flight to Amsterdam, which was leaving from a different terminal. But I made it through customs quickly, got my luggage, caught a cab, and arrived at the KLM flight just in time. I am exhausted but happy to be on my way to Holland.

Geysteren, Holland, Thursday, December 21

My nephew Reinier was at the airport to take me to my father's home in Limburg, a two-hour ride. The first thing my ninety-three-year-old father said was "Well, you badly need a haircut." I will make an appointment with the barber for both of us, so we will look decent on our trip! Then he said, "You better go to bed right away, so you can catch up with your sleep." A father is always a father!

It was good, though, very good, to see my dad in good spirits and eager to go to Germany with me on a Christmas vacation.

Friday, December 22

Getting ready! Going to the barber! Sleeping! Packing! Making phone calls! Tonight my sister, Laurien, and her partner, Henri, came to say hello, and we all went to Horst, a nearby small town, for dinner.

Freiburg, Germany, Saturday, December 23

During the night my father had an upset stomach, as often happens after good but too greasy food. As I heard him go back and forth to the bathroom, I worried about his ability to survive it all. He is so terribly thin, his heart is weak, and his body so worn out! I am afraid that he will die on the spot.

But at 9:00 a.m. he was all set to go on the trip and hardly mentioned his stomach troubles. Joe, a friend and distant relative of my father, drove us to Venlo, where we caught the train to Cologne. At noon we left Cologne, and at 4:00 p.m. we arrived in Freiburg. Franz was at the station and drove us to a small, intimate hotel close to the Münster (Freiburg's cathedral). While my father rested, I made a quick trip with Franz to his home to greet Reny, his wife, and pick up two suitcases with clothes and books I had left there two years ago. After a good meal at the hotel my father and I retired to our rooms. I am feeling very tired.

Sunday, December 24

At 9:30 p.m. Franz and Reny came to the hotel to take me to the Christmas mass at their parish church. My father, who had stomach problems again, decided to stay at the hotel and go to bed early.

I was surprised to see that the church was far from full. I am so used to the overcrowded services in Richmond Hill that I expected the same here. But it was a rather small "crowd."

The pastor welcomed us warmly and invited me to concelebrate with him. The assistant pastor gave a lovely reflection about God's desire to move from power to powerlessness, from strength to weakness, from being creator to being creative, from greatness to smallness, from independence to dependence.

It brought me back to my musings earlier this week. I think that we have hardly thought through the immense implications of the mystery of the incarnation. Where is God? God is where we are weak, vulnerable, small, and dependent. God is where the poor are, the hungry, the handicapped, the mentally ill, the elderly, the powerless. How can we come to know God when our focus is elsewhere, on success, influence, and power? I increasingly believe that our faithfulness will depend on our willingness to go where there is brokenness, loneliness, and human need. If the church has a future it is a future with the poor in whatever form. Each one of us is very seriously searching to live and grow in this belief, and by friendship we can support each other. I realize that the only way for us to stay well in the midst of the many "worlds" is to stay close to the small, vulnerable child that lives in our hearts and in every other human being. Often we do not know that the Christ child is within us. When we discover him we can truly rejoice.

Monday, December 25

Shortly before 10:00 a.m. my father and I took a cab to the cathedral (Das Münster). It was packed, but I was able to get my father a seat in the front row, which was reserved for the elderly. The service was festive, solemn, and very "royal" — processions, incense, candles, and many servers.

The archbishop of Freiburg presided and gave the homily. "Does this cathedral help or hinder us in understanding the mystery of Christmas?" he asked. I was fascinated by the question, since I had just been thinking about the fact that such a hidden and poor event as the birth of Jesus had inspired the creation of such a majestic building and such a rich liturgy. What had all the Gothic splendor, the paintings and sculptures, the robes, staff, miter, and long ceremonies to do with the little baby born in Bethlehem twenty centuries ago?

The bishop "defended" his cathedral, but afterwards my father said, "He has a very optimistic view of human nature. He didn't mention all the human evil that causes so much suffering in our world." I realized that perhaps the cathedral is as much a product of human pride, arrogance, and desire for power, influence, and success as it is of deep faith, piety, adoration, generosity, and the love of God. The Freiburg Münster is one of the best places to see in stone the place where power and piety meet.

I had a splendid view of the majestic church. It is without any doubt one of the most beautiful Gothic churches ever erected. It took five cen-turies to build. In November 1944 the city of Freiburg and most of the cathedral were destroyed by Allied bombing. Happily the unique cathe-dral tower, with its beautiful filigreed spire, was spared. It took more than twenty years to restore the cathedral to its present glory.

Tuesday, December 26

At 11:00 a.m. an influential priest in the diocese came to the hotel for a visit, and I was moved by our conversation. He was very honest about his feelings concerning being a prominent member of the church hierarchy while being mostly interested in the spiritual formation of religious and laypeople. During the week he is quite busy with the administration of the diocese, but on the weekend he escapes to a spiritual center an hour away from the city to spend time in prayer and solitude. He is a kind, warm, open-minded person, with an obvious love for Jesus and the church. But he also realizes that high liturgies, miters, purple cassocks, lots of incense, and clerical formality are no longer speaking to young people in search of meaning.

This priest reflects my own struggle to be in the church without being caught in many complicated structures. The question for him as well as for me is, how can we love the church today? He said to me, "I am always happy when I can get out of my purple robes and look like a normal person again." But then he went on to say, "I have to live day by day, be faithful to my call, and trust that my life will be fruitful, even when things don't change as fast as I would like." I really liked this simple, honest man of the church.

This afternoon I wrote many postcards. While writing I experienced a deep love for all the friends I was writing to. My heart was full of gratitude and affection, and I wished I could embrace each of my friends and let them know how much they mean to me and how much I miss them. It seems that sometimes distance creates closeness, absence creates presence, loneliness creates community! I felt my whole being, body, mind, and spirit, yearning to give and receive love without condition, without fear, without reservation.

Why should I ever think or say something that is not love? Why should I ever hold a grudge, feel hatred or jealousy, act suspiciously? Why not always give and forgive, encourage and empower, give thanks and offer praise? Why not?

I thank God for this little glimpse of eternity in my own heart. I pray that I can hold on to the truth of what my spiritual eye sees and find the strength to live my life according to that vision.

Wednesday, December 27

A very quiet day. There are many things to do and to see in Freiburg, but both my father and I enjoy just being here, with ample time to sleep, to have a relaxed breakfast, to celebrate the Eucharist, and to just rest. There were times when I could hardly be in a foreign city without wanting to see every church, every museum, and every ruin, but these days I am very satisfied to be in my room, read a little, write a little, and pray a little.

It is good for both my father and me to be together without any special agenda. I don't think that we ever before spent such unscheduled time together. We have no great subjects to discuss, but our conversations are alive and pleasant. I keep being surprised by my father's interest in religion, literature, art, and politics. Even though his body is worn out and he can hardly walk, his mind is as clear and sharp as ever, and his ideas, judgments, and opinions are to the point and often astute. For me it is a unique privilege to have this time with him, and I can see that he too is glad we are together.

At 5:00 p.m. Franz and Reny took us to the home of friends I came to know during my previous visits to Freiburg. There we celebrated the Eucharist and had a light meal. My father, who seldom prays aloud, prayed with great fervor that his grandchildren would give God a place in their lives and not be totally preoccupied with material concerns. I experienced much inner peace and joy as I listened to his "free" prayer. For someone who keeps the mass book always in his hands to follow carefully all the words of the liturgy, saying spontaneous prayers is quite a leap.

Thursday, December 28

Five years ago when my father and I were also together for a few days in Freiburg, we went to the circus, and during the performance I was so moved by the Flying Rodleighs, a group of South African trapeze artists, that I introduced myself to them. That little event had many consequences for me. I became friends with the Rodleighs, traveled with them through Germany, interviewed them at length, wrote articles about them, and made a documentary film with them, which will be shown on Dutch TV next Monday night, New Year's.

My father must have been thinking of the Rodleighs when he said, "There is a circus in town again. I wonder if you would like to go." It is the Christmas Circus Festival, a program with the Chinese People's Circus and artists from Moscow, Paris, and Freiburg.

At 4:00 p.m. Franz, my father, and I drove to the great circus tent at the marketplace in Freiburg and saw the show. No animals, only acrobats! There were some dazzling jugglers, a fabulous wire dancer, a great cradle trapeze artist, and spectacular "teeter-totter" jumpers. But I was most fascinated by another act, with three men who combined clowning, dancing, and athletics accompanied by music from the film *Chariots of Fire*. There was much self-mockery in their act. While performing the most amazing athletics, they looked at the audience and at one another as if they were making fools of themselves. Hilarious.

But, spectacular as it was, nothing happened in me comparable to what happened five years ago. Then I was "hooked" by the Rodleighs and felt nearly driven to see them again and again and enter deeply into their world. Now I saw a good show and went home without many afterthoughts or after-feelings. Then I saw something that opened in me a new inner place. Now I just enjoyed some unusual sights and had a few hours of good entertainment. Then I experienced a personal transformation.

Today's circus experience made it clear to me that what really had touched me last time was the very personal quality of the Rodleigh's trapeze act. I had been able to identify with the artists and came to think about them as people I'd like to become friends with. Indeed, they have become friends, and I have discovered the many ways my world and theirs interconnect. The people I saw today remained somewhat abstract to me. I wasn't curious about how they live their daily lives, as I was with the Rodleighs. I didn't think beyond their performance and forgot about them when it was over.

But Franz, my father, and I had a very pleasant afternoon. Back at the hotel we had a nice dinner together.

Friday, December 29

Today Franz took us on a little trip to Bernau, known for its wood-carving workshops, and to Sankt Blasien, known for its high-domed church. Most beautiful, however, was the trip itself, through the snow-covered Black Forest. It felt like driving through a very romantic Christmas card. The view into the valleys with their little villages and charming church towers, the winding roads, the white and green fir trees, and the heavy clouds moving between the hills and mountains was so pleasant to the eye from a well-heated Mercedes.

What I will probably most remember of our trip was a woman called Ursula. She was sitting alone in the restaurant where we went for lunch. When she noticed us she offered us a glass of red wine. I accepted her offer, and as a result she joined us a little later, obviously in need of company. Ursula is an astrologer who tried to convince us of the importance of her gifts to determine our personalities on the basis of the year, the day, and the minute of our birth. She spoke intensely, intrusively, and hardly gave us a chance to respond.

Soon she was busy attacking the Vatican, calling the Pope a poisonous influence, and telling us that she believed in God but had no use whatsoever for the church. She also declared that all the good Popes had been murdered, John Paul I being one of them, that the crusades, Inquisition, and pogroms showed how evil the church is, that Leonardo Boff was her hero, and that most theologians didn't know what they were talking about.

After listening to her tirade for ten minutes, I felt an unusually strong desire to put a needle in her balloon. So I looked her straight in the eyes, asked her to listen to me for a change, and told her that I was a Catholic priest, worked with handicapped people, had met the Pope himself, knew all about Leonardo Boff, and considered her tirade insensitive, simplistic, trendy, and very arrogant. I went on to say to her, "You are a person who has influence on people. What you say is important. Please mind that your words don't wound those you speak with, and please realize that the history of Christianity cannot be summarized in two or three condemnations."

Ursula fell completely silent. She hadn't expected such a strong response. She accepted my words as well as she could, asked me for my name, and wrote her name down for me. I am not sure if I did the right thing. Franz said, "I never heard you defend the Pope in such an unconditional way." I realized that Ursula's simplistic criticism of the church had made me a somewhat simplistic supporter. I don't think I was able to change her mind, but she certainly made me aware of my own mind!

Saturday, December 30

Ever since we left Holland, my father has been saying, "You should buy a new cap." I had accidentally left my cap in the car after Reinier had picked me up at the airport and had been wearing one of my father's old, worn, and much too small caps. "When are you going to buy a new cap?" he kept asking. Today was my last chance, since tomorrow and on New Year's Day all the shops will be closed. The city was so crowded that it was hard to walk at a regular pace through the streets. It seemed that everyone was in a hurry to buy something before New Year's.

I ended up in a department store in front of a large table stacked with caps. I asked one of the attendants, "Can you help me to find a cap my size?" She said, "No, no, look for it yourself. There must be one of your size in this stack, but I can't keep sorting them out according to size. Too many people are messing them up. You are on your own." Surrounded by men and women grabbing caps, putting them on, looking in the mirror, making funny faces, and throwing them back on the pile, I tried to find something halfway decent for myself. Finally I felt so oppressed by the whole scene that I left and went to another store, with fewer people and higher prices. Then I bought a "Harris tweed, hand-woven in the Hebrides" cap for twice what it would have cost me at the previous department store. But at least I can tell a story about it!

At 4:00 p.m. my father and I celebrated the Eucharist in the hotel room. This regular time of prayer together has become an important part of our day. My father, who was reading a Dutch book of essays about religion and visions of life in a postmodern time, said to me, "There is a good piece on the sacraments in it. You must certainly read that." For him the article and our celebrations supported each other.

The article was indeed a spiritually helpful essay. Influenced by Martin Heidegger's philosophy, the author sees the sacraments as an entranceway to a new experience of the potential sacredness of the ordinary. For her the sacraments are the true treasure of the church.

As I celebrate with my father in the hotel room, I sense the truth of that. The beautiful, simple, and deep intimacy between the two of us is made possible by the simple, deep, and intimate presence of Christ with us. Long after my father has left this world, these sacred moments will continue to nurture my heart.

Sunday, December 31

Tonight Hermann and Mechtilde invited us to celebrate "Silvester Evening," New Year's Eve, with their family. We started with the Eucharist in the living room. There were quite a few people. The liturgy was homey but also quite solemn. The most intimate part was the time of intercession, in which several members revealed their very personal concerns.

After the Eucharist we had a dinner à la bourguignon, in which each person could cook his own piece of meat in small pots of boiling oil and dip it in several sauces. It's the kind of meal that keeps you busy and encourages small talk.

At 10:00 p.m. a cab came to take my father and me back to the hotel. Soon after we got there the fireworks began, and they kept my father, whose room looks out on the square, awake for most of the night. On the garden side of the hotel, where my room is located, the New Year's noises weren't so bad, and I slept pretty well.

January 1996

Monday, January 1, 1996

After a very quiet and peaceful day in the hotel, we had a lovely farewell dinner with Franz and Reny, Hermann and Mechtilde. The manager of the hotel had done every possible thing to please us. The table was beautifully decorated, and for my father she had ordered a light meal.

The dinner was in honor of Hermann, who celebrates his seventieth birthday on January 17, and of my father, who celebrates his ninety-third on January 3. I had bought a silver letter opener for Hermann and an etching of the hotel square with the Schwabengate for my father. For Mechtilde I had a "consolation prize," a little bookmark in the form of an owl.

My father enjoyed himself very much and actively participated in these "cultural" discussions. It was truly a warm, charming, and intelligent conclusion to our Freiburg time.

Geysteren, Tuesday, January 2

The trip home went very well with the exception of the change of trains in Cologne. Since the train from Freiburg arrived ten minutes late, we had only seven minutes to move with all our luggage from Platform 2 to Platform 9.

Both my father and I were quite nervous. Just after my father had left the train, he stumbled over his suitcase and fell on the platform. His walking stick went flying and landed on the rail underneath the train. Happily my father got up soon without breaking a bone or getting hurt. The conductor who had helped us leave the train was able to grab my father's stick and get us ready to move again. Loaded with five suitcases and my father following me through the crowd, we went down and up again by moving stairs and made it to our train just one minute before it left for Holland.

In Venlo, Joe, and Tilly, my father's housekeeper, welcomed us and drove us home. We had left Freiburg at 1:00 p.m. We were home at 7:30. A good and comfortable trip, but I realize that not much has to happen to have a fatal accident. I remember how my grandfather, who was a healthy man in his eighties, died shortly after a rather minor accident in front of his house. My father is so thin and fragile that a small fall can be enough to break not only his bones but his spirit as well. I am happy that we are both home safe and well and that my father is grateful for the trip.

Wednesday, January 3

Today is my father's ninety-third birthday. He received many phone calls and a few visitors. On Saturday everyone in the family will come to celebrate, so today we enjoyed a quiet, pleasant day together.

At 4:00 p.m. Robert, the son of Franz, came with his fiancée, Susanne. Both Robert and Susanne are medical doctors specializing in internal medicine. It was a real joy to meet them. They are two self-confident, intelligent, and spiritually open people. They both work long hours and have to struggle to find time to develop their relationship. They are both Roman Catholics with a minimum of resentment against the church. Neither has been married before, even though they are in their early thirties. And they both have very warm relationships with their families. Relative to those of other postmodern professionals, their lives are exceptionally uncomplicated. Not easy, not without the normal tensions of career people, not without serious questions about living an intimate family life in a not-so-intimate medical world, but still lives with clear goals, clear commitments, clear values, and a clear love for each other and for God.

Both my father and I enjoyed their visit. They had come to ask me to marry them on June 15. I was quite honored by their invitation and accepted it wholeheartedly. We spent an hour discussing the details of the ceremony and ways to prepare for it. Then we all went to dinner in a nearby restaurant. At 8:00 p.m. they were on their way back to Germany. Robert and Susanne's visit was, in a way, a beautiful conclusion to our "German experience."

Friday, January 5

During dinner Kathy called to let me know that my friend Timothy is dying. I immediately phoned Tim in Toronto and was amazed to be able to speak to him directly.

"The chemotherapy didn't work," he said. "Things only got worse." I asked him about his "spirits." He said, "There is much, much peace. Phyllis and I pray a lot together, and we have committed ourselves fully to Jesus and the blessed Mother." There was a certain joy in his voice, even though it was clear that he had become very weak.

I spoke also for a moment with Phyllis, his wife, and his dearest friend, Paul, who happened to be there when I called. I said to Phyllis, "I am so grateful that Tim has become part of my life. His deep faith and radical trust are a great inspiration to me, and I am sure that Tim's life will bear many, many fruits." She said, "Thank you so much for saying this. Your concern and interest means so much to Tim. I know that your call made his day." Paul said, "I'll keep you informed, but I don't think Tim can live longer than two weeks."

I have been thinking much about Tim since that call. His communion with God is so deep that all the pain, worries, and fears seem to recede into the background. Seldom if ever have I met a man who embraced his approaching death with so much love and so much confidence. What a grace to know this man!

Saturday, January 6

A very special day. The celebration of my father's ninety-third birthday! He had invited the entire immediate family: my brother Paul; my brother Laurent with his wife, Heiltjen, and their three children, Sarah, Laura, and Raphael; my sister, Laurien, with her companion, Henri, and her three children, Frédérique, Marc with his companion, Marije, and Reinier; and myself. Also present were my father's sister Hetty with her husband, Jan; his sisters Ella and Truus; Cathrien, the daughter of his deceased brother Sef, with her husband, Chris; Elisabeth, a friend of his deceased sister Corrie; and his relative Jo, who is his present driver and tour guide. Together we were twenty-two.

Since my father comes from a family of eleven children and my mother from a family of eight, this family reunion made us very conscious of the many members of our family who have died during the last years. My father asked me to celebrate the Eucharist in memory of my mother, who died eighteen years ago, and also in memory of all the other deceased members of the family.

We all sat around the living-room table in double rows. In sharp contrast to the liturgies I celebrate elsewhere, this was rather formal as many of the people present do not go to church. Sarah, Raphael, and Reinier did the readings. I felt that people seemed uncomfortable.

For me it is hard to celebrate the Eucharist in a formal or ritualistic way. I so much wish that we would feel more connected and inspired, but it seems that their spirituality and my own are miles apart. I spoke about God revealing himself to us in weakness, not only a long time ago in the birth of Jesus but also today wherever people are sick, elderly, de-

pendent, and out of control. I also said that we only live our weakness as
a place of God's appearance (it was the day of Epiphany!) when we truly
believe that we have been loved since before we were born and will be
loved after we have died. If we do not believe this, our weakness easily
leads to bitterness and hardened hearts. Although I felt deeply convinced
of what I was talking about, my words did not seem to be very deeply
received.

After the Eucharist we went to my mother's grave. We were reminded
of that foggy morning in October 1978 when we walked from the church
to the cemetery to lay her to rest. Most of us had been there, except for
Sarah, Laura, and Raphael, who were all born after her death. How much
she would have loved them!

The dinner at a nearby restaurant was quite festive. My brother Paul
was master of ceremonies. Sarah spoke on behalf of the grandchildren,
and both my sister, Laurien, and my brother Laurent offered humorous
but affectionate reflections on my father's life and virtues.

During the dinner the local band walked in dressed up as kings to
commemorate the Feast of the Three Kings, played "Happy Birthday" and
a few other pieces, and passed the hat. A colorful musical interruption.

At 6:30 the dinner was over, and although the roads were very
slippery, everyone made it to their cars and finally home!

My time with my father in Germany and his ninety-third birthday will
always stay with me as a precious memory. It is for me the best time we
have ever had together. Maybe he had to be ninety-three and I had to be
sixty-four to make this possible! Thirty years ago the closeness that now
exists between us was unthinkable. Then it was my mother who offered
closeness, affection, and personal care. My father seemed more distant.
He was the provider who loved his wife, expected much of his children,
worked hard, and discussed important issues. A virtuous, righteous man,
but I found it difficult to feel intimate with him.

I realize that I have lived for a long time with a deep respect for, as well
as a certain fear of, my father. When my mother died, I suddenly became
aware that I hardly knew him. But as we both grew older and a little
less defensive, I came to see how similar we are. As I look in the mirror
today, I see my father when he was sixty-four, and as I reflect on my own
idiosyncrasies — my impatience, my inclination to control things, and my
style of talking — I quickly see that the main difference between us is age,
not character! Few adult sons have the opportunity to come to know their
fathers and spend time with them. It is a special grace that is given to me

during this sabbatical. We like to be together. My father likes his place
as the patriarch, he likes good hotels, good restaurants, and good art. He
likes interesting conversation, good manners, preferential treatment, and
excellent service. And he likes for me to pay the bills! Not because he
has no money or is stingy but because he likes to have a son who can
pay for his father.

My father is interested in me, but more in my health than in my work,
more in my clothes than in my books, more in my German friends than
in my American friends. He is a real European from the old school. A
long time ago when we had a conflict, he said, "As a psychologist you
know everything about authoritarian fathers. Try to be happy that you
have one, but don't try to change him!"

Today I enjoy being with my father. The less I want to change him the
more he enjoys being with me and sharing his vulnerability. As we both
have become "elders" our needs have become quite similar. We both like
solitude, quiet time, restful spaces, good friends, good food, and a peaceful
atmosphere. Our common interests in art, literature, and the spiritual life
give us a lot to talk about. When I was thirty-two and my father was sixty-
one, we belonged to different generations and we were far apart. Today it
seems that we have become part of the same generation and grown very
close, close to death and close to each other. I thank God for my father.
Whatever happens to him in the coming year, I will always be grateful
that we had this unique time together.

Utrecht, Holland, Sunday, January 7

It was a real surprise when a few days ago Rodleigh called. "Where are
you?" I asked. "We are in Zwolle," he said, "and we have been trying to
reach you ever since we came to Holland. Can you come to visit us?"

I was so excited to hear from my trapeze friends. The last time I saw
them was a year ago. Now the question was how to make it to Zwolle
before Sunday night, when the Flying Rodleighs would all leave for their
vacations in South Africa and the United States. This morning was the
only possibility. I called Jan and asked him whether he would like to come
with me.

At 10:45 this morning Jan and I found each other at the train station
in Zwolle, and ten minutes later we were sitting with Rodleigh and his
wife, Jennie, in their caravan. Soon we also saw Jonathon, Karlene, Kailene, Slava, and John. It felt so good to see them all again. I realized how
much I had missed being with them.

Rodleigh told us about the hard times they had recently lived through:

complicated problems with their caravans, serious health problems, and most of all the death of Raedawn, Rodleigh and Karlene's sister, in Italy. After hearing about Raedawn's death, Rodleigh had bought a car and driven alone to Reggio, where the funeral and burial were to be. There Raedawn's friends had taken him to the morgue to see his sister. He didn't want to go, since he had never seen a dead person and wanted to remember his sister the way she was during her last visit, but they didn't let him break their traditions. Seeing his sister's emaciated body so shocked Rodleigh that he wept for two days. Listening to all of this, I was amazed that the Flying Rodleighs hadn't canceled a single performance. Recently Jennie stopped working in the act, but Kerri, a sixteen-year-old girl from South Africa, had been trained to take her place.

As always, Rodleigh explained things with great clarity and systematically, like a teacher. He wanted me to know everything and took his time recounting it, even though a few hours later the troupe would be on their way to Hannover to park their caravan there until March.

At 12:30 Rodleigh took Jan and me to the show. It was a very fine show, but few people came to see it. Uncharacteristically the Rodleighs performed poorly. Because of the hall's low ceiling, the whole act had been toned down, and the two most spectacular tricks failed. Both Slava and Rodleigh missed their catcher, John, and ended up in the net. The huge, largely empty building didn't offer a worthy context for these very artistic performers.

Between the Flying Rodleighs' act and the finale, Jan and I had tea with Karlene and Jonathon in their caravan. Since I last saw them Karlene and Jonathon have fallen in love and become a couple. Kailene, Karlene's daughter, was happy to have a real family now. We had a good and lively visit.

Before the second show started Rodleigh drove Jan and me to the station. As I reflected on this short visit, I realized how good it had been for me. I am looking forward to being with the Flying Rodleighs again in June or July . . . and to realizing my long-held dream to write a book about them. The desire to do this had even grown after I listened to Rodleigh and Jennie's negative response to the New Year's TV program. They felt that their act was poorly shown and poorly integrated into the whole of the program. Since I haven't seen the program yet I couldn't respond well, but I experienced a new impulse to write about the troupe in ways that they themselves could appreciate.

At 5:30 p.m. we arrived in Utrecht. Jan took me right away to Pays Bas, the hotel where he had made a reservation for me. I really liked my room there and decided to stay for a week.

Monday, January 8

A quiet day. I worked a little, but I was so tired that I felt like sleeping constantly. At 1:00 p.m. I gave in and slept until 4:00 p.m.

I was invited for dinner and the Eucharist at the Ariensconvict, the formation center for future priests for the dioceses of Utrecht and Groningen. I was very glad to go there and connect with my own diocese in that way.

What a contrast with the time I was at the seminary! In those days there were hundreds of eager candidates. I lived in the same large building for six years. The discipline was strict, the lifestyle simple and solid, the teaching very traditional and conservative. I could only leave the building in the company of others. My great contribution to the "liberation" of the seminary was bicycles! I convinced the staff that having bikes was good for seminarians. Anyhow, those were the '50s, and the Second Vatican Council was still far away.

The Ariensconvict is a beautiful old-fashioned house in downtown Utrecht where theology students live with their rector while studying theology at the university. All together there are thirty-six students, and there is a concern that few new men are applying and that in the future fewer and fewer priests will be ordained.

During dinner I had an opportunity to introduce myself to the students. The atmosphere was quite friendly and relaxed. Although the institutional quality of the large seminary was gone and the atmosphere was more like a family, it was clearly a miniature seminary, and the discussions, interests, and preoccupations were similar to those of my time. The only woman was a sister who did the cooking.

The Eucharist was lovely but was a miniature of the old high church liturgy. It felt like an adaptation for a small group of a ceremony meant for large crowds. The celebrant, dressed in rich vestments, stood behind a stone altar in a cryptlike chapel. The students sat in a circle facing the altar. There were songs indicated on a board, readings from behind the lectern, a fine homily, and the seminarians received Holy Communion with much devotion. However, I doubt that a stranger would be able to guess that these people live together, eat together, and study together. The formality of the ritual appears to create distance in word, gesture, and movement that does not exist among these men immediately before or after the liturgy. In the celebration one seems to enter into a behavioral world that is separate from normal life. To see these men shaking hands with each other as a sign of peace when they had just finished dinner together was somewhat unreal to me, especially because nobody was leaving the building after the celebration! The homily seemed to be directed to strangers as opposed to those present who all live in the same house. That anyone would spontaneously speak or respond to the readings, or that there would be some kind of sharing seemed far-fetched in this context.

After the Eucharist we had coffee and tea "under the Christmas tree" with gentle conversation about books and teachers of theology.

I did feel quite welcome at the Ariensconvict, and I enjoyed speaking with the men who are there. I hope to go there often during this week.

Tuesday, January 9

This morning I took the train to Haarlem to spend the day with my friend Jurjen. Jurjen is a capable, very intelligent, and deeply committed pastor who works in the inner city of Haarlem with the homeless, AIDS patients, and the poor, and who dedicates much of his time to writing and publishing about contemporary religious issues. His main focus is the integration of spirituality and social action in the pastoral work of the church. It is these themes that brought us together many years ago and continue to inspire us in our discussions: What is the place of prayer, contemplation, meditation, and the interior life in a ministry that responds to the immediate needs of the poor and oppressed? Can you be a monk as well as a social activist? Jurjen's history as a pastor in the Dutch Reformed Church has made him known as a significant social critic who calls the church to step out of its isolation and respond to "real problems." In this context a life of solitude, silence, and prayer easily looks "escapist."

Jurjen, who feels that I have influenced him deeply, has been planning for a few years now to write a small book about me. There is no doubt that nobody else is as qualified to do it as he. He has read every piece I ever wrote, he knows me well personally, he is very familiar with the Dutch "religious scene," and he is a highly respected pastor. Although I feel hesitant about a "biography" at this time of my life, I am glad that Jurjen is the one doing it.

We had a good day together. I was able to give him some factual information about my life and help him a little with some of the "themes." But I tried not to get too involved and I tried to encourage him to feel completely free to write a critical evaluation.

Wednesday, January 10

This afternoon I spent a few hours at the Pax Christi Center with my friend Jan. He showed me around.

The location itself is intriguing. It is a huge shopping center built around the railroad station: a place always crowded with travelers and shoppers — busy, noisy, and very commercial. The Pax Christi Center is like the silent center in the midst of the storm. As soon as you enter it, you experience another world. There is a beautiful chapel where people can drop in, pray, and light a candle. There are several meeting rooms in which people who come by train from different parts of the country can work quietly together. There is a reception hall where homeless people are welcomed. Finally there are the offices where the Pax Christi staff does its work. There are projects for the former Yugoslavia, especially Bosnia; there are projects for Latin America, particularly Colombia, Cuba, Ecuador, and Brazil. There is a Middle East project, several African projects, and a Chechnya project. Pax Christi also leads a campaign against land mines, a pilgrimage to Auschwitz, an extensive youth program, and a large communication and formation department; it publishes several magazines and offers courses and interreligious dialogues. The staff of committed men and women live their work as a mission and are open to sharing their vision.

It was quite symbolic to see this center, with its silent chapel and its many activities, in the midst of the "marketplace." It proclaims intimacy as well as solidarity in a world that lacks both. A very hopeful place — small, hidden, simple, but with the potential of a mustard seed.

Friday, January 12

This morning I took the train to Amsterdam to visit the senior editor of *Trouw,* a Dutch Christian newspaper in which one page is dedicated to the life of the churches in the Netherlands. Although its origin is Protestant, it has developed an ecumenical character and includes news and ideas from all Christian churches.

For a long time I have been wondering where in Holland I could best publish some of my writings. The magazines and journals that have previously published my reflections are reaching a very small and mostly very traditional Catholic readership. My friends have strongly urged me to find a better "forum" and to prevent myself from coming to be seen as an ultraconservative Roman Catholic. "You need to take some initiative," they said. "Otherwise you will not be taken seriously by your own people."

A few days ago I called the editor to ask him if I could visit. We had a very pleasant meeting. When I showed him my reflections for every day of the year and asked him if they might interest him for a daily feature, he responded with great interest. He told me that I had come at the right time since the staff had been discussing a new format for their page on the life of the churches and they were considering publishing more reflective and formative material.

It was a valuable visit for me. I have no idea whether my reflections will be used or whether anything else will come from our conversation, but it feels good to be connected with people in the Dutch publishing world who are on the same wavelength I am.

Saturday, January 13

Finally I am getting to the Winnipeg manuscript. Bill, my editor at Doubleday, is interested, so I am back reading my journal from one of the most difficult times of my life, when I suffered a depression between Christmas 1987 and the spring of 1988. I can see that some more work is necessary. I hope to have the time and energy to do it while in Holland. But it is hard to find the rest and peace this type of work requires.

Rotterdam, Holland, Sunday, January 14

This morning I took the train to Amsterdam to attend the Sunday morning worship. As I entered the Westerkerk I realized that this was the first time I had set foot in this most famous and prestigious church of the city. What simple, dignified beauty. It all radiated a sober solemnity. The general atmosphere was formal, polite, and a little stiff. There were a few hundred people, most of them over age forty.

I realize how I desire more warmth, intimacy, fellowship, sharing, smiles, laughter, and celebration. Everything was meticulously planned and performed, and everyone was well dressed and behaved, so that I didn't feel I had become part of a community of people on a journey to God.

Afterward Jurjen, his wife, Willie, and I went to a coffeehouse. I tried to convince Jurjen that he would preach better and more convincingly if he didn't use a written text and spoke more spontaneously, but he didn't feel ready for that. I understand. When I saw him in that high pulpit looking at all these well-educated and well-groomed middle-aged Dutch men and women, I could sense that there was little space for spontaneity and immediacy. "This is one of the most prestigious Protestant pulpits in the country," Jurjen said. "You'd better know beforehand exactly what you are going to say." I am still convinced, though, that Jurjen should trust his own intellectual and spiritual gifts more and that a less "perfect" sermon might touch hearts more deeply.

At 2:30 p.m. I took the train to Rotterdam to visit my brother Laurent, his wife, Heiltjen, and their children, Sarah, Laura, and Raphael. It was good to see them all. In the evening I finally had a chance to see the video of the TV program with the Flying Rodleighs. It was a lot better than I had expected. Less reflective than the English version and a little more fragmentary, but certainly lively and with many interesting connections between a life with handicapped people and a life with great athletes.

My main criticism is that footage of another trapeze act was used as if they were the Rodleighs. I could well understand Rodleigh being offended that his act was mixed up with that of another, unknown troupe. I could also understand Rodleigh's unhappiness that twice they showed a fall in the net, giving the impression of regular failure. But for outsiders all of this is quite secondary. The people who saw the program were enchanted. Laura, my niece with Down's syndrome, played her role beautifully. Her smile, her total absorption in the performance, and her spontaneity were delightful.

After watching the video we sat around the kitchen table drinking tea, wine, and juices, and we talked about many things. It is good to be together.

Tielt, Belgium, Tuesday, January 16

This morning I took the train from Rotterdam to Ghent to visit my Belgian publisher. Lieven Sercu, my editor there for ten years, was at the station and drove me to Tielt, where the company has its headquarters.

As always I was received with great kindness and warm hospitality. Most of the afternoon was spent on "business." Presently fourteen of my books are in print in Dutch translations with Lannoo. Sales have increased remarkably during the last year, mostly in Holland. During the first eight years of my association with Lannoo, most of my books were sold in Belgium. Although the Flemish and Dutch languages are practically the same, there is not only a physical but also a psychological border between Holland and Belgium. Books published in Belgium have had a hard time "making it" in Holland. Therefore, it was a joy for me to see that interest in my books was gradually growing across the border.

At 7:00 p.m. Godfried Lannoo, the chairman of the board of Lannoo, and his wife, Maria, invited me for dinner. Godfried's sister, Godelieve, and his son, Mattias, who will succeed Godfried, were also at the table. We had a lively discussion about religion, art, history, and publishing.

Wednesday, January 17

This morning I went with Godelieve to the little convent of sisters to celebrate the Eucharist. Most sisters were age sixty and older. They still wear their full habit and live in strict seclusion. The altar was placed in front of a large open "window," through which I could see the sisters. There was no personal contact, only distant smiles. I gave a rather long homily in response to the readings, since I felt the sisters' great desire to hear something encouraging. I have no idea what they felt or thought.

Utrecht, Thursday, January 18

A quiet day. Gied from the Dutch Pax Christi came to the hotel for an interview. We talked for two hours, had lunch, and talked a little more. It was more a friendly conversation than an interview. But I have the feeling that Gied will write a good article based on what we spoke about.

After celebrating the Eucharist with the rector and students of the Ariensconvict, I visited Piet, the vicar general of the archdiocese, at his home.

When Piet asked me if I would be willing to speak to the diocesan council during one of their biweekly meetings, I responded that I wasn't sure the council was really interested in being with me and began to complain that I didn't feel welcome in the diocese. I expressed my disappointment that I had never been invited to preside over a liturgy, never been asked to say a word to the students at the Ariensconvict about L'Arche, never been treated as a brother.

I was somewhat surprised by my complaints, but I realized that they were based on my feelings of having been completely ignored by "my own" ever since I left Holland twenty-five years ago. I realize how ambivalent I feel about this. On the one hand, I want to go my own way, and I am grateful for the freedom I have been given. On the other hand, I still desire to be acknowledged as a priest of Utrecht, informed about what's going on, and invited to make a contribution. I do regret my complaints because they come from my little hurt self and do not go anywhere. I even wonder if I would truly enjoy more attention and not resent a greater role.

Piet is an honest, caring, and correct man who seemed a little puzzled by my negative feelings. He said, "You are one of us, and you know you are always welcome." I knew that he meant it but that my long life in

the USA and Canada has made me used to an exuberant and affective
hospitality I cannot expect from my countrymen.

Meanwhile Piet told me about the restructuring of the diocese, the
different tasks of the chancellery office, the hope for new ordinations,
and the struggle to live his job in a spiritually authentic way. I felt
grateful for his kindness and a little angry with myself for acting as the
"neglected one."

Prague, Czech Republic, Friday, January 19

This morning Jan and I took a KLM flight from Amsterdam to Prague.
At the Prague Airport, Peter, a Dutch friend of Jan who lives and teaches
in Prague, was waiting for us. Peter will be our guide for the next three
days. He speaks Czech fluently, knows Czech history from Wenceslas to
Havel, has many contacts with Roman Catholic and Protestant groups,
and is active in the Czech Pax Christi.

As we drove to the center of the city, Peter tried to answer my many
questions about Jan Hus and the Hussites, about the violent struggles
between Reformers and Counter-Reformers, about the influence of the
Habsburgs, the Nazi domination, the Communist period, the final independence of Czechoslovakia in December 1989, and the split between
the Czech Republic and Slovakia in 1993. In that short cab ride the
names of the writers Max Brod, Franz Kafka, and Jaroslav Hašek, and the
composers Bedřich Smetana and Antonín Dvořák were also mentioned.
I realized that my head was full of little fragments of Czech history and
culture. Peter helped me to put the pieces together and rediscover the
mosaic.

After lunch in a very pleasant restaurant, Peter went home and Jan
and I walked past the National Theatre, along the Moldau, and over the
famous Charles Bridge, flanked by large Baroque statues of Christ and the
saints. Walking over the bridge gave me the feeling of becoming part of a
very painful period of history. The triumphalist Catholic statues erected in
the seventeenth century speak of the victory of the Counter-Reformation
over the reform movements that started with Jan Hus at the end of the
fourteenth century. Talking to Peter later, I realized that even today the
Catholic Church is perceived by many of Prague's now secularized citizens
as a foreign, power-hungry institution. The hierarchy's desire to reclaim
the St. Vitus Cathedral after the Communist domination is looked at by
many with great suspicion.

After our walk we returned to the hotel and went from there to Peter's
house, where we met with the Pax Christi group in Prague. We sat around

the living-room table and exchanged ideas and experiences. After a while Peter asked me to lead a short prayer service. We sang Taizé songs, read passages from Scripture, offered short reflections, prayed together, and concluded with the Our Father in our different languages. It was a good, prayerful time, although I regretted that the three women hardly participated. They let the men do the talking! Before midnight Jan and I were back at the hotel. The last sixteen hours have been very full, very rich, and very challenging. I am ready for a long and deep sleep.

Saturday, January 20

Since I have been in Prague I have learned a new word: *defenestration*. It means "throwing your opponent out the window." There is something of a tradition of defenestration in Prague. It happened on July 30, 1419, when the Hussites stormed the Town Hall and threw three consuls and seven citizens out the window, thus starting the Hussite wars. It happened again on the twenty-second of May 1618, when enraged citizens threw three councillors out the window of the Hradčany Castle into the moat (all of them survived because they landed in a dung heap). This confrontation led to the Thirty Years' War. It most likely happened again on the tenth of March 1948, when Jan Masaryk, the foreign minister of the Czech Republic, the only non-Communist cabinet member, was found dead in the courtyard. I had never heard of this strange "custom," but I have decided to keep my windows closed as long as I can here!

After a very nice dinner and a few hours of rest, Peter took us to his house and showed us the film *The Unbearable Lightness of Being*, based on the book of the same title by the Czech writer Milan Kundera. Seeing this film, which speaks about love and sexuality in the context of the Prague Spring of 1968, was a deeply moving experience. After only a day and a half in Prague, we could see Kundera's story with new eyes.

Sunday, January 21

Before Jan and I came to Prague, Peter had spoken to Tomáš, the former secretary of the Czech bishops' conference and presently university chaplain, about our visit. Since three of my books, *The Genesee Diary*, *The Way of the Heart*, and *Life of the Beloved*, have been translated into Czech, he and several students knew about me. Tomáš invited me to concelebrate the 2:00 p.m. Eucharist in the San Salvador Church right across from the Charles Bridge and to give an afternoon conference for anyone who wanted to come.

The large Baroque church was extremely cold, and I wondered if any-one would come to Mass in such low temperatures. In the large sacristy, which was pleasantly heated, Tomáš greeted us. He impressed me as a strong personality — open, direct, and clearly progressive in church mat-ters. He seemed to feel quite at ease with his role and gave me a few instructions about my place in the liturgy.

When we entered in a long procession with acolytes carrying the cross, candles, and the book, the church was packed with students, visitors, and friends. Many people had to remain standing during the service. It was so cold that I wondered if we would make it through the hour-long service. Happily, just before the procession the sacristan offered me a fur vest to wear under the alb. Without it I probably would not have been very attentive to the liturgy.

The Eucharist was simple. Everything happened reverently and tradi-tionally. There was no difference between a Sunday Mass in Richmond Hill and this Sunday Mass in Prague, except for the language. Before the final blessing I introduced myself with a few words about my life at L'Arche Daybreak.

After the Eucharist about eighty people gathered in the large sac-risty for the talk. The discussion afterwards was quite lively. People were very gentle, kind, open, and attentive. They gave me great authority and hardly criticized my ideas. In contrast to my homeland, where most of what I say or write is subjected to critical scrutiny and is seldom ac-cepted at face value, here everybody received my words more as support for their spiritual life than as something to be discussed. There was a certain obedient passivity in the audience but also a loving receptivity.

Afterwards, one of Peter's friends said, "Some students felt you were too American — too much walking around, gesturing, and dramatic ex-pression. We are not used to that here. We are more quiet and sedate." It is interesting for me, a Dutch man living in Canada, to be considered "too American." They should have said, "You were too Henri Nouwen!" They are right: I tend to exaggerate with my voice and overdramatize things, always afraid of boring people. But notwithstanding the criticism I had the sense that most people found the meeting inspiring and uplifting.

Utrecht, Monday, January 22

After a farewell cup of coffee with Peter, Jan and I took the little van to the airport. At noon our KLM flight left Prague, and at 1:15 p.m. we were in Amsterdam. I keep being surprised that it is possible to have coffee in the center of Prague at 11:00 a.m. and be sitting at my desk at the hotel in Utrecht before 3:00 p.m.

The trip to Prague will always remain in my memory as a time in which friendship, education, beauty, history, good conversation, and relaxation were all part of the experience. It feels as if I had a short look into the heart of central Europe and glimpsed the great story of the making of the culture I am part of.

One thing is clearer to me than ever: What I think, say, and do makes a difference. I come back from this trip with a new sense of responsibility. On the one hand, I am only a little man in a large crowd of voices. On the other hand, my voice is important, as are the voices of Jan Masaryk, Alexander Dubček, Václav Havel, and many others. Havel's call to "live in the truth" has become a great challenge to me. More than ever I realize that I have to keep writing and thus serving the truth in simplicity, honesty, and humility.

I am deeply grateful to Jan and Peter, who opened my eyes and ears to many new visions and new sounds.

Kathy called to tell me that Tim died last Saturday at 3:00 p.m. Although I was prepared for the news I felt much inner sorrow. A beautiful man of God has left us — his wife, his three little children, and his many close friends. I spoke to Phyllis by phone and later to his best friend's wife. There was so much pain and sadness. I sat down at my hotel desk and wrote a letter to Tim's family and friends explaining how he had deepened and strengthened my faith. What a grace to have known him. I wish I could go to the funeral, but I will feel very close to all who mourn Tim's death.

Geysteren, Tuesday, January 23

This morning I took the train to Venray to be with my father. I had five suitcases with me. When I had to change trains and platforms in Nijmegen two conductors, a man and a woman, helped me with this luggage. I was deeply grateful for their kindness but also reminded that I am going to be sixty-four tomorrow!

My father was very glad to see me again and cares for me as if I am ninety-three and he is sixty-four! His heart, however, is very weak, and suddenly around 8:00 p.m. he looked completely spent. He could hardly breathe and walked with great difficulty. When I saw him so small, bent over, wrinkled, and pale, I wondered if he would make it through the night.

Wednesday, January 24

My sixty-fourth birthday. I am really glad to celebrate this day with my father. He felt well again and even took the car to go to the bank. Later we went to a friend's home to see the Rodleighs video. My father loved it. Meanwhile the heating system failed, so we had to keep ourselves warm with the open fire. Two old men sitting close to the fireplace warming their hands.

I feel happy on this day. Grateful to God and my family and friends for all the graces that have come to me during these sixty-four years. I look forward to the years to come as time to deepen my life with God and my friendship with people. I especially hope that I will have more space and time to write. Deep within myself I feel that something new wants to be born: a book with stories, a novel, a spiritual journal — something quite different from what I have done in the past. There is a sense of conclusion and new beginnings. This sabbatical year seems to be the year of transition from an active traveling life to a life of contemplation and writing. I realize, though, that it will require a lot of discipline to refocus my life. But without such a refocusing I will end up busy, restless, and always looking for human affirmation. It's time to make a radical choice for solitude, prayer, and quiet writing. I will need a lot of support to make this happen.

At 6:00 p.m. my father and I had dinner together in a nearby restaurant. We were the only guests! It was a delicious dinner, and we both enjoyed the quiet time together and all the attention we got from the waiter, who had only us to worry about!

This was probably the most quiet birthday of my life. But I will always remember it as the most peaceful.

Friday, January 26

Underneath all the activities of this month I have felt quite anxious about the manuscript of the Winnipeg journal. Although most of the text is finished, it still needs lots of work: corrections, changes, a new introduction, a new conclusion, and so on. I feel a certain fear about working on the manuscript. Maybe I am afraid to reenter that extremely painful experience. But today I felt the courage to take on the project, and suddenly new words seemed to come easily. I wrote the introduction and conclusion, and made various changes in the main text. It was a real relief.

Tomorrow I will leave Geysteren and spend the evening with my sister to celebrate my birthday. My father is too tired to come. A lot of talking people completely exhaust him. So this is my last full day with my father until I come back in June. I hope and pray that I will see him again in good health and good spirits.

Rotterdam, Saturday, January 27

A very special day! My sister, Laurien, organized a birthday party for me at her home in Nijmegen. She had invited several Dutch friends whom I had come to know at different stages of my life, but most of whom I had not seen for several years or even decades.

It was a unique evening for me, especially since everyone was in a very good mood and was eager to meet everyone else. Obviously the main question was, "What has happened with you since we last saw each other?" A lot had happened: most of all children and grandchildren. And jobs: Ferry a computer expert, Toon a businessman, Arnold a doctor, Louis a director of a TV and radio station, Wim a professor of child psychology, Jurjen a minister. Although all in the party were younger than I am, three of them — Ferry, Toon, and Henri — had already retired, and one of them, Louis, is going to say good-bye to his work at the end of next month.

What surprised me was that my friends were still in their first marriages and had also maintained some relationship with the church.

Obviously there were many "do you remember" stories. Most interesting for me was that each had stories to tell about me which I absolutely could not remember. Events that some of my friends remember with great vividness seem to have completely dropped out of my mind. And I carried ideas and images of my friends that were quite different from theirs.

The memories that we all most had in common were of our travels. Our bike trip to Belgium, our car trip to Germany, our boat trip to the island Spetsai in Greece, our plane trip to Israel, and all the events connected with these adventures.

At the end of the evening Louis, Wim, and my brother Laurent gave little speeches full of good humor and loving expressions of friendship.

It was a great birthday party. Good wine, an excellent meal, but most of all precious friendship. At 11:00 p.m. Laurent, Heiltjen, and Raphael took me and all my suitcases to their home in Rotterdam.

Monday, January 29

Today I decided to take the train to Oss, where my eighty-year-old pen friend Antoinette lives. When I called her a few days ago she was disappointed that I hadn't planned to visit her. Since then I have been wondering how I could find an opportunity to go to Oss.

It took me two hours (two taxis and two trains) to make it to Antoinette's apartment. We had a good conversation, and it was clear that I had made her day. She also made mine! It fills me with much satisfaction because now I can return to Boston having seen her and received from her. I know that I have a happy friend in Oss. Her love for me and her friendship make me grateful indeed!

Once I was home my brother Paul called from his car to invite me for dinner. An hour later, at 7:00 p.m., he made it to Rotterdam and took me to a very pleasant restaurant. It was good for us to have some time to catch up with each other and talk about family matters.

Tuesday, January 30

This was my last day in Holland. Tomorrow I am flying back to Boston. I am ready to return. Although I have enjoyed my time with my father and my several visits with friends and family, I did miss the regular writing and experienced this time as somewhat fragmented and unfocused. I look forward to a regular life with many hours at my desk.

Watertown, Wednesday, January 31

My brother Paul took me to the airport at 7:00 a.m., "before the traffic gets heavy," he said. We arrived at Schiphol at 8:00 a.m.

Jonas welcomed me in Boston at 1:30 local time and drove me to my home away from home in Watertown. It is good to be back with Jonas, Margaret, and Sam.

Although I had been able to sleep a little on the plane, I was so tired that I went right to bed.

February 1996

Thursday, February 1

Many letters, and many birthday gifts to open. Many phone calls to make and many little things to arrange for the move to New Jersey on Sunday.

The special event of today was Borys's visit. Since we last saw each other Borys has been in Ukraine, Italy, California, and many places in between. Just as I returned from Holland he returned from a monthlong retreat with the monks of the Ukrainian Monastery in California.

It was very good to be together again. Our friendship becomes deeper and stronger as the years pass. Borys, who often looks exhausted and over-worked, now looks rested and relaxed. It became clear to both of us how important we are for each other. "One day we should travel together," Borys said. I could hear his desire for a companion on his many journeys, someone to pray with, to talk with, and just to be with. I felt quite grateful to be and become more and more a true spiritual partner with him.

The retreat had given Borys a new focus, a new perspective, and a new energy. "Somehow I nearly lost God in my busy life for God," he said. "I am so glad to have refound my first love." I often wonder where we both will be ten, twenty, or thirty years from today. I hope and pray we will still be together and close to God.

Friday, February 2

The Feast of the Presentation of Jesus in the Temple. Borys, Jonas, and I celebrated the Eucharist together in the Empty Bell. Very quiet, very peaceful, very serene. Jonas played the shakuhachi to put us in a spirit of prayer and focus our minds and hearts on God. We read the moving story of old Simeon, who recognized the child Jesus as the light coming into the darkness, and we shared the bread and cup as signs of God's presence among us.

The rest of the day was quite tedious. Susan, my editor in Boston, had done very good work on the reflections, and she raised countless questions in the margins. So I had my work cut out for me today, going from page 1 to page 387! I now realize that there is a lot more to do on the manuscript, but after four hours I decided to let the whole thing rest for a while. I am not in a hurry to get this finished, and I had better not push it.

Tonight Borys will be here again. I look forward to a restful evening.

Saturday, February 3

This whole day I spent packing. It feels as if my "property" has tripled since I came here. More books, more sweaters, more papers! Christmas and my birthday certainly have been times of many gifts. What should I keep? What should I give away? At times I was irritated by the amount of "stuff" I carry around! Why can't I travel light?

At 11:30 a.m. Jutta came for a farewell visit. We had a lovely lunch at a nearby diner. Hamburgers! As always Jutta came with many gifts. Tulips, chocolates, coffee, and a book of essays about May Sarton. I am deeply grateful for Jutta's faithfulness to me even when I am such a poor friend.

This was such a hard week for her in the nursing home. Two people to whom she was very close died. She gave them and their families all her attention. But who is there for her when she comes home at night? Who cares for her in the way she cares for others? Her loneliness is deep and painful. She knows it and she accepts it, but it is a great cross to bear.

Peapack, Sunday, February 4

After the Eucharist in the Empty Bell, Jonas and I drove to Peggy's home in Peapack, where I will stay for the second part of my sabbatical. We had a joyful trip, and I am so grateful for Jonas's willingness to go with me. It was very cold but sunny. The roads were clear even though the meadows and hills were all still covered with snow.

It took us less than five hours to make it to Peggy's home. Dorothy, Peggy's housekeeper, welcomed us kindly and showed us the little house that will be my place for the coming months. It is quite spacious: a living room with kitchen and two bedrooms. Jonas took a walk while I tried to find places to put my things. I am really glad to have a new home and a quiet place to write. January was a good month, especially the time with my father, but it will be good to be in the same place for a little longer and to sit at a table again, working with ideas and the words to express them.

Monday, February 5

After we celebrated the Eucharist together I took Jonas to Bernardsville, where he caught the bus to New York. He will visit Crossroad, who are publishing his "Rebecca" book, before returning to Boston.

I spent all day finding my way around the area: the food store, post office, bank, gas station, and so on. I also made many phone calls: to get a fax installed, to work out arrangements with Federal Express, to plan a visit to Doubleday, to let friends know my new telephone number, and to tell Kathy about my setup.

Peggy is still away. She plans to be back on Friday. Her absence forces me to find my own way around. I am glad I don't have to bother her with my many questions about where things and places are. When she comes home I will know a bit about my new surroundings. They certainly are beautiful.

Tuesday, February 6

My Boston editor, Susan Brown, gave me a copy of an excerpt from Mark Epstein's book *Thoughts Without a Thinker: Psychotherapy from a Buddhist Perspective*. I found it a true eye-opener.

Epstein writes about the first cross-cultural meeting of Eastern masters and Western therapists, where the Dalai Lama was incredulous at the pervasiveness of "low self-esteem" that he kept hearing about. It seems that in the Tibetan cosmology, such feelings represent "the hungry ghost realm," not the human realm. In Tibet one assumes a positive sense of self, which is inculcated early and supported through all of the interdependent relationships that are established by the web of family. So a person is expected to maintain this positive feeling about himself, and if he cannot, he is considered a fool.

I find the concept of "hungry ghosts" fascinating. Epstein's theory is that Western feelings of unworthiness are rooted in the "hungry ghost" scenario because we are prematurely estranged in our childhoods. Thus, many of us are unable to find or sustain intimacy in our adult lives so we become preoccupied instead with the unresolved frustrations of our past. Indeed, it seems that many of us hope to find a solution to our low self-esteem by exploring our past, but in doing so we often drown in the many complicated waves of our personal histories. It is the hungry ghost, looking for a satisfaction that cannot be found.

The hungry ghosts, Epstein says, "are probably the most vividly drawn metaphors in the [Buddhist] Wheel of Life." He describes them as "phantomlike creatures with withered limbs, grossly bloated bellies, and long, narrow necks." In addition, the ghosts, when they eat or drink to satisfy their hunger, suffer from terrible pain and indigestion. Their throats burn, their bellies are unable to digest food, and they cannot take transitory satisfaction. So they remain obsessed with a fantasy of finding complete freedom from pain, especially the pain of the past, but they are ignorant of the fact that this desire is a fantasy.

When Jesus appears to his disciples after his resurrection, they think they are seeing a ghost. But Jesus says, "Why are you so agitated, and why are these doubts stirring in your hearts? See by my hands and my feet that it is I myself. Touch me and see for yourselves; a ghost has no flesh and bones as you can see I have" (Lk 24:38–39).

The Buddhist vision of hungry ghosts and the Christian vision of the resurrection supplement each other. By claiming our presence here and now, and by acknowledging our unfulfilled needs without wanting to fill them up with "food" from the past, we too can come to the joy the disciples experienced when they saw the risen Lord, who took grilled fish and ate it before their eyes (see Lk 24:43).

I am increasingly convinced that it is possible to live the wounds of the past not as gaping abysses that cannot be fulfilled and therefore keep threatening us but as gateways to new life. The "gateless gate" of Zen and the "healing wounds of Christ" both encourage us to detach ourselves from the past and trust in the *glory* to which we are called.

Wednesday, February 7

It seems that I evoked the hungry ghost in me while writing about it! This whole day I felt like a hungry ghost: hungry for attention and affection — telephone calls, letters, and so on. I ended up angry, not only at all those who didn't give me what I craved but also at my own hungry spirit for being so needy. I know that, after all the traveling and moving around of the last two months, it is time for silence, prayer, quiet writing, and just being alone. But my hungry ghost kept me restless, looking for little distractions, and thus avoiding a direct confrontation, which would make that ghost stop complaining so much.

After spending some time in the nearby town of Chester and buying a few things I really don't need, I sat down in front of the galleys of my cup book, which was a setup for frustration! All the way through I knew that the problem was not the book; it was my hungry ghost, feeling abandoned, rejected, forgotten.

Happily I found some consolation in my evening prayers. Somehow, saying them out loud, nearly screaming in the empty house, I started to experience little bits of inner peace.

I ended up the day with a glass of wine in one hand and the wartime journals of Thomas Mann in the other. Reading about Mann's intimate struggles with his writing, as well as his agony over the Hitler regime, helped me to put my little depression in perspective and make it to bed in relative peace.

Thursday, February 8

A difficult day again. I feel lonely, depressed, and unmotivated. Most of the day I have been fiddling around with little things. The same old pain that has been with me for many years and never seems to go completely away.

Meanwhile I have been playing with a new fax machine, which arrived yesterday. I was able to put the pieces together by following the instructions in the booklet, and to my great surprise it worked! I drove to Flanders, a little town ten miles from Peapack, to find a stationery store and buy the right kind of paper for it.

I realize that my busyness is a way to keep my depression at bay. It doesn't work. I have to pray more. I know that I need to just sit in God's presence and show God all my darkness. But everything in me rebels against that. Still, I know it is the only way out.

A few very kind letters gave me a little light.

God help me, be with me, console me, and take the cloud away from my heart.

Friday, February 9

Tonight Peggy and her friend Phil returned from their trip.

Peggy called as soon as she was home and invited me for dinner. It was a joy to see her again and to get to know Phil, whom I had met for only a minute at the Newark Airport a few months ago. It was a delicious dinner (meat loaf and rice pudding) with much conversation about our faith: married priests, women priests, the decline of the nuclear family, the attitude of the Pope, and so on. Peggy was quite clear about these issues and pleaded for radical renewal in the church. Phil was a little more hesitant but open to Peggy's arguments. Being a traditional Catholic, he needed some space and time to move in Peggy's direction.

I am glad that Peggy is back and that we can start creating a small community of friendship, prayer, and common vision in the Peapack Valley.

Saturday, February 10

At 9:00 a.m., Peggy, Phil, and I celebrated the Eucharist together in the second bedroom of the guesthouse where I am staying. It was a beautiful, intimate prayer time.

The whole day I have been working on the Winnipeg manuscript. During breaks, I went through the hundreds of Christmas and birthday greetings that Kathy sent me in a big box. Reading these cards and letters, I became aware of how many people carry me in their hearts and prayers. There were many photographs of newborn babies, and deceased parents and friends, and I have replaced the icons in my breviary with these pictures so I can more easily pray for all these good people.

At midday Nathan called from Calgary. It was a hard but good conversation. I told him about my depression and my deep feelings of loneliness and even rejection during the last few days. I told him that I felt disappointed because we haven't had a good talk recently.

Nathan responded with great love. He wasn't defensive or angry but simply said that he wasn't aware how intense my feelings had been and that he wanted to support me wherever he could. His own week — in contrast to mine — had been very full, with family visits and many intense conversations. He clearly had been living on a different wavelength than I and, of course, didn't realize my anguish. Our conversation made me experience gratitude for friendship. My feelings of anger, depression, anguish, and rejection gradually disappear as the snow is melting in the fields. Thanks be to God.

Sunday, February 11

This morning I celebrated the Eucharist in the living room of my little guesthouse. Peggy had invited a few of her neighbors, and Phil had asked his oldest son to come with his family. I realize that this little group of friends and family can easily become the core of a small liturgical community. It looks as if we are already moving in the same direction as at the Empty Bell.

Richmond Hill, Ontario, Monday, February 12

This morning after the Eucharist, Kathy called from Toronto to tell me that Adam Arnett had had a severe setback — a possible heart attack combined with an epileptic seizure — and had been rushed to the hospital. Shortly afterwards I talked to Nathan, and I realized that Adam was dying. I wanted to fly home immediately, and Nathan encouraged me to do so.

Adam is one of the men who introduced me into the community of L'Arche Daybreak and led me into a whole spirituality of weakness which has transformed my life. Living together with Adam at L'Arche Daybreak has profoundly influenced my prayer, my sense of myself, my spirituality, and my ministry. Adam, the man who suffers from severe epilepsy, and whose life has seemingly been limited because of his many disabilities, has touched the lives of hundreds of L'Arche assistants, visitors, and friends. As my friend and housemate he has reached into the depths of my heart and has touched my life beyond words.

Arriving in Toronto I was held up in immigration since I had been out of the country for so long. But finally I made it through all the checkpoints. Nathan was waiting for me and told me what he knew about Adam's situation. We drove directly to the hospital.

Rex and Jeanne, Adam's parents, greeted me, and we were happy to see each other. Several members of the Daybreak community were there to support Rex and Jeanne and to stay close to Adam in these last hours of his life.

When I walked into Adam's room, he was breathing rather regularly with the help of an oxygen mask. Ann, the person responsible for Adam's home, said, "This morning, shortly after he was brought to the hospital, Adam's heart stopped, and the doctor declared that he had died. But after several minutes his heartbeat and breathing returned. It seemed he was not yet ready to die. I'm sure he was waiting for Rex, Jeanne, and you."

I was deeply moved to see my friend Adam lying there, obviously living his final hours with us. I kissed him on the forehead and stroked his hair.

After half an hour just looking at Adam and talking quietly with Rex and Jeanne, I invited all those in the waiting room to gather around Adam's bed. We held hands and prayed for Adam, for his parents and family, and for his many friends. After that we just sat with him, following his breathing.

An hour later Michael, Adam's brother, came. It was clear that Michael was suffering immensely, and when he saw his brother he began to cry. His father embraced him. A few minutes later, when he saw me, he threw his arms around me and cried. I held his shaking body for a long time and then went with him again to Adam's bed.

Michael is also a member of Daybreak and, like Adam, suffers from epilepsy. I asked Michael to hold the little container with sacred oil, and, while everyone gathered again, I anointed Adam's forehead and both of his hands, praying fervently that God would give him the strength to make the passage to his final home in peace.

"My, my, my...brother...is going...to heaven," Michael said through his tears. "My heart is broken. My heart is broken, Father." I held him again, and we cried together.

Around 6:00 p.m. Nathan and I went to the Church Street House to fetch the food that the assistants had prepared for Jeanne and Rex, and then we had a quiet supper at a nearby restaurant.

When we returned to the hospital, Adam was in a different room because he no longer needed the heart monitors. Adam was now close to death, and the only thing to do was to make him as comfortable as possible. He was still wearing a face mask to help his breathing, but it seemed to make little difference. Finally Rex and Ann removed the mask so that Adam could be free from all unnecessary support systems. His breathing was slow and deep; once in a while it stopped but then started again. Now he was clearly struggling. Although it seemed that he was not having any pain, it was painful to see Adam fighting for every breath. Jeanne said, "With a weak heart like his, I can't understand how he can do it...it is such a struggle." Rex knelt beside the bed and held Adam's hand; Jeanne stood on the other side with her hands on his knees. I sat on the top of the bed caressing his head and hair, and once in a while holding his face between my hands.

The hours went by, and by midnight it seemed that Adam would make it through the night. Nathan and others from Daybreak had gone home, and I started to feel my own exhaustion. Ann said, "Go home now and get some sleep. Rex, Jeanne, and I will be here, and we will call you when Adam dies."

Just after I had fallen asleep at the Dayspring, Ann called and said, "Henri, Adam has died." Adam's life — and mission — had come to its end. I thought of Jesus' words "It is fulfilled." Fifteen minutes later I was back at the hospital. Adam lay there, completely still, at peace. Rex and Jeanne and Ann were sitting beside the bed touching Adam's body. There were tears, tears of grief but also of gratitude. We held hands, and, while touching Adam's body, we prayed in thanksgiving for the thirty-four years of his life and for all that he had brought to us in his great physical weakness and incredible spiritual strength.

I couldn't keep my eyes away from him. I thought, here is the man who more than anyone has connected me with God and the Daybreak community. Here is the man whom I cared for during my first year at Daybreak and have come to love so much. Here is the one I have written about, talked about all over Canada and the United States. Here is my counselor, teacher, and guide, who never could say a word to me but taught me more than anyone else. Here is Adam, my friend, my beloved friend, the most vulnerable of all the people I have ever known and at the same time the most powerful. He is dead now. His life is over. His face is still. I felt immense sadness and immense gratitude. I have lost a companion but gained a guardian for the rest of my life. May all the angels guide him into paradise and welcome him home to the embrace of his loving God.

As I looked at Adam, I saw how beautiful he was. Here was a young man at peace. A long, long suffering had come to an end. His beautiful spirit was no longer imprisoned in a body that could not help to express it. I asked myself about the deepest meaning of these thirty-four years of captivity. But that will only gradually be revealed. Now we simply have to trust and to rest.

Tuesday, February 13

At 8:30 a.m. we celebrated the Eucharist in the Dayspring chapel. Before that I had gone to the Red House to tell Michael and all his housemates that Adam had died. I also went to Adam's house to be for a moment with his housemates, and to the Green House to talk to the people there, especially Bill and David, who had been very close to Adam. There were many tears and long embraces. We so need one another at moments like these.

During the Eucharist Michael was sitting on my right. He had put on his alb and kept holding my hand. Gordie and Francis had also vested themselves to be altar servants. I chose to speak about the resurrection of Lazarus. Somehow our faith in the resurrection of the body is very important at this time. Adam's body, which we all had touched and held so often in his long struggle for survival, will be renewed. In the resurrection he will be dressed with a body that will allow him to express the deepest stirrings of his heart. We are full of tears as Mary, Martha, and Jesus were at the death of their brother and friend, but it is not the end. It is the passage to glory, to victory, to freedom. I could see how we all experienced enormous sadness because of Adam's leaving but also an immense joy that he was finally free.

At the end of mass, Gordie got up and addressed Michael directly: "I know your heart is broken, Michael, but I'd like you to have this." Then he hung a Special Olympics medal, which was dear to him, around Michael's neck. Michael was visibly moved by Gordie's kindness.

Being back at Daybreak means seeing many friends again. Kathy and Timmy, Carl, Kathy and Margaret, Joe and Stephanie, and many others. Sue is away but will return tomorrow.

It happens that the men's group of which I am a member was planning to meet tonight. I was really glad because it would offer me an opportunity just to be with close friends and talk about my own feelings and emotions. Carl and I drove to downtown Toronto, where we were going to have dinner and our meeting. On the way we stopped at the office of the architect Joe, who had sent me the drawings for the little house I hope to build for myself after I return to Daybreak. We spoke for half an hour about it, and it was a good and helpful meeting.

At 6:00 p.m. Joe, Carl, Nathan, and I had dinner. I was fighting fatigue since I had hardly slept last night and was wondering how to stay awake and alert through our meeting. But somehow being with good and caring friends energized me and made the tiredness move to the background of my consciousness.

When we came to the apartment for our meeting, Francis (who was a part of our men's group) joined us. For the next two and a half hours the five of us "checked in" with one another and shared how we were doing "inside." Although I had missed many meetings because of my sabbatical, I soon felt warmly welcomed. I expressed my concern about reconnecting well with friends I had not been with for quite some time, but these concerns vanished quickly when people in the group reassured me about how glad they were to have me there again.

I spoke a little about my good feelings about my writing so far, my anxieties about returning to Daybreak without getting drowned in countless things, and my excitement about having a small house for myself, where I could continue to write without needing to leave the community. Through it all I felt Adam's presence. He had helped me to find roots in Daybreak, and many of my hopes, desires, and plans are somehow connected with him.

It was after 11:00 p.m. when I came home and fell into a deep sleep.

Wednesday, February 14

Today at 2:00 p.m. I went to the funeral home in Richmond Hill. Seeing Adam's body in his casket touched me deeply. He looked so peaceful, like a young man who had just fallen asleep. Tears filled my eyes. Our relationship has had such a deep impact on my life journey. I looked at his beautiful and gentle face, and I felt profoundly humble and grateful to have been in his circle of friends. I couldn't stop looking at him. He looked so normal, so healthy, and so handsome. It was as if he was giving me a glimpse of the new body he would have in the resurrection.

Most of the Daybreak members came during the afternoon just to be with Adam one more time. There was such deep grief. It is hard to imagine how life can go on in the New House without Adam. In his great weakness, Adam called all those who had shared his home to a life of reconciliation, healing, and unity, and thus had become their peacemaker.

Within an hour the room where Adam's body was laid out was full of people from the community, family, and friends. I was touched to recognize that Greg who had lived with Adam for a few years, had come with his wife Eileen, from Chicago, that Steve who had grown close to Adam when he was an assistant at the Day Programme, flew in from Seattle, and Peter who had accompanied Adam for two years in his home, had traveled from Nova Scotia to be with us all at this time. At 3:00 p.m. we formed a large circle and prayed. Then I asked whether anyone wanted to tell a story about Adam, and various people spoke of special moments in their relationships with Adam. Rex's and others' "little stories" brought smiles and laughter, and made us aware of how, beyond all words, all memories and images, this simple, poor man had shown us the gentle face of God.

When at 7:00 p.m. many of us gathered to be with Adam for two more hours, the mood was different: more relaxed, more festive, more playful. As we formed another circle, Kathy and Elizabeth, two community members, told moving stories, not about what they had experienced with Adam but about how they would see him again. Everybody listening felt the joy and peace that came from their words. Here we were, standing around Adam's body, imagining his newfound freedom and celebrating his newfound life. Then we sang "Peace Is Flowing Like a River."

Adam, the peacemaker, is finally free from all captivity. In his brokenness he has shown me my own brokenness, and thus set me on the road to healing and new life. Now he will receive a new body, full of light, full of love, full of glory, the reward of his remarkable mission.

After the visitation I went to Kathy and her son Timmy's house for a brief visit. Kathy had worked with Adam during the last five years in the Day Programme. Kathy made me aware of how much the people there were suffering because of Adam's death. They had walked with him, given him massages, taken him swimming, helped him with his lunch, and had always been with him when he had a seizure. They and the other members of the Day Programme — Michael, Alia, Janice, Rosie, and Tracy — had come to love Adam as a very dear friend. Adam's absence will create a huge emptiness, not only in their tightly knit community of care but also in their hearts. Their grief is deep, and in the weeks and months to come they will have a painful struggle to discover the new way Adam continues to be present in their life and work together.

Kathy is expecting her new baby soon. It's going to be a girl, and her name is going to be Sarah. While Timmy was trying to put a large Batman puzzle together, I recounted the story of Abraham, Sarah, and the three angels who came to tell them that in their old age they would have a baby. I told Timmy that at first Sarah didn't believe the angels because she was so old, but that a year later she had her son, Isaac, who became the father of Jacob, who became the father of Joseph, and so on.

Timmy looked at me and said, "Cool, really cool." Then he said, "Mom, did you know all that about Sarah?"

Kathy answered, "Yes, but I didn't tell you all of it because you and I were still debating whether Sarah would be the best name!"

Timmy replied, "Well, I think so. Don't you think so too?"

Then Kathy turned to me and said, "Timmy and I would like you to be the godfather. What do you think? You can take your time to think it over. We want to be sure she has a good godfather, and we both hoped you would be willing to be that."

Quite touched, I said, "I don't need any time to think it over. I am very happy to be Sarah's godfather... unless you change her name!"

Death and birth. So close to each other. In our community of Daybreak, when Maurice died, Monica was born. Now that Adam has left us, we are waiting for Sarah! I felt a deep joy being so close to that mysterious place where death and life embrace.

Thursday, February 15

When I woke up this morning, I was deeply fatigued. My stomach was upset, and my head felt dizzy and unfocused. But I knew that I had to "step over" all these feelings and be as well as possible for the funeral service. Just thinking about the many details and about the homily I wanted to give made me nervous. I decided to try not to think too much but to get up and do it all in good order.

By 9:00 a.m. I was in St. Mary's Immaculate Catholic Church with my suitcases full of chalices, patens and colorful altar cloths, plus my homily notes written out in my journal book. By 9:45 several hundred people from all over had gathered to celebrate the life and death of Adam Arnett.

As eight of Adam's close friends accompanied the casket to the front of the church, we all sang "The Beatitudes" and during the service we listened to the words of St. Paul, "God chose those who by human standards are weak to shame the strong" (1 Cor. 1:27).

Adam didn't need a eulogy. His simple, hidden life had no impressive curriculum vitae. But Adam deserved to be praised for the miracles he had worked in our hearts. His father, Rex, Ann, his long-time friend and head of his home, and Bill, one of his housemates, spoke about these miracles in a simple and moving way. All three of them told stories about how Adam had reached a deep place in them that few people had been able to reach and he had planted there little seeds of hope.

As I have lived these last three days, I've come to see with a clarity I never had before that Adam was the living Christ among us. Where else did we have to go to be with the man of sorrow and the man of joy? Where else did we have to look for the presence of God? Yes, Adam was loved by God long before his parents, his brother, or we, loved him. Yes, Adam was sent by God to live among us, a hard but blessed life for thirty-four years. And yes, Adam, after completing his mission, was called back home to God to live a new life in a new body. That's the story of Jesus. That's the story of Adam too!

I know, too, that L'Arche became my community and Daybreak my home because of Adam — because of holding Adam in my arms and touching him in complete purity and complete freedom. He called me home. It was not just a home with good people, but it was a home in my own body, in the body of my community, in the body of the church, yes, in the body of God. Without him I do not know where I would be today.

As I was holding the bread in my hands, standing in front of Adam's body, and speaking Jesus' words "Take and eat, this is my Body given for you," I saw, in a whole new way, the mystery of God, of Adam, and of each one of us. Indeed in Christ, God had taken a body so that we could touch God and be healed. I sensed today that God's body and Adam's body are one, because, as Jesus says, "In so far as you did this to one of the least of my brethren you did it to me" (Mt 25:40). In Adam, indeed, we touched the living Christ among us. And, as with Jesus, everyone who touched Adam was healed.

At the cemetery the pallbearers carried Adam's body to the burial site and placed it on the metal structure above the grave.

After a short prayer, I gave Michael the holy-water sprinkler, and, while I held him tightly, he bent over his brother's casket and carefully blessed it, slowly walking from one side to the other. Then I prayed: "Dear God, into your hands we commend our son, brother, and friend Adam. Welcome Adam to paradise, and help us to comfort each other."

Adam's casket was lowered into the grave, and I was hit by the finality of his death. He was gone and would never be with us again. St. Paul says it with so much conviction: "What is sown is perishable, but what is raised is imperishable; what is sown is contemptible but what is raised is glorious; what is sown is weak, but what is raised is powerful; what is sown is a natural body, and what is raised is a spiritual body" (1 Cor 15:42–44). It was right in front of that big hole that I was confronted with the finality of death as well as with the hope in the resurrection.

Clara sang the beautiful blessing we had sung in the church, and when everyone had been able to throw some sand on the casket, I said, "Let's now go in peace." Then we left the place where Adam was laid. Some lingered a while, as if it was hard to leave this lovely man all alone there, but after a few minutes there was complete solitude. Adam has left us, and we have to continue to live in hope.

At 4:00 p.m. Sue took me to the airport. It was good to be away from the crowd and just feel my own grief and deep fatigue. Sue thanked me for coming back to Daybreak in this time of mourning. I was very glad that I had come. But now it was time to go away and be alone. At 6:20 I arrived at La Guardia Airport, and a half hour later I was at Jay and Wendy's home. Wendy was waiting for me and gave me some supper, meanwhile asking everything about Adam. I was glad to be with her in her warm home.

When I finally stretched out on the large bed in Wendy's guest room, I felt as if I would be able to sleep for days, even weeks.

New York, Friday, February 16

At 8:00 p.m. Wendy, Jay, Jonathan, and I had a cozy dinner. After the full and intense week at Daybreak, it was a real gift just to be with a few friends and enjoy a good meal.

I still feel the loss of Adam in my heart. It is as if things just aren't the same anymore. I keep thinking about his youthful face lying in the casket. I pray for him and all the people in Daybreak who are in grief.

Peapack, Saturday, February 17

Jay took me to the Port Authority bus station, where I caught the 10:00 a.m. bus to Bernardsville. Peggy was there to take me home.

I was really glad to be back in my little house. After a lovely lunch with Peggy and Phil, I slept most of the afternoon, deeply feeling the weight of the (exhausting) fatiguing week in my body, mind, and spirit.

In the evening, I tried to write a little bit about Adam, but I had to force myself to stay awake. It feels as if I am crying inwardly because of Adam. Every part of my being seems to be mourning his death.

Monday, February 19

Today's Gospel is about the cure of a boy possessed by a demon who makes him dumb and throws him constantly into fire and water.

Two aspects of healing are clear here. First of all, we have to trust in the healer. Jesus says, "All things can be done for the one who believes" (Mk 9:24). Second, the healer must be a person of prayer. When the disciples ask Jesus, "Why could we not cast it out?" Jesus says, "This kind can come out only through prayer and fasting" (Mk 9:29).

I am touched by this mutuality between the healer and the person who needs healing. Healers must be in communion with the source of all life and healing so that they can be true mediators of the healing power, which is larger than themselves. People who seek healing must surrender themselves, trusting that the healer can indeed mediate that healing power to them. The humility of the healer and the faith of the sick person are both central to the work of healing.

Tuesday, February 20

Most of the day I spent writing about Adam's death and funeral. Although my emotional and spiritual fatigue is still with me, I am able to write a bit, and to use my writing as a way of grieving.

At 6:30 p.m. I went to Peggy's house for a Mardi Gras dinner. Peggy's son Steve and several friends were there. As always when Peggy invites family and friends, our conversations were interesting, focused, and primarily meant to help someone in his or her personal life.

The theme that ran through most of our conversations was interiority. Steve told about several people he had met who seemed to have hardly any inner life and often dealt with their emotions and feelings through harmful acting out. This led to a discussion about the meaning of being in touch with your own soul, knowing your passions, emotions, and feelings before acting them out and wounding others. In our outer-directed society, with so many people who feel threatened and are primarily concerned with their own survival, getting and staying in touch with one's interiority seems increasingly difficult.

Considering this was a Mardi Gras dinner, our conversation was quite serious. But there was a lot of laughter amid all the serious talk.

Tomorrow will be Ash Wednesday already.

Wednesday, February 21

I am certainly not ready for Lent yet. Christmas seems just behind us, and Lent seems an unwelcome guest. I could have used a few more weeks to get ready for this season of repentance, prayer, and preparation for the death and resurrection of Jesus. But this morning quite a few gathered for the Eucharist. Peggy had brought some ashes, and I put on my alb and Guatemalan stole to mark the special quality of the day.

I spoke about how Jesus stressed the hidden life. Whether we give alms, pray, or fast, we are to do it in a hidden way, not to be praised by people but to enter into closer communion with God. Lent is a time of returning to God. It is a time to confess how we keep looking for joy, peace, and satisfaction in the many people and things surrounding us, without really finding what we desire. Only God can give us what we want. So we must be reconciled with God, as Paul says, and let that reconciliation be the basis of our relationships with others. Lent is a time of refocusing, of reentering the place of truth, of reclaiming our true identity.

After the reflections on the Gospel, we put ashes on one another's foreheads. Later when I came to the post office, I saw Eugene, the postmaster of Peapack, with a big black mark on his forehead. For a moment I had forgotten all about ashes and thought he had hurt himself, but then I realized that he and I had the same mark, and we laughed together seeing it!

Strangely enough this became a busy day: many faxes, phone calls, letters, et cetera. The best thing was that I could finish writing briefly about Adam's death and funeral and send it to Kathy. Writing it has really helped me to deal with my sadness and pain.

Thursday, February 22

When you can say to Jesus, "You are the Messiah, the Son of the living God," Jesus can say to you, "You are the rock on whom I will build my church." There is a mutuality of recognition and a mutuality of truth here. When we acknowledge that God has come among us through the Messiah — his anointed one — to free us from our captivity, God can point to our solid core and make us the foundation for a community of faith.

Our "rock" quality will be revealed to us when we confess our need for salvation and healing. We can become community builders when we are humble enough to see our dependence on God.

It is sad that the dialogue between Jesus and Simon Peter has, in my church, been almost exclusively used to explain the role of the papacy. By doing so, it seems to me that we miss seeing that this exchange is for all of us. We all have to confess our need for salvation, and we all have to accept our solid center.

And the keys of the Kingdom? They too belong first to all who confess Jesus as their Christ and thus come to belong to a community of faith in which our binding and unbinding happen in the Name of God. When indeed the body of Christ, formed by believers, makes decisions about its members, these are Kingdom decisions. That is what Jesus refers to when he says, "Whatever you bind on earth will be bound in heaven, and whatever you loose on earth will be loosed in heaven" (Mt 16:19).

These thoughts came to my mind on this Feast of the Chair of St. Peter, as we were gathering around the table with several people who had left the Catholic Church because they saw it as too authoritarian. More than ever it is important to realize that the Church is not simply "over there," where the bishops are or where the Pope is, but "right here," where we are around the table of the Lord.

Most of the day I was busy giving titles to the 387 reflections I wrote before Christmas. I also had a good telephone conversation with Jan van den Bosch, who wants me to come to the Hermitage in St. Petersburg in September to make a three-part television program of my book on Rembrandt's *Return of the Prodigal Son.*

New York, Friday, February 23

Today is Wendy's birthday. I took the bus from Bernardsville to New York to be with Wendy and Jay, and their son, Jonathan. Wendy had asked me to celebrate the Eucharist at 6:30 p.m. for the small circle of friends she had invited for dinner. Many of them belong to her prayer group. I met some remarkable people.

As we reflected on the readings and expressed our need for God's healing grace, it became clear how much suffering there was in the little group — depression, loss of family members through an accident and through AIDS, conflict with authorities, a close relative with a mental handicap, and the great stresses of New York City life. I spoke a little about the ways absence and presence touch each other. Precisely where we feel most present to each other we experience deeply the absence of those we love. And precisely at moments of great loss we can discover a new sense of closeness and intimacy. This is also what the Eucharist is about. We announce the presence of Christ among us until he comes again! There is both presence *and* absence, closeness *and* distance, an experience of at-homeness on the way home.

I was struck again by the paradox that loving someone deeply means opening yourself to the pain of her or his absence. Lent is a time to get in touch with our experience of absence, emptiness, unfulfillment, so that in the midst of our overcrowded lives we can remind ourselves that we are still waiting for the One who has promised to fulfill our deepest desires.

Peapack, Saturday, February 24

On the bus from New York City to Bernardsville, I became completely absorbed in the American journal of Thomas Mann. I have been reading this journal since I bought it in Utrecht and have become increasingly interested in it. I am reading his notes written during the end of the Second World War. While carefully following all that is happening in Europe, from his home at Pacific Palisades, he maintains his work on the novel *Doctor Faustus*. This discipline as a writer astonishes me. Mann certainly was not alone. His wife, Katia, his children, and his wide circle of relatives created a busy social life. His German friends living with him in exile formed a lively artistic community, full of music, literature, and art. Still, in the midst of it all, even during emotionally intense days, such as the day Germany fell, he kept working on his novel. It is exciting, encouraging, and very inspiring to get such an intimate look into the life of such a great novelist.

After I got home I contacted Ginny, asking her if she would be open to doing some typing for me. There is more to type than Kathy alone can do, and I foresee that the work will steadily increase. Ginny was willing and eager to help. She said that she had just been thinking about finding something new to do. I am very happy to have this unexpected support.

Today is my brother Laurent's fifty-first birthday. I called and realized that many family and friends had gathered in his home and were planning to go to the show *Evita* in Rotterdam. I wished I could be with them.

Sunday, February 25

The Eucharist this morning brought quite a few people together. The Genesis reading about the creation and fall of Adam and Eve, and the Gospel reading about the temptation of Christ spoke to me in a new way.

Adam and Eve were tempted to be like God. Jesus was tempted to deny his divine Sonship. When we act as if we are God, we cause war, but when we act as God's beloved children, we create peace. When we acknowledge God as our creator and Lord, we open ourselves to the news of Jesus that indeed we are God's children, eternally beloved, destined for a life eternal.

What especially struck me were the serpent's words "Your eyes will be opened, and you will be like God." When Adam and Eve do eat from the tree the storyteller says, "Then the eyes of both were opened, and they knew that they were naked" (Gen 3:5–7). But Jesus came to open our eyes to the deeper truth that, even though we are sinners, we are still God's beloved children. "Blessed are your eyes because they see," he says (Mt 13:16).

Both temptation stories are about our true spiritual identity.

Monday, February 26

Today's readings complement each other in a remarkable way. In the first reading, Moses says, "You shall not steal; . . . you shall not defraud. . . . You shall not revile the deaf. You shall not render an unjust judgment. . . . You shall not hate in your heart," and so on (Lv 19:11–17). The *nots* sound harsh and forbidding, like gunshots. But in the second reading, Jesus says, "I was hungry and you gave me food, I was thirsty and you gave me something to drink, I was a stranger and you welcomed me. . . . Just as you did it to one of the least of these brothers and sisters of mine, you did it to me" (Mt 25:35, 40).

This is the great movement from "you shall not" to "you may." We may care for the poor, the sick, and the dying, and meet God there. Instead of a distant God, whom we must please by not doing evil things, Jesus reveals to us a God who is as close to us as the poorest person is.

I keep marveling at the radicality as well as the simplicity of Jesus' message. He breaks right through all the questions about what to do in order not to offend God and places the poor in front of us, saying, "This is me...love me." How radical and how simple!

Tuesday, February 27

Translating my own reflections from English into Dutch is quite an interesting job. I have never done any translating. But the people of *Trouw* want me to do my own translating. They chose 40 meditations from the 387 I had given them and faxed them to me so I could translate them and fax the translation back.

I find myself doing a lot more than translating. Since I don't have to be faithful to the author, I can make all the changes I want! And I make many because the Dutch language has its own beautiful idioms worth using. A lot of the Dutch idioms come from the seafaring world. The verb "to reject" can be translated by *afstoten*, which literally means "pushing away" and refers to pushing a boat away from the pier. I am also discovering that I need a lot more words in Dutch than I do in English to say the same thing! It's like a little word game, which I enjoy.

At 8:00 p.m. Jeffi, one of the Daybreak assistants, called to tell me about Alia, one of the core members of Daybreak, who lives at the Corner House with her. Alia has been at Daybreak since 1988, and although she has quite severe leukodystrophy, she has been doing remarkably well. She is a beautiful young woman, deeply loved by everyone. She cannot walk, speak, or see, but she radiates immense peace and joy. In the musical *One Heart at a Time*, which the community performed last year for its twenty-fifth anniversary, Alia had a central place. Hundreds of people saw her onstage in the large beanbag, and dancing in the arms of an assistant, Ben.

Jeffi told me that Alia can no longer swallow food and had to be taken to the hospital to be fed intravenously. On Thursday the doctor plans to put a tube into her stomach so she can receive liquid food without having to swallow. It is clear that Alia has entered a new phase of her illness. Jeffi spoke with much tenderness but also sadness about the seriousness of her illness. Alia's father has been coming to the hospital often. He is a wonderful man, who on several occasions has spoken to us about his Muslim faith and prayer. It is so hard for him, as it is for all of us, to realize that his dear Alia might not be with us for very long. At moments like this I wish I wasn't so far from home.

Wednesday, February 28

"This evil generation ... asks for a sign," Jesus says in today's Gospel (Lk 11:29). But what we are looking for is right under our eyes. Somehow we don't fully trust that our God is a God of the present and speaks to us where we are. "This is the day the Lord has made." When the people of Nineveh heard Jonah speak, they turned back to God. Can we listen to the word that God speaks to us today and do the same? This is a very simple but crucial message: Don't wait for tomorrow to change your heart. This is the favorable time!

The people sitting around the little table in my living room were very excited about this idea. Just being here together in the presence of God, listening to God's Word, breaking bread together and drinking the cup — this is the moment of salvation; this is the moment of God's appearance among us. All we need is *right here.*

One person, who hadn't been to our Eucharist celebration before, was deeply moved by what the readings were telling her. She was struggling with her addiction to smoking and had been feeling miserable and depressed. She said, "I can't believe this. Everything you all are talking about speaks directly to me. This is more than a coincidence. God must have called me to this place to hear this."

The rest of the day I have been busy with the manuscript of the reflections for every day of the year. If all goes well, I will have a final manuscript for the publisher very soon.

En route to Santa Fe, New Mexico, Thursday, February 29

Last year when I was planning my sabbatical, Malcolm, a dear friend from Texas, said to me, "If you ever want to spend some time in my house in Santa Fe, just let me know." It felt like a wonderful idea. Although I have been in Santa Fe a few times on my way to the Benedictine Monastery of

Christ in the Desert in Abiquiu, and once to preach at the ordination and installation of my friend, Wayne, as a pastor there, I really hardly know the city or the state. But everyone who knows Santa Fe has told me, "Go, you will enjoy it. It is one of the loveliest places in the United States."

I took Malcolm up on his invitation. He suggested March first through tenth as the best time, and here I am, flying to New Mexico. Malcolm will meet me at Albuquerque Airport and drive me to Santa Fe. He and his daughter Alison will get me settled in their house and leave me there on Saturday. But I won't be alone. My longtime friend Frank, a Presbyterian minister from California, will join me on Saturday and we will spend the week together. I am excited, full of expectation, and open to new things.

March 1996

Santa Fe, Friday, March 1

Last night Alison and Malcolm were waiting for me at the Albuquerque Airport. It was good to see them again. Around 11:30 p.m. local time we made it to his house in Santa Fe. A small, intimate, romantic adobe condominium. An ideal place to spend a week.

After a good night's sleep Malcolm took me to a popular breakfast place and later to some of the art galleries on Canyon Road. After dinner at a nearby restaurant Alison rented a video and Malcolm and I went to a piano bar. I got to bed feeling very tired, but grateful for Malcolm and Alison and for their generous care of me.

Saturday, March 2

At 10:00 a.m. Malcolm, Alison, and I celebrated the Eucharist in the living room and at 11:30 left for the Albuquerque Airport. Malcolm and Alison took the plane to Dallas from Gate 3, and Frank arrived from San Francisco at Gate 4! It was so good to see him again. We haven't been together since August.

Frank and I rented a car and drove back to Malcolm's house. At 6:00 p.m. we went grocery shopping. I hope we bought enough for the week so we don't have to go back! These huge stores make me tense and nervous.

Malcolm's house is so cozy and efficient that I can imagine being happy just staying here reading, writing, talking, praying, and watching the sun go down from the roof. But I guess we will do other things as well, considering we are in one of the most historic places in the USA, with a rich culture and a great variety of art and music.

Sunday, March 3

As we walked through Santa Fe this afternoon, Frank and I could see the remarkable intermingling of the three cultures that have shaped the city: the Pueblo Indians, the Hispanics, and the Anglos. We saw the jewelry, weavings, and pottery of the Indians, the Spanish architecture, and the mostly American art galleries.

I was quite overwhelmed by the beauty of the Indian jewelry and the black-on-black pottery. Frank, who recently spent a few months in Saudi Arabia, found the Indian jewelry quite similar to that of the Bedouins.

It was harder to find a way to appreciate the modern art displayed in the various galleries. Much of it is inspired by New Mexico's turbulent history, the magnificent, clear sunlight, the rich flora, the picturesque adobe houses, and most of all the awe-inspiring desertscapes. Many of these paintings are very large, as if the painter wanted to express the immensity of what the eye sees, and very expensive. It was hard to decide what really spoke to me.

But this town certainly puts you right in the center of much of what America is about.

Monday, March 4

At noon Frank and I visited Jim, who is the president of a small publishing house in Santa Fe. Jim is a longtime friend of my friend Fred, who had said to me, "When you go to Santa Fe, be sure to visit my friend Jim." It was a delightful visit. During lunch we spoke about our personal histories, spirituality, books, and of course, Santa Fe.

I was deeply touched by Jim's kindness, openness, honesty, and intelligence. He loves his work, is very committed to his role as editor and publisher, has a great interest in spiritual subjects, and radiates humility as well as self-confidence. One remark he made shows his personality. He said, "I love to help people, but I get very embarrassed when they thank me."

I very much hope that this visit can be the beginning of a new friendship.

Tuesday, March 5

Last week when I was talking to my friend Joan in San Diego, she said, "When you are in Santa Fe I would like to come to visit you, just for a chat." But shortly after I arrived in Santa Fe she called again and said, "Could you come to me instead?" Today was the day for my lunch with Joan.

We were happy to see each other, and after a short conversation in the living room we went to the same restaurant where Sue and I and her other guests had dinner last December. It was so good to connect with her again. We talked about many things. After lunch we went back to her home and admired her splendid garden in full bloom, driving around in a golf cart.

Returning home I reflected on our friendship. Joan is a beautiful, wonderful, and incredible woman. Our conversation reflects our desire for safe, trustworthy, and spiritually helpful company. This is not so easy to find for a person in her situation. When we had arrived at the restaurant a letter was laying on Joan's plate. The writer said, "Since I do not know how to reach you but have heard that you often come to this restaurant, I decided to send my letter to you there in the hope you will find it and read it." The letter asked for a very large sum of money to prevent the closing of a home for disadvantaged people due to temporary government cuts.

I said, "Don't you sometimes feel overwhelmed by these requests for money, and a little lonely in the midst of them?" She laughed and said, "Well, Henri, that seems to go with the territory." Although she might have been a little irritated by getting such a letter with her lunch, I realized that the writer's courage and strategy would probably be rewarded.

Wednesday, March 6

Tonight at 6:00 Jim came for dinner. Frank and I had so much enjoyed our time with him last Monday that we invited him to spend the evening with us.

After dinner I showed Jim the video *Angels* over the Net about the Flying Rodleighs and told him that I wanted to write a book about them but still hadn't found the right form. It has been five years since I met the Rodleighs. I have collected many notebooks of information about their lives, their art, and their ideas, but whenever I start to write I experience an enormous hesitation, even fear.

Jim responded quite radically: "You must write the book because you have given it so much of your energy and attention. You have to trust your intuition that your friendship with these trapeze artists allows you to say something very important."

I said, "Yes, that intuition is strong, but I am afraid. When I first saw the Rodleighs, something very deep and intimate within me was touched. They brought back in a vivid way the longings I had had as a seventeen-year-old boy for communion, community, and intimacy. Many of these longings went underground during my time at the seminary and the university and my years of teaching. They only manifested themselves in occasional mental wanderings, curiosities, and feelings of anguish. When I went to L'Arche I allowed all these feelings and emotions and passions to reemerge. But seeing the Rodleighs catapulted me into a new consciousness. There in the air I saw the artistic realization of my deepest yearnings. It was so intense that even today I do not dare to write about it because it requires a radical new step not only in my writing but also in my life."

Jim said, "I knew all this. The video showed it to me. The Rodleighs are completing something within you that for many years remained uncompleted. It has to do with your search for community and your deep yearning for completeness. If you do not write the book you will deny yourself an enormous opportunity for growth. Yes, it feels risky, and it is difficult, but you really have no choice."

I said, "But what is the book finally about?"

He answered, "About community, in the most universal sense. Through the Rodleighs' story you can express the longing of all people. It is not just about flying and catching but about that invisible community that undergirds all you are seeing in the Rodleighs. You see friendship, family, cooperation, artistic expression, love, commitment, and much more. It all has to do with community. And that's your final subject. It is like DOS in the computer world: the invisible force that keeps everything together. It is a metaphysical principle that holds the stars, the sun, and the moon in their orbits, that connects God with humanity, that allows people to fall in love and bring forth new life. It is the mysterious, ungraspable, and inexpressible reality on which everything else is based. It is that reality that you must touch through the image of the trapeze. Your life now is already very much involved in all of this. You cannot ignore it for much longer. You have to express it. For you that means writing about it."

I felt deeply challenged by Jim's insights. Maybe he is the one I have been looking for to help me give birth to this book. After he left I said to Frank, "We have to talk more with him. Maybe I came to Santa Fe to meet Jim so that I can finally get moving on this long-delayed project." It is an exciting thought.

Thursday, March 7

A very quiet day. We went shopping in the town and dropped in at Jim's to say hello. I came to the conclusion that Jim would be the ideal man to help me write the book on the Rodleighs. No one has ever responded so positively, enthusiastically, but also critically to my desire to write this book. So I asked him if he would be willing to visit again to discuss the possibility of becoming my editor and publisher for the book. He said he would love to do it.

Santa Fe, Friday, March 8

At 9:30 Wayne, a friend from my Harvard days, came for a visit. We had not seen each other since 1988, when I came to Santa Fe to preach at his ordination and installation. Presently he is the director of "Bread for the Journey," an organization that supports various projects to help the poor in New Mexico.

It was very good to see him again. He is an affectionate, caring man with a great heart and a beautiful laugh. After an hour "catching up" with each other, Wayne invited Frank and me to take a trip to the shrine of Chimayó.

We drove for a good half hour through the desert and arrived around noon at the charming-looking church of Chimayó, a small adobe structure with two towers and a lovely walled-in courtyard in front of it. The intimate building is often called the Lourdes of America. Every year close to three hundred thousand people come from far and wide, often on foot, to pray for peace in the world and in their hearts, to fulfill a promise, or to seek healing.

The miraculous crucifix found around 1810 forms the center of the shrine. There also is an adjacent room with a little well, El Pozito, with "holy dirt" that people cross themselves with and take home. Like Lourdes water, the holy dirt of Chimayó helps people in their prayers for healing.

When Wayne, Frank, and I entered the little church we were engulfed by an atmosphere of prayer. You could feel that for more than a century and a half people had filled this intimate space with their cries, tears, and words of thanks and praise. The crucifix on the main altar surrounded by a reredos of painted symbols is deeply moving. The face of Christ is gentle and loving even in his agony. We prayed for a while and went to the El Pozito, where people were kneeling and crossing themselves with the dry sand.

After lunch we made a second visit to the shrine. We just wanted to be there a little longer.

Around 3:30 p.m. we were back home. I took a nap, and Frank started to prepare the meal. Jim was joining us again for dinner.

The evening with Jim was very amicable. We shared our personal stories and discussed plans for the trapeze book. Jim was quite open to working with me on the book and eventually publishing it. When he left I felt that I had started a precious friendship as well as an exciting writing project.

Sunday, March 10

At 10:00 a.m. Frank and I walked up to the Martyrs' Cross, a large white cross that sits on top of a small hill overlooking the city.

After attending Mass at St. Francis Cathedral, we bought some posters and art cards. In a secondhand bookstore I saw a beautiful color engraving of the Church at Chimayó. Looking at it for a long time, I experienced a deep attraction to it. It brought back all the feelings and emotions I had had during our visit there on Friday. It felt like something of spiritual value. After some hesitation I decided to buy it thinking that it is probably the best possible way to remember our visit to Santa Fe.

We were back at the house in the early evening. After a light meal and evening prayers we went to bed early, planning to leave at 5:00 a.m. tomorrow to be on time for our flights to San Francisco and Newark.

Peapack, Monday, March 11

It was still dark when Frank and I left the house in Santa Fe. We had a quiet, peaceful drive and we prayed together on the way.

I always want good-byes to be special but they are hard for me. At the airport I somehow got in a complaining mood and it seemed that a little demon was invading me, wanting to destroy all the good things we had lived.

We had decided to go early to the airport to have time for a cup of coffee. But when we got to the little restaurant close to the gate, Frank didn't seem to want any coffee or food and he seemed to me to be quite flat. I felt that he was overly concerned with getting his boarding pass and making a call to friends in Albuquerque. Suddenly I had the experience of being left alone. I felt as though we were just going through the motions, and that, in reality, Frank wanted to be by himself.

Although I knew in my heart that much, if not most of this was pure projection, and said more about my state of mind than about Frank's, I couldn't keep it to myself and started to complain: "Where are you?" I said. "You are no longer here. I had hoped we could have a good chat and a warm farewell. I feel as if you are happy that the vacation is over."

Frank reacted strongly. "Don't deny the good week we lived together," he said. "Don't ruin it all. Yes, I did have to make a phone call, and I didn't want to drink coffee, but you make a lot out of nothing. I just find it hard to talk in airports."

I felt embarrassed and sad. I didn't want to spoil the good week we had had, but here we were, having an argument about nothing.

Shortly before my plane left I was able to get a hold of myself and thank Frank for his friendship. Still, I felt very disappointed and for the whole trip I kept thinking about my inability to step through my feelings. It was good to be home again and even though I soon became involved with unpacking, letters, and faxes, I had an uneasy feeling about the morning.

Later Frank called. I asked him for forgiveness and we talked for a while which helped me to reclaim the good week we had had together. Just before going to bed I realized that the Gospel for tomorrow is about forgiving from your heart.

Tuesday, March 12

The days in Santa Fe, simple and unpretentious as they were, revealed to me in a new way the beauty of life. Friendship, art, nature, history, and the tangible presence of the immanent as well as transcendent love of God filled me with gratitude for being alive and being alive with others.

In Santa Fe both agony and ecstasy are imprinted on the buildings and monuments and reflected in the many adobe houses. I well understand why painters, sculptors, writers, and musicians like to live there. Many great people have left their spirits in Santa Fe to protect as well as inspire them. During this short stay I experienced the presence of these spirits and got a glimpse of the permanent reality shining through the impermanence of all created things. Malcolm, Alison, Jim, Wayne, and most of all Frank became the ones who helped me to keep the heavy curtains of life's theater slightly open and encouraged me with their love and affection to trust that there is a great show being prepared for us.

A very full, somewhat intense, but also joyous day. This was going to be a publishers' day in New York City.

After meeting with my Crossroad publishers Gwendolin and Bob about my writing, we went to dinner at Gwendolin's apartment on Front Street, south of the Brooklyn Bridge. Friends came and we had a very pleasant evening. I was carried away a little with too many funny life stories, but we had a good time, with much laughter and camaraderie. I was so grateful to Gwendolin for not taking us to a restaurant but inviting us to her own place. Even though we talked a little about books and publishing, it felt more like a happy family reunion than a business dinner. It was one of those rare occasions when good working and good living come together. It seemed like a European evening, reminding me of my evenings with Gwendolin's parents, Hermann and Mechtilde, and with Franz and Reny in Freiburg, and of the dinner with the Lannoos in Tielt. Writing books, making friends, creating community, sharing stories all merged into one event. I will always remember this as the European evening in New York. I now see what Gwendolin has brought from Germany to her colleagues. She herself said as much when we walked along Front Street: "I chose to live here because it feels a little like Europe, and I like it here."

Wednesday, March 13

I feel a new energy around the book about the Flying Rodleighs. Today the print center in Bernardsville copied and bound all the interviews I had done in November 1992, which Connie, my former secretary, had typed out. I am amazed how much material I had collected: three volumes of notes. Tomorrow I will send them all to Jim in Santa Fe. Kathy will send him all the photographs from Toronto that were taken in June 1993. I am very curious about Jim's reaction.

Thursday, March 14

Jesus says, "Whoever is not with me is against me, and whoever does not gather with me scatters" (Lk 11:23). These words frighten me. I want to be with Jesus, but often it feels like I want to be with many others too! There is within me a strong tendency to play it safe. I want to stay friends with everyone. I do not like conflict or controversy. I hate divisions and confrontations among people. Is this a weakness, a lack of courage to speak out forcefully, a fear of rejection, a preoccupation with being liked? Or is it a strength that allows me to bring people together and be reconciled, to create community, and to build bridges?

Jesus also says, "Do you think that I have come to bring peace to the earth? No, I tell you, but rather division! From now on, five in one household will be divided, three against two and two against three" (Lk 12:51–52). What do I do with all these harsh words? Isn't there enough religious conflict? Isn't Jesus inciting me here to a confrontational life and stirring me up to create separation between people? I still remember Pasolini's movie *The Gospel According to St. Matthew.* There Jesus is portrayed as an intense, angry rebel who alienates everyone in sight.

I have made an inner decision to keep looking at Jesus as the one who calls us to the heart of God, a heart that knows only love. It is from that perspective that I reflect on everything Jesus says, including his harsh statements. Jesus created divisions, but I have chosen to believe that these divisions were the result not of intolerance or fanaticism but of his radical call to love, forgive, and be reconciled.

Every time I have an opportunity to create understanding between people and foster moments of healing, forgiving, and uniting, I will try to do it, even though I might be criticized as too soft, too bending, too appeasing. Is this desire a lack of fervor and zeal for the truth? Is it an unwillingness to be a martyr? Is it spinelessness? I am not always sure what comes from my weakness and what comes from my strength. Probably I will never know. But I have to trust that, after sixty-four years of life, I have some ground to stand on, a ground where Jesus stands with me.

And when divisions arise against my desire, I have to find the courage to live them as lovingly as I tried to prevent them; then Jesus' harsh words might prove consoling.

Friday, March 15

Last night I watched a television conversation between Bill Moyers and Joseph Campbell. It was a rerun of a series of programs made in the eighties.

I was struck by Campbell's remark that we serve the world by being spiritually well. The first questions are not: "How much do we do?" or "How many people do we help out?" but "Are we interiorly at peace?" Campbell confirmed my own conviction that the distinction between contemplation and action can be misleading. Jesus' actions flowed from his interior communion with God. His presence was healing, and it changed the world. In a sense he didn't do anything! "Everyone who touched him was healed" (Mk 6:56).

This morning during the Eucharist we discussed the great commandment. The same theme came up. When we love God with all our heart, mind, strength, and soul, we cannot do other than love our neighbor, and our very selves. It is by being fully rooted in the heart of God that we are creatively connected with our neighbor as well as with our deepest self. In the heart of God we can see that the other human beings who live on this earth with us are also God's sons and daughters, and belong to the same family we do. There too I can recognize and claim my own belovedness, and celebrate it with my neighbors.

Our society thinks economically: "How much love do I give to God, how much to my neighbor, and how much to myself?" But God says, "Give all your love to me, and I will give you your neighbor and yourself."

We are not talking here about moral obligations or ethical imperatives. We are talking about the mystical life. It is the intimate communion with God that reveals to us how to live in the world and act in God's Name.

Saturday, March 16

In one of Jesus' stories a Pharisee, standing by himself, prays to God: "God, I thank you that I am not like other people" (Lk 18:11).

That's a prayer we often pray. "I'm glad I'm not like him, her, or them. I am lucky not to belong to that family, that country, or that race. I am blessed not to be part of that company, that team, or that crowd!" Most of this prayer is unceasing! Somewhere we are always comparing ourselves with others, trying to convince ourselves that we are better off than they are. It is a prayer that wells up from our fearful selves and guides many of our thoughts and actions.

But this is a very dangerous prayer. It leads from compassion to competition, from competition to rivalry, from rivalry to violence, from violence to war, from war to destruction. It is a prayer that lies all the time, because we are not the difference we try so hard to find. No, our deepest identity is rooted where we are like other people — weak, broken, sinful, but sons and daughters of God.

I even think that we should not thank God for not being like other creatures, animals, plants, or rocks! We should thank God that indeed we are like them, not better or worse but integral parts of God's creation. This is what humility is all about. We belong to the humus, the soil, and it is in this belonging that we can find the deepest reason for gratitude. Our prayer must be, "Thank you, God, that I am worthy to be part of your creation. Be merciful to me a sinner." Through this prayer we will be justified (see Lk 18:14), that is, find our just place in God's Kingdom.

Anthony Heilbut's biography of Thomas Mann reveals an incredibly complex character. He describes him as disciplined and sensual, artistic and political, expansive and depressive, imaginative and narcissistic, married and homosexual, self-revealing and deeply hidden, famous and anxious to be praised, immersed in religious themes and a confessed unbeliever. Mann had to flee Germany because of his strong antifascism, but he ended up "fleeing" the United States because of being on McCarthy's list as a Communist. I am quite overwhelmed by all the animosities, jealousies, hatreds, and petty rivalries in his circle of artists and the pains and tragedies in his family. And then the suicides! Heilbut writes, "The rate of suicides among émigrés grew epidemic."

It seems that Mann never became free from the inner and outer clouds that darkened his heart and his society. His was a very long, extremely productive, but deeply tragic life. It is as if redemption never came to him and if he wanted to redeem himself he never could. Tonight I pray for Thomas Mann. Lord, have mercy upon him, whether he is as great as Goethe or not. Give him the love that he yearned for all his life but that even the Nobel Prize couldn't bring him. Keep him safe in your all-forgiving, all-embracing love.

Sunday, March 17

To the question who was to blame for the tragedy of a man born blind, Jesus replied, Nobody. "He was born blind so that God's works might be revealed in him" (Jn 9:3).

We spend a lot of energy wondering who can be blamed for our own or other people's tragedies — our parents, ourselves, the immigrants, the Jews, the gays, the blacks, the fundamentalists, the Catholics? There is a strange satisfaction in being able to point our finger at someone, even ourselves. It gives us some sort of explanation and offers us some form of clarity.

But Jesus doesn't allow us to solve our own or other people's problems through blame. The challenge he poses is to discern in the midst of our darkness the light of God. In Jesus' vision everything, even the greatest tragedy, can become an occasion in which God's works can be revealed.

How radically new my life would be if I were willing to move beyond blaming to proclaiming the works of God in our midst. I don't think it has much to do with the exterior of life. All human beings have their tragedies — death, depression, betrayal, rejection, poverty, separation, loss, and so on. We seldom have much control over them. But do we choose to live them as occasions to blame, or as occasions to see God at work?

The whole Hebrew Bible is a story of human tragedies, but when these tragedies are lived and remembered as the context in which God's unconditional love for the people of Israel is revealed, this story becomes sacred history.

I talked to my father today by phone. I asked him, "What do you think of my daily column in the Dutch newspaper?" He paused and said carefully, "Some are better than others.... It is not easy to write a column." Although his response was not very different from his responses to my high school performances, and quite in character, I still felt a little hurt. So I called a friend in Holland, who said what I wanted to hear, "Very good," and that made me feel better. My mind is quite funny: I say that I want to hear the truth, but then I keep begging for compliments!

I guess my father was right. Some *are* better than others.

Monday, March 18

I had many telephone conversations today: first with Jim, who had received all the trapeze material. He was quite enthusiastic and told me that I wouldn't need to spend any more time with the Rodleighs to be able to write the book. That is very encouraging. Then I talked to Carl, who asked me for a short article about Adam for the Daybreak newsletter. I wrote it tonight, and I hope Carl likes it even though it might need many revisions. Then I made a call to Wayne in Santa Fe to thank him for our good trip to Chimayó and to ask him if I could use the name of his organization, Bread for the Journey, as the title for the yearbook of reflections. This morning this title came to mind, and I wondered why. Then I realized that it was Wayne who had planted the seed. He was very happy to let me use "his" words.

A good, even though somewhat fragmented day.

Tuesday, March 19

Today is the Feast of St. Joseph, the righteous man. Often the family of Jesus is portrayed as the model for all families. But a closer look at the way Joseph, Mary, and Jesus lived together evokes little desire for imitation. Indeed, Joseph was a very decent man. He didn't want to give his pregnant girlfriend a bad reputation, and after a reassuring dream, he married her. But was it a happy life? When Jesus was twelve they lost him in the crowd, and when they found him, after three days of anxiously looking, their question: "Why did you do this to us?" was answered with something close to a reproach: "Did you not know that I must be in my Father's house" (Lk 2:49)? This response, "But didn't you know I have more important things to do than pay attention to you," is hardly consoling.

All the other references to Jesus' family life are more disturbing than consoling. At Cana when Mary asks for his help, Jesus says, "What do you want from me? My hour has not come yet" (Jn 2:4). When, later, Jesus receives a message saying, "Look, your mother and brothers and sisters are outside asking for you," he replies, "Who are my mother and my brothers?" (Mk 3:32–33). Finally we find Mary standing under the cross. Seeing his mother and his beloved disciple, John, Jesus says to his mother, "Woman, this is your son" (Jn 19:27). About Joseph there is no word. What happened to him? Did he die?

In this time of broken families, of separation and divorce, of children with only one parent, and of mothers and fathers in great anxiety about their suicidal or drug-using kids, the seemingly quite dysfunctional family of Jesus may offer us some solace! It is clear to me that Jesus is quite ambivalent if not negative about so-called family values such as family harmony, filial affection, staying together at all costs. I wonder if our church's elevation of celibacy, especially for those who want to serve God, does not have its roots in the quite disturbing situation of Jesus' own family.

But Joseph is a saint! He lived it all in a great hiddenness. Ignored by the Gospel writers, and by the early church, he emerges today as a man trusting in God even when there was hardly anything for him to hold on to.

Wednesday, March 20

These days I feel strong, alive, and full of energy. Still, I am aware that much of that well-being is the direct result of the loving support of many friends. At the moment I do not experience any anger or hostility directed toward me. I feel in gentle harmony with my family, the people in Daybreak, especially Nathan and Sue, and the many friends close by and far away. In situations like this I easily forget how fragile I am inside, and how little is needed to throw me off balance. A small rejection, a slight criticism might be enough to make me doubt my self-worth and even lose my self-confidence.

I had been thinking about this when I read Michelangelo's poems to Tommaso Cavalieri, the young Roman nobleman whom he first met in 1532, when he was fifty-seven years old. His love for Tommaso, and Tommaso's affection for him, made him feel fully alive. He writes:

> With your bright eyes, I see the living light which my blind eyes alone can never see; and your sure feet take up that load for me which my lame gait would let fall helplessly.
>
> My very thoughts are framed within your heart.

These words evoke deep feelings in me. They reveal my true dependence on human affection and love. I know how many of my thoughts are framed in the hearts of those who love me.

Thursday, March 21

The first day of spring. It still is chilly, cloudy, and wet, and the heat is still on in the house. But at least there is the promise of new color, new sunshine, new leaves on the trees. I can't wait to see it all happen.

Tomorrow Nathan is coming, and that makes me happy. He will be here until Palm Sunday. What a joy it will be to welcome him, show him my new home, and celebrate our friendship in prayer, meals, trips, and good conversation during the next eight days.

Friday, March 22

I was nervous driving alone to Newark Airport to welcome Nathan. I wanted to be so sure that I would find my way and be on time that I ended up getting to the Air Canada gate an hour before his arrival time.

I spent my time wandering through Terminal C, a huge place, with thousands of people coming and going, urgent announcements, little bars and restaurants packed with patrons, bookstores, newsstands, and lines of waiting travelers. Walking through the large concourses I kept being surprised by how many people there are and how few people I know. I suddenly had this feeling of aloneness, of being lost in the crowd, of being a stranger in a strange land.

At 4:45 p.m. Nathan arrived. I was happy when I saw him emerging from the gate. His was one out of the million faces that smiled at me and knew me.

Saturday, March 23

Most of today was spent showing Nathan around. I thought it would be good for him to know the area so he will be free to take the car and go where he wants. It is a joy for me to be able to have a friend who offers me trust, love, and safety and from whom I have no secrets.

Sunday, March 24

The resurrection of Lazarus is one of the most complex stories of the New Testament. It has many levels of meaning. This morning I found myself speaking about it without always fully knowing on which level I was moving.

First of all, there is the contrast between the death threat against Jesus and the calling to life of Lazarus. When Jesus says to his disciples, "Lazarus is dead. For your sake I am glad I was not there, so that you may believe. But let us go to him." Thomas says to his fellow disciples, "Let us also go, that we may die with him" (Jn 11:14–16). Going to Lazarus meant going to Judea, where Jesus' enemies were trying to kill him. But going to Lazarus also meant going to the place of life. The resurrection of Lazarus becomes the event where death and life touch each other. After Lazarus was called back to life, the leaders became determined to kill Jesus (Jn 11:53). All of this can be seen as Jesus' way to prepare his friends and disciples for his own death and resurrection. By resurrecting Lazarus, Jesus shows that he is indeed the resurrection (Jn 11:25) and that his own death, which will happen soon, is not a final death.

Second, there is a love story here. Lazarus was one of Jesus' closest friends, and his deep compassion for Lazarus's sisters, as well as his great love for Lazarus, moved Jesus to call Lazarus back to life. Whenever Jesus calls someone to life — the son of the widow of Nain, the daughter of Jairus — we always see an immense love and compassion. It is this love and compassion that is the source of new life.

Third, there are Jesus' words when he first heard of Lazarus's illness: "This illness does not lead to death; rather it is for God's glory, so that the Son of God may be glorified through it" (Jn 11:4). As in many other situations Jesus sees a tragic event as the opportunity to reveal God's glory.

How do all these levels belong together? Maybe the best way to answer that question is to look at Jesus' own death and resurrection. There we see that the final power of death is overcome. There we see that this overcoming of death takes place in the context of love of those who knew Jesus intimately. There we see the greatest tragedy of human history become the occasion for the salvation of the world.

Wednesday, March 27

Quite a large group of neighbors came to the Eucharist this morning. It seems that a little community is emerging. So far the focus is still very much on me, but I hope that gradually people will discover the mystery of the Eucharist and be nurtured by the real presence of Jesus, visible in the gifts of bread and wine as well as in the gifts of one another.

The rest of the day was full of frustrations, all related to photocopying, faxing, binding, and sending. Hardly any time for writing, praying, and just reflecting. The day gets taken up with countless little things, necessary, time-consuming, and utterly distracting.

I am enjoying Nathan's visit so I do not totally 'lose it' over the little things.

Thursday, March 28

During the Eucharist this morning we talked about God's covenant. God says, "I am your God and will be faithful to you even when you won't be faithful to me." Through human history, this divine faithfulness is shown to us in God's increasing desire for intimacy. At first God was the God *for* us, our protector and shield. Then, when Jesus came, God became the God *with* us, our companion and friend. Finally, when Jesus sent his Spirit, God was revealed to us as the God *within* us, our very breath and heartbeat.

Our life is full of brokenness — broken relationships, broken promises, broken expectations. How can we live that brokenness without becoming bitter and resentful except by returning again and again to God's faithful presence in our lives? Without this "place" of return, our journey easily leads us to darkness and despair. But with this safe and solid home, we can keep renewing our faith, and keep trusting that the many setbacks of life move us forward to an always greater bond with the God of the covenant.

Nathan and I did some shopping, but we spent most of the day at our desks writing. At 7:00 p.m. we went to Peggy's home, where we had a delicious dinner and a very animated — as always with Peggy — conversation. Peggy was eager to know Nathan better, and he was very happy to tell her about his life, his vocation, and his great love for L'Arche. I could see a new and beautiful friendship emerge. A joy to behold!

Friday, March 29

Tonight when Nathan and I went out for supper we had a very honest and direct conversation about life and the ups and downs of our own relationship.

Our friendship began in France and grew strong over the first year. Later, at Daybreak there were many stresses, and because I became too dependent, the friendship finally broke. This breakage triggered many things in me, and the pain of our separation was so deep that I had to leave the community for six months to try to rediscover trust and to re-find hope. Without any doubt those were some of the hardest and most agonizing months of my life. During that time I wondered if I would ever return to Daybreak and live in the same community with Nathan.

When the time was right I did return and ever-so-gradually the friendship was restored, and even deepened. Today we are committed friends, as people of faith, as coleaders of Daybreak, and as men committed to share with and support each other.

During our supper Nathan challenged me to be less complaining and more affirmative. "When you say 'yes' to an invitation, don't complain that you are too busy, and when things go well for you, don't make ambivalent statements about it as if you still need some special sympathy." I thought I was beyond my complaining attitudes but he was pointing out that they keep creeping up and preventing me from fully claiming the joy and peace that is mine.

Well, a lot to think about and to work on.

Tomorrow Sue, Carl, and John, who have been giving a short retreat in New York City, will be coming for a visit. It will be great to see them.

Saturday, March 30

At 3:30 p.m. Sue, Carl, and John arrived by bus in Bernardsville. They were in a good mood and quite happy with the miniretreat they had given.

After getting settled in Peggy's house, they came over to the little guesthouse, and we all had a nice chat, catching up with the "latest from Daybreak." Then John went off for a rest, Carl for a walk, and Nathan, Sue, and I spent a good hour talking about my place in Daybreak after September. It is becoming clear to me that I would love to continue my writing after September while also having some kind of pastoral presence in the community. Presently Sue is the interim pastor. Would she be willing to stay in that role for another year? Would the community be open to letting me stay away longer, with regular visits to Daybreak? Should I go forward with my plan to build a small house for myself in Daybreak, or should I simply take over the present Dayspring when the new Dayspring is built? These were some of the questions we talked about in preparation for the Council meeting in Daybreak on Thursday.

Today I received news that Claire, a friend of mine, had died. I had hoped to visit her because I knew that she was ailing and now I am sorry that I did not get there.

Quite a few years ago, Claire had come to Daybreak to ask for some spiritual support. She had been struggling with deep feelings of rejection and depression and had been seeing a psychiatrist for many years without much result. Although she had lived in "high society" and had known many of "the great" of our world, she often felt very lonely and even unappreciated. Underneath it all was the question: "Do people really love me for who I am?"

Sue and I had both talked with her several times during her visit, but what really deeply affected her was her dinner at the New House, where she met Adam, Rosie, John, Michael, Bill, and their assistants. It was a completely new world for her. During her time at the New House, something happened within her that had a radical effect on her inner life. She felt accepted for who she was. Nobody there knew about her life, her notoriety, her fortune, or her many connections. She was simply Claire but the people around the table made her feel that she was special to them.

After her visit to Daybreak I called Claire often and visited her several times. Every time she said again, "At Daybreak my depression left me. I have many problems with my health, and I often have to go to the hospital but I know now that God is close to me and that I am loved."

Now Claire is dead. Her body was finally no longer able to hold on to her spirit. I am glad she had such an easy death, without long suffering. She died at peace with God, her husband, her children, and her many friends. Her daughter asked me to celebrate the Eucharist and give the homily at her funeral. I hope and pray that the many people who will be there will get a glimpse of the immense love of God that Claire experienced through the broken people of Daybreak.

Sunday, March 31

After a very animated Palm Sunday Eucharist in the living room, with about twenty people, and a pancake breakfast at Peggy's home, Peggy drove Nathan, Sue, Carl, John, and me to Newark Airport. Shortly after Nathan, Sue, Carl, and John left for Toronto, I was on my way to Boston.

In Boston, Jonas was waiting at the airport. It was really good to see him again. The main purpose of my visit was to be part of an evening at St. Paul's Catholic Church in Cambridge to celebrate Jonas's book, *Rebecca*.

It was a beautiful evening. Close to five hundred people came. Both Jonas and I gave short presentations about the loss of a child and the journey from grief to gratitude. This being the first day of Holy Week allowed us to make the evening into a spiritual preparation for entering deeply into the paschal mystery. We sang several Taizé songs. Jonas played two pieces on his flute, and after a short intermission several people spoke about their own pain connected with the loss of a child, a family member, or a friend.

One woman touched me very deeply. She told us that long ago she had given up her baby son for adoption because of the shame of being pregnant without being married. Twenty years later, while trying to get in touch with her son, she discovered that he had died in an accident when he was eight years old. Upon hearing this she experienced an immense sense of loss and grief. But gradually she was able to live through her pain. The experience brought her to study theology, and today she is close to getting her Master of Divinity Degree.

This and many other stories made the evening special. We concluded with a prayer and the Our Father. Many people stayed after the presentations, talking to one another. All of Jonas's books at the church were sold.

It was a wonderful evening. I felt very grateful to be there with Margaret, Jonas, and many old friends. There was a spirit of love and joy in the midst of the tears that were shed. I was especially happy because Margaret and Jonas shared their feelings about Rebecca and they were so available during the question and answer time.

April 1996

New York, Monday, April 1

Somehow yesterday completely exhausted me. Today I slept as long as I could. At 11:00 a.m. I was still walking around Jonas's house in a bathrobe, hardly willing to get dressed and start the day.

At 6:00 p.m. Krister and his wife, Brita, came for dinner at Jonas and Margaret's home. Krister, while Dean of Harvard Divinity School, had invited me to join the faculty. I had accepted his invitation, but shortly after I came to Harvard, he became the Lutheran bishop of Stockholm. When Krister and Brita returned to Cambridge after four years in Stockholm, I had left to join L'Arche. Krister may have felt a little guilty about getting me to Harvard, because he knew that my time there had been quite hard for me, and in many ways disappointing.

I was happy to have the opportunity to tell him that there was no bitterness in me about my time at Harvard, and that there was no reason for him to feel guilty. I told him that during my three years at Harvard I had made some beautiful friends, especially Jonas and Margaret. I said I had discovered that although the academic life had been a good life for me, my deep desire was for a life with the poor in a community with a contemplative dimension. Without Harvard I wonder if I ever would have been able to choose for L'Arche. It was a real joy for me to reestablish my friendship with Krister and Brita after a twelve-year interruption.

At 9:00 p.m. Jonas drove me to the airport. By 11:45 p.m. I had arrived at Wendy and Jay's home in New York. I am a little nervous about Claire's funeral tomorrow.

Richmond Hill, Tuesday, April 2

A little before 9:00 a.m. I arrived at the church for Claire's funeral. The sanctuary was nearly full by the time the casket was brought in. The liturgy was very gentle in mood. In the homily I spoke about Claire's poverty — her wounded heart searching for love — and about the blessings she received. I tried to express how her real blessings were hidden, not in her fame, wealth, or success but in her little, often lonely heart.

At 2:00 p.m. I was on my way back to Toronto to celebrate Holy Week and Easter with my community. When I arrived at Daybreak, Sue, Carl, Nathan and his parents, from Calgary, joined us for dinner at the Dayspring. It is very good to be back home again.

Wednesday, April 3

A busy day with work in the office, several planning meetings, dinner at the Church Street House, and other events. But what dominated my day emotionally was news of the suicide of a man that I barely knew.

The first time I had met him, about four years ago, his kindness had touched me in a deep way. In the following years I lost contact with him, but I was grateful to see him turn up at a lecture recently. He looked very good, in fact, open and radiant. We embraced, and I said, "It's so good to see you again after all these years." There were so many people crowding around us at the moment that that was all I could say.

The next day I realized that I had no plans for lunch, so I had called his home but all I got was the answering machine. I didn't know his work number, so I left a message hoping that someone would pick it up and let him know that I was free for lunch. Nothing happened.

Last night his friend Vincent called and told me that he had committed suicide on Monday afternoon by jumping from the roof of a building.

My whole interior flooded. I didn't even know what to think or feel, but I was overwhelmed. What had happened? Why did he kill himself? Where was his partner? And, beyond all these quick, stormy thoughts, there was the sense of loss: he is gone. I will never see him again, never get to know him. His young life so full of promise is cut off, suddenly, desperately. I hardly knew him, but he had touched me and I remembered him well. I had not been aware of any depression, inner anguish, or despair. He had looked so well on the night of the lecture. He had seemed so attentive and free. When a woman in a wheelchair wasn't able to reach the lecture hall, he was there to offer his help. There was no sign of self-absorption or inner pain. Now he is gone, forever. My heart turns, turns, turns....

Tonight I talked to his partner for nearly an hour. He was deeply shocked but able not to let his grief overwhelm him. He told me about their long relationship. He told me about his friend's long struggle with depression, how he had often spoken about his desire to kill himself, about his many fears, especially about being a disappointment to others. He told me that last year during Holy Week he had attempted to kill himself by jumping from the same building.

I just listened. It was a story of love and pain, communion and separation, intimacy and distance. So strange! This was someone that I saw only twice, but he rooted himself somewhere in my heart.

Holy Thursday, April 4

The whole community met at 2:00 p.m. in St. Mary's Anglican Church for the foot-washing service and again at 8:00 p.m. we came together in the Dayspring chapel to celebrate the Eucharist. Daniel, the youngest son of one of the Daybreak families, received his first communion.

I carry in my heart a jumble of images: many, many people, young and old, strong and weak, happy and depressed — talking, asking, laughing, crying — confessing their sins, expressing their gratitude, kissing, hugging, singing, washing each other's feet, listening to words of reassurance, receiving the Body and Blood of Jesus — giving gifts, decorating, flowers in vases, wheelchairs, purple and white vestments and robes — Holy Thursday, Claire and her grieving family, Peggy and Phil, Jonas — Holy, Holy week, leading to Easter — pain in the world, plane accidents, murders and tragedies — a big snowstorm, slippery road — having dinner with friends — Kathy and Timmy waiting for her baby soon — little Daniel, beautiful eyes, eager to receive Jesus, and many presents, especially a watch, knowing all about the Son of God and the Son of Mary, who died for us and rose from the grave — many children listening, getting distracted — community, friendship, fund-raising and planning, the architect, new buildings — calling home to Holland. Phone calls from publishers, letters with invitations to come here and there to speak, just to be present, to write forewords and recommendations — Holy Thursday, Holy Week — Peace, Joy, Hope, Trust — God and all the people — just one day, only one day.

Good Friday, April 5

About a hundred of us walked from the meeting hall to the Dayspring chapel, each carrying a stone to symbolize our burden and our brokenness. We stopped three times to remember how Jesus is condemned to death, Simon of Cyrene is forced to carry the cross when Jesus falls, and Veronica wipes Jesus' face with her towel. Jesus is nailed to the cross.

Michael, Adam's brother, dressed in an alb and with a crown of thorns on his head, is Jesus. An assistant helps him to carry the cross. At the third station there is an armchair for him to rest in. We sing and listen to reflections on the passion of Jesus. In the chapel we place our stones on or around the cross. Sitting together in chairs and on the floor we sing, "Behold, behold, the wood of the cross." Lorenzo hammers three big nails in the cross, piercing the silence. Then we sing again: "Were you there when they crucified my Lord? . . . Were you there when they nailed him to the tree? . . . Were you there when they laid him in the tomb? . . . Sometimes it causes me to tremble, tremble, tremble."

Yes, it is a good Friday. In the midst of all the grief and mourning, there is sweet consolation. We are together, and there is love pouring out from our broken hearts and from the pierced heart of God.

Tonight we met again to listen to John's story of Jesus' passion, to pray for the church and the world, to venerate the cross, and to receive communion. The cross is in the center. As I look at the large crucifix, I remember how it came to us. Four years ago a Franciscan priest, Father Pancratius, whom I met in Freiburg while he was dying of cancer, said to me, "Henri, I want to give you this crucifix before I die. I want you to give it a place among your people with disabilities."

He told me the story of the crucifix. When many years ago he went to Croatia with a group of young Germans to help restore a church that was destroyed during World War II, they found the crucifix under the rubble. The pastor, grateful for the German gesture of reconciliation, gave it to Father Pancratius. There were no crossbeams, just the wood-carved body. When the dying priest gave it to me for my community, I felt as if I had been given a mandate to connect the suffering that comes from hatred, violence, and war with the suffering of people with physical and mental disabilities.

Joe, the leader of Daybreak's woodworking shop "The Woodery," together with the men with disabilities who work with him — Bill, John, David, Gordie — made two large, finely polished crossbeams on which the body was hung. For three years now the large cross has been on the wall of the vestibule of the Dayspring chapel. Today we brought the cross into the chapel and placed it on the lap of Michael, who was resting in his beanbag. Michael, who has severe cerebral palsy, was glad to "hold" the cross and let people come to it to pray. Michael's spastic body and the body of Jesus on the cross became like one body. As people formed a line to kiss the feet of Jesus on the cross, they realized that Jesus continues to suffer until the end of time in the countless people whose hearts and bodies are broken.

Good Friday is much more than reliving the passion of Jesus; it is entering into solidarity with the passion of all the people of our planet, whether
in the past, the present, or the future. In Jesus all human suffering is collected. The broken heart of Jesus is the broken heart of God. The broken
heart of God is the broken heart of the world. "Behold, behold, the wood
of the cross on which is hung our salvation. Oh, come let us adore."

Holy Saturday, April 6

Most of the day I spent preparing — with other members of the community — for the Easter Vigil celebration. As we all gathered, we were
ready: flowers, music, decorations. The little basement chapel was packed
to capacity as we brought in the Easter candle, listened to the readings,
renewed our baptismal vows, and celebrated the Eucharist.

After the Gospel reading I reflected on the significance of our faith in
the resurrection of the body. As a community of people conscious of our
disabilities, we are held together not so much by the Word as by the body.
Although we use many words and there is a lot of 'talk' among us, it is
the weak bodies of our core members that create community. We wash,
shave, comb, dress, clean, feed, and hold the bodies of those who are
entrusted to us and thus build a communal body. As we claim our faith
in the resurrection of the body, we come to see that the resurrection is
not simply an event after death but a reality of everyday life. Our care
for the body calls us to unity beyond organization, to intimacy beyond
eroticism, and to integrity beyond psychological wholeness.

Unity, intimacy, and integrity are the three spiritual qualities of the
resurrected life. We are called to break through the boundaries of na-
tionality, race, sexual orientation, age, and mental capacities and create a
unity of love that allows the weakest among us to live well. We are called
to go far beyond the places of lust, sexual need, and desire for physical
union to a spiritual intimacy that involves body, mind, and heart. And we
are called to let go of old ways of feeling good about ourselves and reach
out to a new integration of the many facets of our humanity. These calls
are calls to the resurrection. Caring for the body is preparing the body
for the final resurrection while anticipating it in our daily lives through
spiritual unity, intimacy, and integrity.

As I talked about these things it seemed that those who were present
at the vigil could recognize some of what I spoke about in their daily
Daybreak life.

As we received the Body and Blood of Jesus, I was struck by the *real* quality of the paschal mystery. We are the people of the resurrection, living our lives with a great vision that transforms us as we are living it.

Easter Sunday, April 7

"Christ is risen. He is risen indeed." We whisper it to each other. We joyfully announce it. We shout it from the rooftops. It was a very colorful and happy celebration this morning. Brian and Nathan played their guitars and led us in song. The small children opened the cocoons, which, on Ash Wednesday they had filled with things we want to let go of and things we hope for, and we all admired the butterflies that came out.

And the flowers were so radiant, especially the flowers that covered the large wooden cross Michael had carried on Good Friday. After we had sung our hearts out with Glorias and Alleluias we all — more than a hundred of us — had an Easter brunch that began with "Christ is risen" in at least ten languages. It all was exuberant, festive, and very exciting.

Then in the afternoon Nathan, his parents, and I went to see the Dutch film *Antonia's Line*. What a contrast! All the issues that haunt our contemporary world were there. Violence, sexual abuse, murderous revenge, accidents, suicide, irrelevant religion, and cynicism were all part of Antonia's life. In and through it there is Antonia, a stoic woman who faces it and chooses her own moment to die, bravely, but without a glimpse of Him who rose from the tomb. For me *Antonia's Line* was a meeting with my own country, culture, and history, especially after the jubilant morning celebration in Canada. I felt like I was in my two homes, L'Arche and Holland, on the same Easter Day. Both the risen Lord and Antonia live within me, and somehow I have to come to love them both. The cover of *Time* magazine this week shows the face of Jesus, half of it holy, half of it sensual, and the cover story wonders whether the resurrection is a fable or a divine truth. All of this is very close to me. I realize that my faith and unbelief are never far from each other. Maybe it is exactly at the place where they touch each other that the growing edge of my life is.

I am very tired after these five days at Daybreak. I am glad that I came, but I have missed my solitude, my time to write, and my moments to read and pray. My body aches and looks for a place to rest. I am ready to return to my little home in Peapack and continue my sabbatical.

Peapack, Easter Monday, April 8

When I arrived in Peapack today at noon, Peggy and I had a nice lunch together, catching up on each other's Holy Week and Easter. Mine was beautiful but exhausting, uplifting but quite overwhelming, prayerful but also distracting. More and more I realize my limitations. Being among people — encouraging, consoling, planning, celebrating, mourning, and dancing from 6:00 a.m. to 11:00 p.m. — is no longer easy for me. My body protests, and my stomach gets upset. I am touching my emotional and physical limits.

Back in my room in Peggy's guesthouse I just sat in my chair, taking in the wonderful silence and solitude. Three full hours alone! I hadn't experienced that for more than a week. What a gift!

My week in Boston, New York, and Richmond Hill informs me that my inner priorities are quietly shifting. Instead of yearning to be among many people, I yearn for intimate friendships. Instead of wanting to lecture to large groups, I desire to speak to a few people. Instead of being excited about huge celebrations and liturgies, I feel inspired by small prayer gatherings, and instead of enjoying traveling and moving around a lot, I feel most happy in my little room writing for long hours.

I know that these shifts are taking place within me, but my old self keeps acting as if they are not happening and I am still planning much more than is good for me. It will probably be a few years before my new self is fully in control.

Easter Tuesday, April 9

A beautiful Easter Tuesday Eucharist at 9:00 a.m., with good conversation about the resurrection, shopping in the morning for office supplies and food, mailing things, sleeping in the afternoon, dinner with Peggy and Phil in the evening, telephone calls, faxes, and so on.

Today I was thinking how nobody recognizes Jesus immediately. They think he is the gardener, a stranger, or a ghost. But when a familiar gesture is there again — breaking bread, inviting the disciples to try for another catch, calling them by name — his friends know he is there with them. Absence and presence are touching each other. The old Jesus is gone. They no longer can be with him as before. The new Jesus, the risen Lord, is there, intimately, more intimately than ever. It is an empowering presence. "Do not cling to me...but go...and tell" (Jn 20:17).

The resurrection stories reveal the always-present tension between coming and leaving, intimacy and distance, holding and letting go, at-homeness and mission, presence and absence. We face that tension every day. It puts us on the journey to the full realization of the promise given to us. "Do not cling to me" might mean "This is not heaven yet" but also "I am now within you and empower you for a spiritual task in the world, continuing what I have begun. You are the living Christ."

While many question whether the resurrection really took place, I wonder if it doesn't take place every day if we have the eyes to see and the ears to hear.

Easter Wednesday, April 10

Several interesting letters today. A friend of mine wrote to tell me about attending a Eucharist that I celebrated with Bill, from Daybreak, assisting me. While at first my friend felt repulsed by Bill's disability, appearance, and behavior, she finally received communion from him and was deeply moved by the look of love and compassion in his eyes. All of this must have taken place at least four years ago, but the letter was written in 1996. A true grace.

Then there was a long letter from Rodleigh of the Flying Rodleighs, full of stories about all that had happened to them since we last saw each other in Holland. Lots of setbacks — cold weather, poor health, failing trapeze tricks, car trouble, and so on. But, as always, Rodleigh remains optimistic and looks forward to a better summer. I look forward to seeing them again in July.

Thursday, April 11

Most of the day I have been busy preparing for my ten-day trip that starts tomorrow — Newark, Chicago, San Francisco, Cleveland, Chicago, Newark. I am looking forward to the several events: Don's birthday, visiting Jeff and Maurice, discussing the book of daily meditations with the publishers, a few days with Frank, Alvaro, and Kevin, preaching at the installation of Jim in Cleveland, and leading a workshop about the inclusion of people with disabilities in the liturgy. It is going to be work as well as vacation.

Tonight I had a lovely dinner with Carol and John in their cozy little home. Carol comes every morning to the Eucharist and has become a real support to me. It was special to be with her and her husband for an evening. Often I think that what we are living these days is very similar to what St. Paul and the apostles lived during the early years of Christianity — intimate celebrations in people's homes, prayers, conversations, and mutual support. Simple but very nurturing.

Chicago, Friday, April 12

When I arrived in Chicago, Don was waiting for me. Twenty minutes later Claude arrived from Portland.

I have known both Don and Claude since 1966, when I came to the University of Notre Dame as a visiting professor in the Psychology Department. Our thirty-year friendship has been very important for us in our personal as well as our professional journeys. Don's sixtieth birthday gave him the excuse to invite both Claude and me for a quiet day at his father's summer house before his birthday party at his father's home in Winnetka. I am really glad to be with Don and Claude and to reflect on our past and future as we enter the "third phase" of our lives.

Saturday, April 13

Don, Claude, and I spent the morning and afternoon telling each other our spiritual stories. We mainly talked about our struggles and needs at this point in our lives and how we can support each other in the years to come.

At 3:00 p.m. we drove to Don Sr.'s house in Winnetka. Around 6:00 p.m. all the family and friends arrived to celebrate Don's birthday with the Eucharist and a meal.

Although Don Jr. was the center of the party, most of the attention went to Don's father, our host. Don's father, who is fondly remembered by hundreds of thousands of elderly Americans as the host of the *Breakfast Club*, a popular radio program from 1933 to 1967, is becoming increasingly dependent on the daily care of family and friends. His various physical ailments keep him bound to his bed and wheelchair. There is much desire among his family and their many friends to offer "Himself," as he is affectionately called, what he needs without having to look for a nursing home.

What fascinated me most of all was Himself's kind, humorful, and even-minded disposition. While the various caregivers worried a lot about many things, Himself was like a peaceful, carefree king making a grateful remark here and there and keeping a sense of humor amidst it all. The immense admiration that has surrounded him during most of his life has not diminished in the least during his "weak years." Now, as in the years of the *Breakfast Club*, Don Sr. continues to draw love, affection, support, and friendship from all who meet him.

San Francisco, Sunday, April 14

This afternoon Don drove Claude and me to O'Hare Airport. The three of us were very grateful for the two days we had had together and were more than ever committed to deepen our friendship and support one another on our journey to "old age."

Guerneville, California, Monday, April 15

This morning I had a fruitful meeting with Tom, John, and Greg, of HarperSanFrancisco to discuss the publication of *Bread for the Journey*. We talked about the contract, serial rights, subsidiary rights, translations, and other business things. For me, however, the main fruit of our meetings was a deeper connectedness with Tom, John, and Greg, and a stronger feeling of their interest in and commitment to me as a person and a writer. In large publishing houses it is hard to have a personal relationship with the editors. But for me part of the joy of writing is precisely the friendships and mentoring relationships that can develop in the context of book pub-lishing. That is why I often prefer small publishing houses. There, people have more time and can pay more attention to what they publish. I have discovered, however, that when I express clearly my own needs and de-sires, there is an honest response. The way Tom, John, and Greg gave me their time and showed a real personal interest in my ideas, plans, and hopes was very encouraging.

After lunch with my Harper friends I met Kevin, Frank, and Alvaro, who were waiting for me to go with them for a few days' vacation. We arrived at our destination on the Russian River around 6:00 p.m., and the small but quite comfortable house is an ideal place for a few quiet days.

Tuesday, April 16

The Easter issue of *Time* magazine had as its cover article a discussion about the "quest for the historical Jesus." In recent years Harper has pub-lished three books on the subject: *Jesus: A Revolutionary Biography* by John Dominic Crossan, *Meeting Jesus Again for the First Time*, by Marcus J. Borg, and *The Real Jesus* by Luke Timothy Johnson. John gave me the three books yesterday, and I have been reading them off and on, here and there.

These books force me to ask again, "Who is Jesus for me?" and "What does it mean when I say: I believe in Jesus?" I very much like what Johnson writes in his conclusion when he talks about the "real Jesus" being "first of all the powerful, resurrected Lord whose transforming spirit is active in the community." But the "real Jesus" also reproduces in our lives a faithful obedience to God as well as loving service to others. Then Borg says "that we cannot understand or explain the post-Easter Jesus by historical facts only because the post-Easter Jesus is the Jesus of tradition and *experience.*"

Reading these studies I experience a deep desire to write more about the meaning and significance of Jesus for my own and other people's daily lives. This year, more than ever, the Gospel stories about the resurrection have deepened my hope and faith and have given me a new vision of the body. Crossan, Borg, and Johnson all have helped me but most of all challenged me to make the true connection between the story of Jesus and our stories.

Wednesday, April 17

Most of the day rain! Except for a little shopping we stayed in the house, reading, writing, having our meals, and praying together.

Guerneville, Thursday, April 18

We spent the morning taking photographs. We drove first through the dark woods with the splendid, tall redwood trees and then curved our way up to the top of the park, where we had a lovely view of the valley with its green meadows and pine tree-covered hills.

Kevin had promised to make some black and white photographs of me that were needed for book covers and for lecture posters. The light on the hill was quite spectacular, and Kevin had a great time placing me against different backgrounds and taking pictures from close by and far away. In between we took photographs of each other with different views of the valley. Soon, however, the clouds came rolling in again, and it began to rain. Back home we made another series of pictures in the living room.

In the afternoon we went to the neighboring cemetery to visit Randy's grave. His books *The Mayor of Castro Street, And the Band Played On,* and *Conduct Unbecoming* made him a well-known author. He died of AIDS in 1994. His grave was a simple black marble stone. On the left side his name was engraved, while the right side was left free for a second name. Another grave nearby showed the names of two young men, one with dates of birth and death, the other with only the birth date.

While the cemetery had many graves of people who had lived in the nineteenth century, mentioning parents, husbands, wives, and children, these end-of-the-twentieth-century graves reveal the face of love in a different way and show that a major shift has taken place in the values of our society.

In the early evening we prayed evening prayers together and spent a good hour talking about our friendship and about ways to support one another. Tomorrow morning we return to Oakland.

Oakland, California, Friday, April 19

Michael, a longtime friend and founder-coordinator of Bethany House, a small Catholic Worker house for people with AIDS joined us on our return to Oakland. My plan was to spend the afternoon and evening with him.

The unexpected surprise of today was that Andrew Harvey, the specialist on Rumi and writer on mysticism, was giving a lecture. It was, for me, an opportunity to meet this spiritual writer, whose life and work have intrigued me from the moment I first heard about him. Tom, a Franciscan priest and friend of Michael, joined us.

The lecture was excellent, and I was moved by it, not just because of its content but because of Andrew's transparent, radiant, free, humorful, and bright presence. Everything about him — the way he looked at his audience, took his glasses off and put them on again, and directed his questions to his listeners as an invitation to personal transformation in which both radical love for God and radical service for others were asked for — made me want to know this "messenger."

After the lecture I introduced myself to him. It seemed that he had never heard of me until he realized that I was the author of *Life of the Beloved*. Then he reacted with excitement. "I have your book right beside my bed, and I read in it very often. I like your style, the way you write about suffering, and the nice size of your books. We should meet." I never asked an author for an autograph before, but now I said, "Please sign your book for me, and let me know where I can write you and send you a few of my own books."

Although Harvey's personal and intellectual history is completely different from mine, I had the deep sense of meeting a soul-friend. I hope he did too.

Before driving home, Michael, Tom and I had a cup of tea at a nearby deli. We discussed at some length the way Andrew's mysticism had touched us.

Cleveland, Saturday, April 20

At 6:30 a.m. Michael drove me to the San Francisco Airport. At 5:15 p.m. local time I arrived in Cleveland, where Jim was waiting for me.

Jim has been a good friend since I met him at Yale Divinity School in the early 1970s. When he was ordained to the ministry in the United Church, he invited me to be part of the ceremony, and when he married Cindy he asked me to preach at the wedding. When their sons, Luke and Mark, were born, Cindy and Jim urged me to baptize them. Meanwhile I followed Jim and Cindy in their careers and visited them in their homes at Northfield, Connecticut, Nyack, New York, and Newton, Massachusetts. And during all these years we talked a lot! Our themes were mainly theology and ministry, civil disobedience and pacifism, formation and education, the economy and ecology, but most of all about how to deal creatively with conflict. I could never have guessed that Jim, this passionate and ideologically intense "rebel," would become the senior minister in such a prestigious church. But I am deeply convinced of the authenticity of his call. Where he is now he must be, and all he has lived in his career and family life will have a chance to bloom here, where he will be installed as pastor tomorrow afternoon.

Richard and Lois and their children, ten-year-old Tim and four-year-old Molly, were my hosts for the weekend. The last time I met Richard and Lois was twelve years ago, when I gave a lecture on peace in Cleveland. Both were at Yale when I taught there. It was great to see them again and meet the children, who had been born since I last stayed with them. Richard and Lois kiddingly accused me of encouraging them to have children during my last visit. It was a happy accusation.

Twenty-five years ago it all started at Yale Divinity School. Now things are coming full circle. Jim, pastor of a large church; Cindy, a Catholic hospice pastoral caseworker; Richard, a Lutheran long-term care ombudsman; and Lois, a Presbyterian minister and pastoral counselor, now have become a small group supporting one another and offering their children a safe environment in which to grow. A marvel in the mystery of friendship and faithfulness.

Chicago, Sunday, April 21

Jim's installation was a joyful and festive event. He had chosen as readings the story of the healing of the commander Naaman (2 Kgs 5:1–14) and the story of the Prodigal Son (Lk 15:11–32). In my sermon I tried to speak about Jim's call to be a compassionate father and to wash himself seven times in the river of his new community.

During the reception I met many old friends from Yale Divinity School and many new friends from the L'Arche community in Cleveland.

Also my dear friend Bob, a former Trappist brother and a retired mail carrier in Cleveland, was there. Bob had put together in 1988 an anthology of my writings, *Seeds of Hope*. What most pleases me is not only that *Seeds of Hope* is still in print and will be reedited soon but also that, through our friendship, Bob has become a fine writer in his own right and enjoys a good readership.

After the reception we had a nice dinner at Jim and Cindy's home, and at 8:30 I was back at the airport to fly to Chicago.

Monday, April 22

Most of this morning I spent working on my talk. Although I was asked to speak about the very concrete matter of including people with disabilities in the Catholic liturgy, I decided to take a much broader approach, offering a theological framework for the question.

After some struggling with different concepts, I decided to speak first about God's vision that our human life is a mission to proclaim the unconditional love of God in this world. I turned next to Jesus' way of vulnerability, which reveals God's love for us in human brokenness. Finally I would speak about the work of the Spirit in the community of faith that comes together as a fellowship of the weak with the poor in the center.

Cardinal Bernardin had asked me to join him for a lunch in honor of the Polish Cardinal of Bratislava and his entourage. It was quite a luncheon! Most of the men wore black suits and Roman collars. There were five bishops, some secretaries, pastoral workers, translators, and myself in blue suit and red tie. Everyone was extremely friendly. The Polish Cardinal poured out many compliments to Cardinal Bernardin about his hospitality and the warm reception he had received on his trip through the United States. Whenever he had a chance he handed out little buttons for the Eucharist Congress that will be held in his diocese in May 1997.

At 3:00 p.m. we left for the conference. After several introductions the cardinal spoke for fifteen minutes and then let me take over. I was moved by the great attentiveness of all who were there. It was easy to speak to such a receptive audience. I offered my three meditations, interrupted with a few songs and a short time for people to speak with their neighbors.

People smiled, laughed, sang, and clapped with great enthusiasm. Three times I invited some of the disabled members of the congregation to come up and interact with me. During the third reflection I asked a teenager who was deaf to come up. I kept forgetting that he was deaf and had to keep his eyes on the sign language translator to understand me. When I was trying to look in his eyes he couldn't see the signer and "hear" me. Finally I put my arms around him while standing behind him and whispering in his ears. Then he could see the signs and respond with movements of his head to what I was saying.

At 8:00 p.m. the Cardinal presided over a very festive Eucharist. Gorbet, one of the men with severe cerebral palsy moving around in a walker, served at the altar. He was happy and smiling as he served. One of the readers came up in her wheelchair and several disabled people helped to distribute communion.

During communion time, the Cardinal who was sitting beside me leaned over to me and said, "Isn't this a beautiful celebration? I am so moved." Then before the final blessing he said to the congregation: "As one who is also disabled I have to say that this Eucharist has truly given me much comfort and hope. Thank you all very, very much." People had tears in their eyes when they saw their spiritual leader being so close to them.

At 10:30 we were back at the Cardinal's residence. He was exhausted. I was glad to be alone again. Once in my room I called Al, Kevin, and Frank, to say hello and ask them their reflections about our vacation time. They seemed to have good memories and gratitude for the opportunity to just be together and deepen our friendship. Then I called Joan in San Diego. I realize how important it is not only to live well but also to remember well what we have lived.

Peapack, Tuesday, April 23

After a one-hour delay I left Chicago late this morning and got to Newark at 1:30 p.m. Peggy was there to take me back to Peapack. We had a lot to tell each other about our "adventures" during the past week. Back in my little red house I spent most of the afternoon reading and answering mail, listening to voice messages, and making phone calls.

Wednesday, April 24

Today I spoke by phone to Art and Dean. I came to know them during my time at Yale Divinity School and was deeply involved in their spiritual journeys. Both Art and Dean are close friends of the Berrigan brothers and have shared with them long periods in jail because of their acts of civil disobedience. Once I visited Dean in the Danbury prison and gave a short retreat to him and his fellow inmates. Presently Art lives and works in Washington, D.C., in the Dorothy Day Catholic Worker House, and Dean is completing his Ph.D. in psychology while spending a few days a week working as a psychiatric social worker.

There is no doubt that the time of the Vietnam War and the pervasive threat of a nuclear holocaust have radically marked the lives of these men. While most people consider the issues of the sixties no longer significant, Art and Dean are convinced that basically nothing has changed and that nuclear destruction is as much a danger today as it was thirty years ago.

Dean and Art are my good friends, and I stand in awe of their commitment, perseverance, and radical witness. Whether their cause is popular or not, they keep prophesying and calling people to conversion. At the same time, within myself, I grapple with a certain ambivalence. Their personal lives have been deeply affected by their prison life and their repeated acts of disobedience, but it sometimes seems to me that without an active protest against the arms race it might be hard for them to be at rest. In working for peace we may make a certain division of the world between the forces of light and the forces of darkness, and if that happens I feel uneasy, mainly because I think that each of us participates in both these worlds. Then I ask myself if such polarization prevents a creative dialogue with the government, the army, and other power groups, and if the "civil disobedience" model is the most fruitful for our decade. What I do know, though, is that I want to stay close to Art and Dean in their journeys and to strengthen our friendship, especially in times when they experience little support.

Tonight at 8:00 p.m. Timmy called to tell me about the birth of his new sister, Sarah. She was born at noon on Monday morning. "I cut the umbilical cord," Timmy said quite proudly. I wondered how it must feel for a ten-year-old boy to see his sister appear from his mother's womb. When I was twelve and my second brother was born I had no idea how that happened. All I remember are cakes, flowers, a nice-smelling room, a little, beautifully dressed baby in a large crib, my mother in bed but clearly not sick, and many visitors. As a young boy, it seemed to me that my father hadn't much place in it all. When he came home from work he had another son! But that was another time and another place!

Kathy came to the phone and told me that the birth had gone well. "Timmy was wonderful," she said. "When I had no energy anymore to push, he said, 'Come on, Mom, you can do it!'" I look forward to seeing Sarah on Friday when I return to Daybreak. I am happy to be Sarah's godfather.

Thursday, April 25

All the popular papers, such as the *New York Post* and the *New York Daily News*, are full of the auction of some of Jackie and Jack Kennedy's personal possessions at Sotheby's. The bids exceeded all expectations. I was quite amazed by the enormous value connected with "who had it and who gave it." When I spoke to Nathan on the phone he said, "Objects that belonged to saints would never sell for that much!"

The only time I met Jackie was at Murray's funeral. Murray was Peggy's husband and my friend for many years. Jackie spoke to me about my homily and especially about the way I talked about Murray's vulnerability. "I never have thought about being vulnerable as something positive," she said. "I should have thought about that earlier."

Richmond Hill, Friday, April 26

After the Eucharist in Peapack with a very lively discussion about the story of Paul's conversion, I got ready to leave again for Toronto.

The two reasons for returning to Daybreak are the meeting of the Dayspring Council and the celebration of Nathan's community leadership for the coming four years. During the past five years the Daybreak community has been planning to build a new Dayspring or spiritual center, which will include a house of hospitality and a new chapel. The present Dayspring building is a small bungalow with five bedrooms and a large basement converted into a chapel. With more than 150 members, the Daybreak community needs more space to pray and to offer hospitality. The Dayspring Council is a small group of people from Toronto and several places in the USA who oversee the project, offer suggestions, and participate in the ongoing fund-raising.

At 8:00 p.m. the community gathered in the Dayspring chapel for the Eucharist. Kathy, Timmy, and the four-day-old Sarah were there. What a tiny and beautiful baby. It was Sarah's first visit to the chapel. She will be there often! After the homily I gave Sarah a special blessing.

It is good to be back in Daybreak. It will be a very busy weekend with the council meeting, Nathan's installation, and discussions with the architect. I hope it will be life giving and hope giving.

Saturday, April 27

The Dayspring Council meeting was very encouraging and unifying. There were many questions and an overall excitement about the plans and the way they fitted in the general vision of the Daybreak community.

I concluded the day with a visit to Kathy, Timmy, and little Sarah.

Sunday, April 28

Having completed one four-year term as community leader, Nathan was asked and agreed to continue in the role for another four years. This afternoon the whole Daybreak community gathered in the meeting hall to celebrate his leadership. It was an afternoon of affirmation, celebration, and encouragement, with songs, speeches, skits, and many blessings.

In my own little presentation I took two triangles, one with the point up and the other with the point down. Nathan is boss but also shepherd, a leader who gives direction but also a leader who listens, a man who talks with the government, is concerned about budgets, and connects our agency with other agencies, but also a man who holds us together as community, prays with us, joins us at the table, and keeps our focus on those who are the weakest among us. The triangle with the point up shows that we are *in* the world as an agency not afraid of competition. The triangle with the point down shows that we are not *of* the world but we are a community of service and care.

After explaining these two triangles, I put them on top of each other so that together they formed a star. I believe that it is precisely the tension between the upward and the downward triangles that creates the light, a guiding and enlightening light. It is very hard these days to be a good leader, prudent as a snake and gentle as a dove but Nathan has a unique ability.

Peapack, Monday, April 29

A very busy day. A morning Eucharist in the Dayspring chapel with close to fifty people, dictating letters to Kathy, visiting the doctor in Richmond Hill to unplug my ears, lunch with Joe, a three-hour meeting with the architect about the plans to build a small house for me connected to the present Dayspring, a visit to the New House for a chat with the assistants about Adam's death and their own plans for the future.

At 6:00 p.m. Nathan took Wendy and me to the airport. At 10:15 p.m, an hour late, Wendy and I arrived at Newark.

A very tiring day, after a tiring weekend. But everything went well, and I am pleased with the results. I am very glad to be back in Peapack, and I look forward to a quiet week of editing and writing.

Tuesday, April 30

While we were in Richmond Hill, Malcolm, one of the members of the Dayspring Council, gave me an article about John Updike's latest book, *In the Beauty of the Lilies*, published in *The Christian Century*. The author, Ralph C. Wood, writes about the loss of religious faith being told in the book with disquieting passivity. One of the main characters of the novel suffers from sloth.

The concept of sloth helps me to understand my own world a lot better. It is not evil or good but the passive indifference toward both that characterizes our attitudes. I can see how hard — yes, impossible — it is to preach to people who are slothful because nothing really matters to them. They don't get excited about a beautiful thought, a splendid idea, or an encouraging perspective, nor do they become indignant about ugly words, sordid ideas, or destructive viewpoints. Evelyn Waugh, according to Wood, once called sloth the besetting late-modern sin. I believe Waugh is right. It seems the sin of a spoiled generation, for whom nothing really matters.

I realize that much of what I want to do is to help people break out of their prison of sloth and become engaged in making the world a better place. I am trying so hard to do this that I am criticized for overemphasizing, exaggerating, and getting too excited. Still, I do feel that it is much better to be hot or cold than to be lukewarm. Lukewarmness creates nausea and an inclination to vomit. I understand why God spits out those who are lukewarm (Rev 3:16).

I wonder if sloth is not a special temptation for elderly people, who have seen so much happen but so little change. I realize that sometimes I am tired of putting up another fight, waging another battle for the good. Sometimes I just want to be left alone. But God does not want me to rest too soon. I have to be faithful to the end, always trusting in the final fulfillment of God's promise.

May 1996

Wednesday, May 1

May starts with a beautiful, bright sun making the Pleasant Valley a little paradise with the daffodils, the blooming cherry and peach trees, and the other budding trees. During the Eucharist we exchanged thoughts about living nonjudgmentally, thus following Jesus, who came not to judge but to give life.

My day was low key: correcting manuscripts, making phone calls, having a relaxed lunch with Peggy and her friend Roma, and getting some extra sleep. Since my busy weekend in Canada, I still feel extremely tired, and my body keeps asking for sleep. Sometimes I worry about the intensity and frequency of my fatigue, but when I give my body the rest it asks for, I start feeling a lot better rather quickly.

This afternoon Frank was promoted in the U.S. Air Force. It was a very important event for him. Regrettably none of his family or friends could be there with him. Part of the problem was that the promotion took place during a week of exercises on the base, and there was no time for celebrations. Still, I wished I could have been there for Frank. There are not too many special occasions in his life, and this public affirmation of his ministry needs to be celebrated. Hopefully we can do it in the future.

When we were in Santa Fe, Frank asked me, "Could you write a prayer for me for my promotion?" I said, "Sure," but later wondered whether he wanted a prayer that I prayed for him or a prayer that he himself could pray. When I finally wrote the prayer, I felt drawn to make it a prayer that he could pray, not only once but often. I tried to crawl into his skin and speak to God from his heart. Frank is not a man of many words, especially words that connect with his feelings. That probably is the main reason why I chose to pray in his name. So this is the prayer I wrote:

Dear Lord,

As I come to the halfway point of my life, I want to enter into your presence and recommit myself to you. During the last four decades, you have guided me and gradually brought me to a mature faith, to a new confidence in my gifts, and to a spiritual adulthood. Along the way I have struggled with many things, trying to find my place in life, trying to find my place in my family, trying to find my place among my colleagues, trying to find my place as your minister. It has been a long journey with many joys and many pains, with many doubts and many hopes, with many moments of loneliness and with moments of beautiful friendship.

Now, as I receive the affirmation of my colleagues in being promoted to the rank of major in the U.S. Air Force, I come again to ask you to lead me always closer to your heart, and to the hearts of those who are entrusted to me. Precisely because I find myself in a secure place, with good health and good friends, I am free to choose you again as my shepherd and my guide. Help me to be humble in the midst of a world that is so full of ambition. Help me to be vulnerable in a world so concerned with power. Help me to be simple in surroundings that are so complicated. Help me to be forgiving in a society where revenge and retaliation create so much pain. Help me to be poor of spirit in a milieu that desires so many riches and aspires to so much success. As I enter the second half of my life, I come to you with an open heart, asking that I may trust in the gifts you have given me and may have the courage to take risks in your service.

I do not know where you will lead me. I do not know where I will be two, five, or ten years from now. I do not know the road ahead of me, but I know now that you are with me to guide me and that, wherever you lead me, even where I would rather not go, you will bring me closer to my true home. Thank you, Lord, for my life, for my vocation, and for the hope that you have planted in my heart. Amen.

I faxed the prayer to Frank's office and sent him a flowering plant. I hope and pray that he finds joy on this special day and especially that his promotion will increase his self-confidence.

Military life, with its countless regulations and ordinances is, in a way, not very different from church life. Both seek to control the whole person, not only in public but also in private. Every time Frank wants to take a few days off, he has to fill out all sorts of forms and get all sorts of permissions. Sometimes it seems that the bureaucracy of military life prevents ministry. Being in the military while serving God in ministry is quite a challenge. In the Dutch Army the chaplains remain civilians even though they wear uniforms and everyone is captain and becomes major at age thirty-five. But in the American services chaplains are real officers, subject to military law. The result is that they are evaluated as much as officers as they are as ministers. For many chaplains this system leads to a great preoccupation with promotion. Being a successful officer can become more important than being a fruitful minister.

When I think about it I realize that the values of ministerial service are radically different from the values of military service. Jesus' way of vulnerability and forgiveness stands in stark contrast to the military way of power and retaliation. I wonder how one can be free to confront the dark side of the "military-industrial complex" while being subject to its laws of reward and punishment. And I am not surprised that chaplains can easily become more concerned with how they are appreciated by their commanders than with how they are appreciated by their moderators or bishops. Still, I believe that just as we are called to be *in* the world without being *of* it, some of us are called to minister *in* the military without being *of* it.

These considerations made me write Frank's prayer the way I did. I am sure that Frank's thinking about all of this is quite different from mine. I know, though, that underneath all the thoughts and ideas about military chaplaincy, Frank experiences every day the heavy presence and pressure of the authoritarian military system and realizes that it is hard to keep claiming his spiritual freedom in the midst of it. That is why I wrote this prayer on the day of his promotion. Frank is a beautiful human being, and I want to rejoice with him today, even while I couldn't be with him.

Thursday, May 2

Eugene, the postmaster of Peapack, showed me a quotation from one of my books, published in the last issue of the *Catholic Digest*. He asked me to sign it. Then he put a thirty-two-cent love stamp on it and stamped it with the date. He was quite excited about his discovery and later showed the page, with quotation, signature, stamp, and date, to Ginny when she came in.

I like Eugene a lot. He radiates kindness and goodness and always has a friendly word for his customers. He told me that he originally had taken a subscription to the *Catholic Digest* to read aloud to his bedridden mother and later started to read it for himself. "It is a nice little magazine with short, uplifting pieces," he said. He was surprised that I didn't know much about the *Catholic Digest*. I asked him for the order form in the issue he had shown me so he tore it out and gave it to me. Now I can write to them.

How wonderful it is to be surrounded by so many kind people. Eugene in the post office and the people of the deli next door... they feel like family. Sometimes I even forget to pay them, as if they do their work all for friendship and the pure joy of doing it. But they are dedicated people working long hours and always on their feet. I wouldn't be able to do it.

Saturday, May 4

This morning I took a plane down the east coast to attend the memorial service for a young man who took his own life. I had a deep desire just to be there and to offer my support to his friends and to his partner.

At 9:30 I was at the chapel. About 150 people came to the service. The atmosphere was very gentle, warm, personal, and prayerful. The homilist spoke very personally about the story of the disciples going to Emmaus, recognizing Jesus in the breaking of the bread, and returning to their community. He showed how each of us is called to live with our grief, loss, anger, guilt, and pain, while we move to recognize that in it all Jesus is present among us. Each of us must find and belong to a community of support, love, and care, where our grief can gradually be transformed into gratitude.

From this memorial service I want to fully claim the mystery of God's love, revealed to me through this beautiful human being.

At 2:00 p.m. I was back at the airport, to await Jonas's arrival. Jonas is returning with me to Peapack to have a few quiet days in the valley. We had lots to talk about on the plane and during our drive home.

For some reason I feel quite anxious interiorly. I realize that I am walking around with some deep, unresolved emotions and that not much is needed to bring them to the surface and throw me off balance. I wasn't expecting this but I feel quite powerless in the face of these free-floating emotions of love, hate, rejection, attraction, gratitude, and regret. I wish I could come to a new peace but after so many years I fear that new tensions instead of peace may be in store. I know that prayer is very important at this moment.

Monday, May 6

We are waiting for the Spirit to come. Are we really? This morning during the Eucharist I spoke a little about preparing ourselves for Pentecost just as we prepare ourselves for Christmas and Easter. Still, for most of us

Pentecost is a nonevent. While on secular calendars Christmas and Easter are still marked, Pentecost is spectacularly absent.

But Pentecost is the coming of the Spirit of Jesus into the world. It is the celebration of God breaking through the boundaries of time and space and opening the whole world for the re-creating power of love. Pentecost is freedom, the freedom of the Spirit to blow where it wants.

Without Pentecost the Christ-event — the life, death, and resurrection of Jesus — remains imprisoned in history as something to remember, think about, and reflect on. The Spirit of Jesus comes to dwell within us, so that we can become living Christs here and now. Pentecost lifts the whole mystery of salvation out of its particularities and makes it into something universal, embracing all peoples, all countries, all seasons, and all eras. Pentecost is also the moment of empowering. Each individual human being can claim the Spirit of Jesus as the guiding spirit of his or her life. In that Spirit we can speak and act freely and confidently with the knowledge that the same Spirit that inspired Jesus is inspiring us.

We certainly have to prepare ourselves carefully for this feast so that we can not only receive fully the gifts of the Spirit but also let the Spirit bear fruit within us.

Tuesday, May 7

This morning during the Eucharist, Don left a message on the phone telling me that his father had died in the night. I immediately called him, and we spoke about Don Sr.'s beautiful life and peaceful death. This is a great loss for Don and his family. Don really loved his father and during the last few years had grown very close to him.

I am so glad that I was with Don Sr. only three weeks ago. Weak as he was, he clearly was the quiet center of the family, and always with a prayer and a smile. Without any doubt he was a great human being. He was a very good husband, a greatly admired father, a generous supporter of the poor and the weak, and a man of deep faith. To me he was always a most gracious host, always interested in my life and work, always supporting my writing, and always eager to pray with me and Don. I will truly miss him.

On Thursday I will fly to Chicago to be at the wake and the funeral. I just want to be close to Don during this time of grief and mourning.

This afternoon I drove Jonas back to the airport. It has been good for us to be together for a few days. I had a chance to talk with him about the anxiety I experienced, and which continues to lurk underneath my exterior presentation. He gave me a listening ear and a caring response. Some of the intensity of my inner turmoil decreased, but I realize that when this wound opens up in me, the healing is slow and requires much patience. Jonas's comforting and consoling presence at least let me experience the beginning of a healing process.

Wednesday, May 8

Finally, I am back to some new writing. The past few weeks have been so fragmented with travel, lectures, visits, correspondence, phone calls, and correction of manuscripts that my plan to write a book about Adam during May keeps being delayed. It is so frustrating to see the days pass by without any inspiring work. I know that my fatigue is connected with my lack of creativity.

But today I am writing about Adam. I am amazed to realize how much is stored in my heart and mind, and how easy it is for me to express it all! The more I write the more I discover I have to write.

It is so clear to me that Adam's story is the story of God, and it needs to be told. Every aspect of Adam's life speaks about God's way of loving. Adam's light, Adam's personality, Adam's hiddenness, Adam's silence, Adam's disabilities, Adam's suffering, and Adam's healing presence — they all reveal the mystery of strength in weakness and power in vulnerability.

Writing about Adam gives me energy and new hope. Even my deep anguish lingering under the surface of my busy life is somewhat alleviated in the writing. Thanks be to God. Thanks be to Adam.

Winnetka, Illinois, Thursday, May 9

I arrived at O'Hare Airport at 6:00 p.m. and immediately found a cab to take me to the funeral home in Skokie.

I knelt in front of the closed casket that held Don Sr.'s body and prayed. My prayers were more *to* Himself than *for* Himself. As I let my head rest on the casket, I asked Don Sr. to send me his spirit of equanimity, kindness, and humor, and to guide me in the years ahead. I especially prayed to him to intercede with Jesus to take my inner anguish away and to lead me to a greater inner peace. I also asked to be a good, faithful friend to Don, his brothers, and their aunt in their grief.

Friday, May 10

At 10:00 a.m. I drove with Don's brother Bob and his wife, Martha, to the funeral home for a final visit. At 11:00 a.m. the funeral procession arrived at the church. Don Jr. led the service in a very personal way, making everyone feel included and appreciated. He made the large and somewhat pompous church into a meeting hall of good friends, where both grief and gratitude could be felt and expressed. In his homily Don spoke about his father as a great host and a great peacemaker, and showed the beautiful unity of his father's professional life, his family life, and his spiritual life.

At the end of the service, Bob asked all people, as his father had done on his radio show for many years, to once more bow their heads in prayer and pray in their own way to God for peace and unity among people. The death of Himself was indeed deepening the community that had grown during his life. I couldn't miss the parallel with Jesus' death. As his death was the beginning of a true community of faith, Don Sr.'s death created new bonds of love and new commitments to care for one another.

Atlanta, Saturday, May 11

Don drove me to the airport at 9:00 a.m. and we spent a little time waiting for my plane to Atlanta. We affirmed our deep and long friendship made strong in this time of grief.

At the Atlanta Airport, Chris was waiting for me. I came to know Chris during my time at Yale Divinity School, where he took several of my courses. He also shared with me some of his struggles as an openly gay man in the church, and as a Presbyterian Christian who desired to become a minister but faced church ordinances that did not allow openly gay men to be ordained.

After graduating from Yale, Chris moved to Los Angeles, where he became a very active lay minister in a church and where he founded the Lazarus Project, focused on spiritual growth for homosexual people. When my travels brought me to Los Angeles, I always tried to visit Chris, and when Chris's travels brought him to Toronto, he came to Daybreak to see me.

During these years Chris wrote *Uncommon Calling*. Several other books followed, including his best-selling book, *Coming Out to God*.

A few years ago Chris met Mark and moved with him to Atlanta. Chris and Mark were married in the sanctuary of a Presbyterian church there in 1994.

I had not seen Chris for at least seven years, and I was glad to meet Mark. It seems that Chris has become much more at peace with himself than he was during his Yale and Los Angeles days. He radiates a beautiful gentleness and kindness that seem to have been covered before.

Monday, May 13

I am glad to be home again. Now I can dedicate the whole week to writing about Adam.

Jesus says, "When the Advocate comes, whom I will send to you from the Father, the Spirit of truth who comes from the Father, this Paraclete will testify on my behalf. You also are to testify" (Jn 15:26–27).

What is the testimony of the Spirit? The Spirit will witness to the unconditional love of God that became available to us through Jesus. This divine love, as it becomes manifest within the structures of the world, is a light in the darkness. It is a light that the darkness cannot accept. The divine love of God reveals to us that fruitfulness is more important than success, that the love of God is more important than the praise of people, that community is more important than individualism, and compassion more important than competition. In short, the light of the Spirit reveals to us that love conquers all fear. But the world rules by fear. Without fear the world doesn't know how to control or govern.

The Spirit's testimony threatens the world. It is not surprising that anyone who testifies with the Spirit is a danger to the world. That is why Jesus predicts, "An hour is coming when those who kill you will think that by doing so they are offering worship to God. And they will do this because they have not known the Father or me" (Jn 16:2–3).

These words are very relevant in our days. When we do not live in deep communion with God — that is, with the Spirit of Jesus within us — then religion is easily put into the service of our desire for success, fame, and stardom. From that place we are willing to "kill" whoever is in the way of reaching our goal. The tragedy is that indeed we quickly convince ourselves that we do the killing in God's name. This is how many Indians, Jews, and Muslims have lost their lives. This is part of what gives a religious rationalization for violence in Northern Ireland, Bosnia, and many other places.

Jesus wants us not to be surprised when these things happen. He says, "I have said these things to you so that when their hour comes you may remember that I told you about them" (Jn 16:4).

We talked about these things during the Eucharist this morning and became aware of how often we, as church, have hurt each other in the

Name of God. Many of the people around the table had had painful experiences in their church, or with their parents and friends. They were surprised when family members and religious people wounded them so deeply. Sometimes, because of the pain, they had left the church, but by doing so they lost contact with the message of Jesus.

The words of Jesus are very important. They warn us that this will happen, and they prepare us for this very experience of pain. Jesus' prediction may help us not to reject the love of God even when we are rejected in God's Name.

Tuesday, May 14

Jesus says, "If you keep my commandments, you will abide in my love, just as I have kept my Father's commandments and abide in God's love" (Jn 15:10). Jesus invites me to abide in his love. That means to dwell with all that I am in him. It is an invitation to a total belonging, to full intimacy, to an unlimited being-with.

The anxiety that has plagued me during the last week shows that a great part of me is not yet "abiding" in Jesus. My mind and heart keep running away from my true dwelling place, and they explore strange lands where I end up in anger, resentment, lust, fear, and anguish. I know that living a spiritual life means bringing every part of myself home to where it belongs.

Jesus describes the intimacy that he offers as the connectedness between the vine and its branches. I have to be grafted onto Jesus as a branch onto the vine so that all my life comes from the vine. In communion with Jesus, the vine, my little life can grow and bear fruit. I know it, but I do not live it. Somehow I keep living as if there are other sources of life that I must explore, outside of Jesus. But Jesus keeps saying, "Come back to me, give me all your burdens, all your worries, fears, and anxieties. Trust that with me you will find rest." I am struggling to listen to that voice of love and to trust in its healing power.

I deeply know that I have a home in Jesus, just as Jesus has a home in God. I know, too, that when I abide in Jesus I abide with him in God. "Those who love me," Jesus says, "will be loved by my Father" (Jn 14:21). My true spiritual work is to let myself be loved, fully and completely, and to trust that in that love I will come to the fulfillment of my vocation. I keep trying to bring my wandering, restless, anxious self home, so that I can rest there in the embrace of love.

This afternoon Ginny took me to the mall at Short Hills. I found two different sizes of unlined blank books, which I would like to fill with my Adam story. Now I feel new motivation. The new books help!

Wednesday, May 15

I am painfully aware that more than eight months of my sabbatical year have passed. When I reread some of my early journal entries about my hopes for long times of solitude, prayer, and writing, I have to laugh at myself. The year has been different from my expectations and has been one of the busiest and most involved years I can remember.

But still, it's been a wonderful year. I did not write as much as I planned, but I wrote a lot, I did not pray as much as I planned, but my experience of God has deepened in my writing. I haven't been as alone as I hoped, but I've had much more solitude than before.

I look with some apprehension toward September, because I feel far from ready to end my sabbatical. My mind is fuller than ever with ideas for my writing. I know that my return to Daybreak is only realistic if I continue to do *some* writing, because without it I will dry up interiorly and will quickly feel tired and depressed. I'm grateful that Sue, Nathan, and others at Daybreak agree with me. I am encouraged that they support my desire to build a small house for myself where I will have some space for writing.

If I look back and compare what happened with what I anticipated, I realize that I can't fruitfully predict what will happen. God must remain the God of surprises.

Thursday, May 16

Jesus said to his disciples, "A little while, and you will no longer see me, and again a little while, and you will see me" (Jn 16:16).

Life is "a little while," a short moment of waiting. But life is not empty waiting. It is to wait full of expectation. The knowledge that God will indeed fulfill the promise to renew everything, and will offer us a "new heaven and a new earth," makes the waiting exciting. We can already see the beginning of the fulfillment. Nature speaks of it every spring; people speak of it whenever they smile; the sun, the moon, and the stars speak of it when they offer us light and beauty; and all of history speaks of it when amidst all devastation and chaos, men and women arise who reveal the hope that lives within them.

This "little while" is a precious time. It is a time of purification and sanctification, a time to be prepared for the great passage to the permanent house of God. What is my main task during my "little while"? I want to point to the signs of the Kingdom to come, to speak about the first rays of the day of God, to witness to the many manifestations of the Holy Spirit among us. I do not want to complain about this passing world but to focus on the eternal that lights up in the midst of the temporal. I yearn to create space where it can be seen and celebrated.

Every day at the communion table I experience unity and peace growing among us. This is a glimpse of the Kingdom during my "little while."

Friday, May 17

Much of today was getting ready for my trip to Santa Fe. Tomorrow I will fly to Albuquerque and drive from there to Santa Fe to spend a week writing under the supervision and mentorship of Jim. I am very much looking forward to seeing Jim again and discussing with him not only the subject but also the craft of my writing.

What I most hope is to learn how to write a good story that engages the reader to the very end. I realize that Jesus told stories and that most spiritual masters told stories. As I am busy writing about Adam and plan to write about the Flying Rodleighs, I know what I want said, but I do not know how to say it. I hope to return with better knowledge about creating a compelling story. So my trip to Santa Fe is a little gift that I give myself to push me into a new dimension of storytelling.

Santa Fe, Saturday, May 18

It gets tiring to write about traveling again. Going from here to there ... to there ... to there. Airports and planes, rent-a-car places and baggage claim areas are boring and somewhat nauseating. Traveling gives me a rubbery feeling inside, a feeling of belonging nowhere. The gates, moving walkways, newsstands with dolls, flags, cups, and long racks of magazines, the unmovable metal chairs depersonalize and deaden my spirit.

Today I flew from Newark to Denver to Albuquerque and drove to Santa Fe in a rental car. When I finally got to Malcolm's condominium, I felt sick from fatigue and from feeling violated in my spirit. There is nobody to accuse. I experience a new, inner understanding of the *"world"* that Jesus talks about. Everything is moving, moving, and moving, but at the same time everything is static.

I *am* glad to be in Santa Fe again and I look forward to meeting Jim tomorrow even though I am somewhat nervous about entering into this relationship. Do I expect too much from him? Can he and will he help me with my writing? Is he going to become a friend? I am too tired to think clearly about it. One thing is clear. I need sleep and a lot of it!

Sunday, May 19

Today I had a memorable lunch with Jim. Although I had come to Santa Fe to ask for Jim's help in my writing, our first conversation has focused on what to do with our lives between ages sixty and eighty.

For me this is an increasingly important question, which is not without anxiety. Over the years I have built up a certain reputation. People think of me as a Catholic priest, a spiritual writer, a member of a community with mentally handicapped people, a lover of God, and a lover of people. It is wonderful to have such a reputation. But lately I find I get caught in it and I experience it as restricting. Without wanting to, I feel a certain pressure within me to keep living up to that reputation and to do, say, and write things that fit the expectations of the Catholic Church, L'Arche, my family, my friends, my readers. I'm caught because I'm feeling that there is some kind of an agenda that I must follow in order to be faithful.

But since I am in my sixties, new thoughts, feelings, emotions, and passions have arisen within me that are not all in line with my previous thoughts, feelings, emotions, and passions. So I find myself asking, "What is my responsibility to the world around me, and what is my responsibility to myself? What does it mean to be faithful to my vocation? Does it require that I be consistent with my earlier way of living or thinking, or does it ask for the courage to move in new directions, even when doing so may be disappointing for some people?"

I am more and more aware that Jesus died when he was in his early thirties. I have already lived more than thirty years longer than Jesus. How would Jesus have lived and thought if he had lived that long? I don't know. But for me many new questions and concerns emerge at my present age that weren't there in the past. They refer to all the levels of life: community, prayer, friendship, intimacy, work, church, God, life, and death. How can I be free enough and let the questions emerge without fearing the consequences? I know I am not yet completely free because the fear is still there.

Jim is sixty-two years old. I am sixty-four. We both are asking the question about how we live between sixty and eighty. The difference is that Jim is bound neither by his reputation nor to any institution, so he is very free, and he loves his freedom. It's quite an experience for me to meet such a man.

Jim seems genuinely interested in my life and writing too, without having any other goal in mind except to help me to claim what is mine. He seems to have no agenda. He doesn't seem to want me to conform to any of his ideas. I trust that God put this man in my path for a good reason.

Monday, May 20

Most of the morning I spent writing about "Adam's passion." Adam's whole life was passion, not action. He could not *do* anything. Everything was done to him. Jesus fulfilled his life in passion. He was handed over to suffering, to the actions of others, which he had to undergo. I keep wondering if Adam's lifelong passion didn't make his life a prophetic witness in a society where all the emphasis is on action even though many people live the greater part of their lives in passion.

After lunch I bought a short biography of the painter Georgia O'Keeffe by Michael Berry. The more I read about O'Keeffe and look at her paintings, the more I feel a deep affinity with her. She struggled in relationships, especially in her relationship with the photographer Alfred Stieglitz. Her struggles to develop her own art form — going back and forth between New York and New Mexico — reveal a person with a great need for love, affection, and personal support, but also for independence, freedom, solitude, and space for creativity. She definitely belongs to New Mexico. As I walk around Santa Fe looking at the sky, the buildings, and the flowers, and letting the colors of this milieu affect me, I realize that indeed nature imitates art. O'Keeffe's paintings make me *see* Santa Fe. Just as Rembrandt and several other Dutch painters opened Vincent van Gogh's eyes to really *see* the landscape he was walking through, O'Keeffe gives me eyes to see the world that surrounds me.

Why is Georgia O'Keeffe so popular? I think it is the combination of her personality and her art. Just as Vincent's story and his art cannot be separated, so Georgia's story and her art belong together. It's not just her paintings that hold me in their grip; it's also this most remarkable woman, whose intense search for intimacy and solitude is part of the art she created. Seeing her art is seeing her life, and seeing her life is helping me see my own.

I realize that my emerging questions and my strong feelings about Georgia O'Keeffe are closely connected. They both reflect my struggle to reach a new integration of solitude, intimacy, and creativity in the decades ahead of me.

It has been good to be with Jim. Our conversations about our lives and our work are open and free. Jim asked me, "What is most important in your life?" I had to think a long time before I could answer this. I said, "Well, three things: living a vision inspired by the Gospel of Jesus; being close to the poor, the handicapped, the sick, and the dying; and finding a way to satisfy my deep yearning for intimacy and affection." Jim laughed at me and said, "Well, you seem to have it all. You are a very lucky man."

Tuesday, May 21

During and after lunch Jim and I talked about the Adam book. Jim was clear that poverty was the most important concept of the book. He said, "Poverty is being empty of adverse human influences. When you are completely free from these influences, you are open to the Divine. In his poverty Adam appears to have been fully open to the Divine, and thus he helped you to become more aware of the Divine within yourself." Jim's Christian Science background made him identify with what I was trying to say about Adam.

Jim feels that Adam's life gives expression to the presence of the Divine in our lives, but he is convinced that the book is not only about Adam but also about me and about my own spiritual search. He encouraged me to share about the ways that Adam touched and shaped my life.

I become aware of how my own needs for friendship, human contact, and intimacy are still part of "worldly" influences. Adam, who appeared so deeply disabled, had a divine gift for me. Others who appear gifted, or who offer me something other than the Divine, leave me finally, with empty hands. Sharing his experiences of human relationships, Jim concluded by saying, "There are no shortcuts to the Divine. Success, sex, power, and fame will not give us what we need. On the contrary, we often have to lose them all in order to discover the truth of the good, present, and active God within us. Your relationship with Adam has taught you a lot about this."

Wednesday, May 22

Today I spent the day with a friend. When I got back to Malcolm's condominium at 7:00 p.m. I discovered that I had lost my house key. I panicked because I had locked the front door and the gate of the house. Frantically I kept going through all my pockets, but no key. Finally I drove to a public phone and tried to call Malcolm in Fort Worth to ask him what to do, but he wasn't home. Then I called Jim, who was busy with a client on another line. I said, "I am home, but can't get in. I have no idea what to do, but I will retrace my steps. Maybe I dropped the key." Jim said, "Keep calm, stay there, and call me back in a few minutes so we can figure something out."

Meanwhile, the sun was going down. I wondered to myself if perhaps the key had fallen in the condominium parking lot, so I decided to go and look while I was waiting. Just before I arrived at the place, I said to St. Anthony, "Please help me find the keys. Please. I promise that I will give a nice gift to someone who needs it." I was surprised by my own prayer. I had not prayed like that since I was a child, and I cannot remember ever praying to St. Anthony before tonight.

It was getting quite dark as I stepped out of my car and let my eyes go over the parking place. I didn't see anything at first, so I kept looking. And suddenly, there was something red on the asphalt. I bent over and picked up my key! I cried out, "Thank you, St. Anthony, thank you, thank you." I called Jim and said, "Please come over to celebrate my key!" He came, and we laughed a lot. I wondered, "To whom shall I give St. Anthony's reward?"

Thursday, May 23

This morning I had a pleasant late breakfast with Wayne, and we talked directly and honestly about our ways of finding new freedom in life. The question of how the institutions that surround us help or inhibit us in our creativity is real for both of us. Although Wayne is twenty years younger than I, we both feel we are in transition. Wayne is moving with his family to California to find a new direction in his life, and I am pondering new writing, new thinking, and a new way of living after this sabbatical is over.

At 5:00 p.m. I drove over to Jim's house. At dinner we talked about Jim's business plans. Not long ago, he had been thinking about selling the publishing house and retiring, but he chose the opposite and is now branching out in new directions and taking new risks. I wonder what we will be talking about ten years from now. When we said farewell I knew that in Jim I had found a new friend and a trustworthy critic, not only of my writing but also of my outlook on life.

It all started with the trapeze book. Jim seemed the ideal person to help me write that book. Right now the book about Adam is more important because I am in the middle of it. But whether it is a book about Adam or one about the Rodleighs, it is always going to be a book about me. It is my experience of Adam and the Rodleighs that finally makes a book about them possible. I wear the glasses through which they are seen. So the question is not simply "Who is Adam?" or "Who are the Rodleighs?" but "Who am I?"

Jim has helped me to take myself seriously in the writing. I know that as long as I am not interiorly free, I cannot let Adam and the Rodleighs come close enough for me to be able to write about them with true spiritual attentiveness.

I am very grateful for Jim and our work together.

Saturday, May 25

The last day of the Easter season. I am deeply moved by the final scene in the Gospel of John. After Jesus has called Peter to follow him, Peter points to the "beloved disciple," and says, "Lord, what about him?" Jesus answers, "If it is my will that he remain until I come, what is that to you? Follow me!" (Jn 21:21–22). How often do I say, "What about him, her, them, this, or that?" I keep raising questions that seem to be expressions of concern but are in fact signs of my lack of trust. There are so many "yes, but" remarks in my life. "Yes, I will follow you, but tell me first what is going to happen with my family, my friends, my career, my future plans." Jesus answers, "Don't worry about all of that. Trust me, follow me, and all will be well." It is not surprising that my life is so fragmented. Many worries keep pulling me away from the center, thus dividing my life. I want to believe in my call to follow Jesus and to trust that everything else will fall into place because I do believe that He holds the whole world safely in the palms of his hands.

This afternoon my sister, Laurien, and her companion, Henri, arrived. The sun was shining brightly and the valley more beautiful than ever. We took a little walk along the river and then had dinner with Peggy.

I am very happy that they have come to visit me, because of my desire to share with my family where I live and what I do. Although I visit them when I am in Holland, we seldom see each other on this side of the Atlantic.

Pentecost Sunday, May 26

In the letter to the Galatians Paul writes, "The fruits of the Spirit are love, joy, peace, patience, kindness, goodness, trustfulness, gentleness and self-control; no law can touch such things as these" (Gal 5:22–23). During the Pentecost celebration we talked about these fruits and their meaning in our lives. Peggy made a large plate with nine fruits, each "named" for one of the spiritual fruits, and the seven-year-old Rush went around the circle inviting each person to take the one fruit that they would most like grow within them.

It was a joyful event. Beautiful flowers, brought by Joanie; altar bread made by Carol and Peggy; readings read by Claire and Jane; plus songs and prayers. It was a very intimate celebration of the Eucharist with about twenty people.

Memorial Day, Monday, May 27

Close to thirty people came to the morning Eucharist! It was clear that this Monday holiday permitted people to come with their families to participate in the morning's celebration.

The Gospel about the rich young man who loved Jesus and was loved by him but couldn't follow him because of his attachment to his many possessions was a real challenge for us. What seemed to impress people was the realization that this story does not imply a huge leap from everything to nothing but rather a long series of small steps in the direction of love. The tragedy for the rich young man was not that he was unwilling to give up his wealth — who would be? The real tragedy for him was that he missed something both he and Jesus desired, which was the opportunity to develop a deep and intimate relationship. It is not so much a question of detachment as it is a question of fully trusting and following the voice of love. Detachment is only a consequence of a greater attachment. Who would worry about his few possessions when invited to be intimate with the Lord of abundance, who offers more fish than we can catch and more bread than we can eat? What would have happened if the young man had said yes to Jesus? Wouldn't he, just like the other disciples, have become a source of hope for countless people? Now he drops out of history and is never heard of again! What a loss! To follow the voice of love, step by step, trusting that God will give us all we need is the great challenge.

Shortly after the Eucharist Laurien and Henri left to continue their visit in the United States. I hope they enjoyed their time with me. It means so much to me that they came. I'm afraid I made the mistake of inviting them to participate with too many people from here instead of spending quality time with them alone. I wanted to share my "natural milieu," but I realize that for such a short visit it was too much. We did enjoy the time, but I have to think about how I would welcome them in the future so that they feel welcome and comfortable.

Joanie invited a large part of the eucharistic community to her birthday. It strikes me that this little community that has grown during the last three months has come to have meaning for her. New friendships have developed through our daily spiritual gatherings, and Joanie has discovered a spiritual community that is giving her energy and hope. For her it was obvious that it was *in* and *with* this community that she wanted to celebrate her birthday.

New York, Tuesday, May 28

This afternoon I arrived at 5:00 p.m. at the Crossroad offices. Gwendolin, Bob, and I talked for a few minutes about the text of the first eight months of my sabbatical journal, which I had sent them a few weeks ago. They both responded warmly to what I had written, gave me some notes they had made about the parts that spoke most to them, and wondered how I could most effectively integrate the best stories with the best meditations. I realize that I still have three months of my sabbatical left and will write a lot more before this journal is finished, but it is good to gradually discover which of all these pages are worth presenting to a large readership.

Peapack, Wednesday, May 29

I stayed in New York with Wendy and Jay, and after a very quiet Eucharist in their living room this morning, I took a cab to Port Authority and a bus back to Peapack. It was a nice day in New York, but I am glad to be back in this quiet place.

Frank called with the news that he was "deployed" to Haiti as chaplain from June until September. He had been planning to visit me in July, but now he may come for a few days before I leave for Holland. I hope that when he does go to Haiti he will get to know the L'Arche community there.

Thursday, May 30

This morning I received a fax from Jan van den Bosch's Dutch Media Production Company, telling me that they plan to make the TV documentary of the Prodigal Son in St. Petersburg from September 10 to 13. I knew that this was coming, but somehow I had put it out of my mind, not really believing that they would be able to make all the arrangements with the Hermitage in such a short time. But here it is! Everything is done, and I am expected to be in Holland before September 9 so I can travel with the crew to St. Petersburg on the tenth.

I keep wondering if it is wise for me to get so involved with television. I never watch TV and hardly see the programs that I am part of. Still, it is a powerful medium. What irritates me most about TV is that the visual so dominates the audio. People say, "Oh, I saw you on TV. I liked your enthusiasm and the way you used your hands." When I ask, "What did you think about the ideas we discussed?" they seldom have a response.

Making a TV documentary is time consuming, fatiguing, frustrating, and often boring. I have to do the same thing over and over again to reduce my "nuanced" ideas to three or four clear, unambiguous sentences. So why do I keep doing it? Well, I like Jan, I want to do something for my country, I get caught up in the excitement of it all, and it is hard to say no to those who have such strong opinions, desires, and visions as the Dutch! So I will go to St. Petersburg in September.

Friday, May 31

Today is the Feast of the Visitation. A very young girl meets a very old woman. Both are pregnant. Both feel misunderstood. Joseph, the young girl's fiancé, is considering separation, fearing scandal. Zechariah, the old woman's husband, has been struck dumb and doesn't understand what's happening. And the women themselves, do they know? Hardly. They are puzzled, confused, and somewhat lost.

Mary, the young girl, needs to get out of the little gossiping town where she lives. She suffers from staring eyes and whispers behind her back. She escapes. In haste she goes over the hills to Ain Karim, where her old cousin Elizabeth lives. She knows deep within her that Elizabeth will understand and offer her a safe place to wait for the child.

As they meet and look at each other, they shout with joy. They embrace, they hold each other, they cry, they laugh. The fear and self-consciousness fall away from both of them.

"The mother of my Lord," cries Elizabeth. "My soul magnifies the Lord," cries Mary. Elizabeth understands, affirms, and celebrates. Her whole body is jubilant. The child in her womb leaps with joy. And Mary realizes her grace, her gift, her special blessing. With a newfound freedom she exclaims, "The Lord has looked with favor on the lowliness of this servant. Surely, from now on all generations will call me blessed, for the Mighty One has done great things for me" (Lk 1:43, 46–49).

Two women who felt oppressed and isolated suddenly realize their greatness and are free to celebrate their blessing. The two of them become community. They need each other, just to be together and protect each other, support each other, and affirm each other. They stay together for three months. Then each of them is ready to face her truth alone, without fear, willing to suffer the consequences of her motherhood.

I can hardly think about a better way to understand friendship, care, and love than "the way of the visitation." In a world so full of shame and guilt, we need to visit each other and offer each other a safe place where we can claim our freedom and celebrate our gifts. We need to get away once in a while from the suspicious voices and angry looks and be in a place where we are deeply understood and loved. Then we might be able to face the hostile world again, without fear and with new trust in our integrity.

June 1996

Saturday, June 1

This morning at noon Lorenzo arrived at the Newark Airport. He is going to stay with me for a week so that we can work on his biography.

Lorenzo and I both arrived at Daybreak on Labor Day 1986. For both of us this was a major decision. For me it was a farewell to twenty years of teaching in universities, and for Lorenzo it was a moving from his family and from studies in California to another way of living.

Lorenzo, after several years as a house assistant, started to work in the Daybreak woodworking shop, and I, after living for fourteen months in one of the Daybreak houses, became full-time pastor of the community. We became friends. During our several get-togethers over the years, the idea arose for me to write a small book about Lorenzo's life and vocation. This seems to be a good way for Lorenzo to reflect on his life, for me to come to know him better, and for us to spend creative time together.

What fascinated me from the beginning about Lorenzo's life was the way this man of noble birth, educated in the high society of Rome, gradually felt drawn to a very simple life with handicapped people in Canada. Lorenzo's physical handicaps, a cleft palate and hip dysplasia, which have required countless hospitalizations and surgeries, definitely played an important role in his final decision to move away from the world of social visibility to the world of marginal people. But the decision was fruitful because it was taken in great faith and with deep love. I trust that it will gradually become clear how Lorenzo's story can be told in a way that reveals God's gentle guidance in our lives.

Sunday, June 2

Trinity Sunday. Beautiful weather. Sunny, cool, no wind, many birds chirping, very quiet. Peggy suggested that we celebrate the Eucharist in Mimi's garden, created in memory of her deceased daughter.

About twenty people sat in a large circle in the lovely fenced-in garden. I tried to explain the mystery of the Trinity by saying that all human relationships are reflections of the relationships within God. God is the Lover, the Beloved, and the Love that binds us in unity. God invites us to be part of that inner movement of love so that we can truly become sons and daughters of the Father, sisters and brothers of the Son, and spouses of the Holy Spirit. Thus, all our human relationships can be lived *in* God, and as witness to God's divine presence in our lives.

I am deeply convinced that most human suffering comes from broken relationships. Anger, jealousy, resentment, and feelings of rejection all find their source in conflict between people who yearn for unity, community, and a deep sense of belonging. By claiming the Holy Trinity as home for our relational lives, we claim the truth that God gives us what we most desire and offers us the grace to forgive each other for not being perfect in love. We had a good discussion about this mystery of love and a joyful celebration of the Eucharist.

Monday, June 3

Lorenzo is a Roman nobleman. Presently he is an assistant woodworker in the Daybreak woodery. Lorenzo is a simple man with deep convictions, a strong prayer life, and a great desire to serve the poor. He is gentle, kind, faithful, and upright in everything he says and does.

The story of his youth in a palazzo in Rome, of his studies in the United States, and of his life with people with mental disabilities in Canada is basically very unsensational. It is the story of a wounded heart in search of a vocation. It is the story of a soul. But in all its simplicity and straightforwardness, it is a story full of light. Francesco, Lorenzo's brother, made an audiotape on which he describes Lorenzo as a man of stability and determination, and as one having clear goals in the midst of a world full of social busyness, partygoing, unfocused living, and spiritual flatness.

Whenever Lorenzo goes home he feels the difference between the lifestyle of his family and his life in the Daybreak community. Sometimes he feels seduced by the many voices questioning why he is wasting his life with such unsophisticated people when in Italy he could enjoy more comforts and pleasures. But when he returns after a visit to Italy he feels at home, surrounded by his people at Daybreak.

I think it is good to write down Lorenzo's story. It is a story of simple sanctity in the midst of an ambitious and competitive world.

Wednesday, June 5

Lorenzo had written a few notes about simplicity to help me in my writing about his life. He feels that simplicity is one of his main characteristics. He wrote, "Simplicity is finding pleasure and enjoyment in the small and ordinary things of life. Simplicity is the total surrender to that inner core where the spirit of each being exists. It enables us to experience being part of creation and its beauty."

What Lorenzo had to say about simplicity clearly comes from his heart. I wonder if *simplicity* is not the core word around which I should write his biography.

At 10:30 a.m. Steve arrived. Steve is a friend and artist from Newburyport, Massachusetts. He made the cover for the book *With Burning Hearts* and has agreed to make cover images for the hardback volumes of my "collected works" that Continuum will publish. The idea is to make a series of drawings of hands: blessing hands, healing hands, speaking hands, giving hands, and so on. Steve wanted to use my own hands for these drawings. So he came to take photographs of my hands.

It was a beautiful day with magnificent light. Steve took hundreds of pictures in the garden. While he was taking these pictures, I became aware of how many things hands can express: joy, anger, love, care, gentleness, support, and more.

After lunch Lorenzo got "into the act," and we made many photographs of our four hands, holding, touching, pulling, pushing, grasping, slapping, et cetera. We also used a cup with wine and a plate with bread, to express giving and receiving.

Steve was in a great mood, full of joy and laughter. He left around 3:00 p.m.

Lorenzo created a wonderful dinner for both of us.

I am tired and ready to go to bed early.

Thursday, June 6

"You shall love the Lord your God with all your heart, and with all your soul, and with all your mind, and with all your strength. You shall love your neighbor as yourself" (Mk 12:29–31). This morning during the Eucharist we reflected on these words. The love of God, neighbor, and self is one love. This great commandment is a call to the most profound unity, in which God, God's people, and we ourselves are part of one love. In this way the great commandment is much more than a moral prescription. It is a mandate to always, in all things, and at all places live and work for oneness. All that exists is one. It is all part of the all-embracing divine love. Our call is to make that love visible in our daily lives.

This unity can be seen in three ways. First, when we direct our whole beings toward God, we will find our neighbor and ourselves right in the heart of God. Second, when we truly love ourselves as God's beloved children, we will find ourselves in complete unity with our neighbor and with God. Third, when we truly love our neighbor as our brother and sister, we will find, right there, God and ourselves in complete unity. There really is no first, second, and third in the great commandment. All is one: the heart of God, the hearts of all people, our own hearts. All the great mystics have "seen" this and lived it.

I spoke for an hour and a half by phone with Sue and Nathan about my return to Daybreak in September and my future role in the community. Sue has been asked to go for one year to Stratford, Ontario, to support the L'Arche community there, so she won't be able to be Daybreak's pastor any longer. We talked about naming another community member to do it whom I could support, which would free me to continue my writing. We are hopeful that my small house can be built during the summer, but much depends on the permissions we need from the town of Richmond Hill. I feel quite good about our conversation.

Friday, June 7

The Eucharist was very special today because of the presence of Amy, a lovely wife and mother of two children who is suffering from advanced brain cancer. Her friend, a medical doctor, brought her in a wheelchair. She was laid on the large sofa right in front of the altar table. Around her was a circle of about twenty people.

After the reading of the Beatitudes I spoke about us as a community of the weak held together by mutual forgiveness and celebration. At the conclusion of the Eucharist we all blessed Amy, asking God for healing in her body, mind, and heart. Amy herself was very open and shared her immense frustration that God had not heard her prayers and performed a miracle. At this moment she was clearly not yet in a spiritual place where she could prepare herself for her death. But she was deeply grateful for the prayers of our little community.

Tomorrow will be a very busy day. I'll be driving Lorenzo to the airport, driving to Princeton for the wedding of Bobby and Anne, bringing the car back to Peapack, packing for the trip to Holland, and going by bus to New York to stay with Wendy and Jay. I hope all goes well, but I get nervous just thinking about it.

I don't feel completely ready to leave this beautiful place and lovely community. I would have loved to stay a little longer, write a little more, and deepen the community. But I will be back on July 15 and have one more month here. I am grateful to Peggy and all her friends who have made this such a special time for me.

New York, Saturday, June 8

At noon I arrived at the Nassau Inn in Princeton, where Fran had invited me for lunch. After many years of not seeing much of each other, we had reconnected at the funeral of Don Sr. in Winnetka. Fran is presently the principal of a school. It was a joy to be with her again and strengthen a long friendship.

A little before 2:00 p.m. Fran dropped me off for Bobby and Anne's wedding. It was a very simple ceremony. I was asked to read the epistle:

> That is why we do not waver; indeed, though this outer human nature of ours may be falling in decay, at the same time our inner humanity is renewed day by day. For we are well aware that when the tent that houses us on earth is folded up, there is a house for us from God, not made by human hands but everlasting, in the heavens. (2 Cor 4:16, 5:1)

While reading these words facing Bobby and Anne, I realized how appropriate they were for the situation. Bobby has experienced so much pain in his life, and he knows about folding the tent that houses us on earth. He needs a strong faith and much hope not to despair but to give his life new energy. His great ambition helps him a lot, but it also makes him very vulnerable.

I was glad to be with him at this moment. I was at his graduation, ordination, and first wedding. I want to be faithful to my friendship with him and to remain present in his life and in the lives of his two boys.

I finally completed all the tasks that were ahead of me in preparation for my trip to Holland. Now the busy day is ending, and I feel happy to be safe and well with Wendy and Jay.

En Route to Amsterdam, Sunday, June 9

After a prayerful Eucharist with Jay and Wendy, I took a cab to Greenwich Village to attend the wedding of Mark and Paul. It was the first time I have attended a same-sex marriage. Although I was warmly welcomed by the rabbi and her husband, I found myself somewhat lost in the event and even somewhat like a stranger among strangers.

Mark and Paul have been living together for twenty years. Only recently did they decide to sacramentalize their relationship. In Saturday's paper there was an article about gay weddings. In the article Paul explains his decision to get formally married with these words: "I got tired of living in sin." That tongue-in-cheek remark summarizes for me the moral predicament of gay and lesbian people. While everyone is discussing the morality of the homosexual life, these two men are discussing the morality of not being married!

Now I am glad to be on the plane, looking forward to another time in Europe and a second vacation with my father.

Geysteren, Monday, June 10

I keep wondering why I take so much luggage with me. I am always determined to travel light, but I always end up with more suitcases than I can carry! When I arrived at Schiphol I realized that I wouldn't be able to carry all my luggage alone. Since a cab to my father's home was too expensive, I took the train. But I had to change trains twice. It was a nightmare to get all my stuff from one train to the other. At the airport, as I was going down the escalator with my loaded luggage cart, all my suitcases fell off, tumbling down the moving steps. I nearly fell over them. People saw me panicking but ignored me. Finally I asked a young man to help me. He was kind enough to take two of the five pieces of luggage and carry them onto the railroad platform.

During the two-and-a-half-hour trip, two people came to my rescue and made it possible for me to catch the connecting train. When I finally arrived at my father's town, I was completely exhausted, more emotionally than physically. Remarkably neither of the two breakable gifts I was carrying was damaged and nothing was stolen. I saved a lot of money by taking the train but lost a lot of energy.

My father and I were happy to see each other. My father looked well and seemed in good health. He was looking forward to our trip to Belgium next week. I was so tired that I went to bed immediately and slept for six solid hours. After I woke up my father and I watched the Scotland-Holland match in the European Cup soccer games in England and had a simple supper. I was back in bed at 9:00 p.m.

Wallenhorst, Germany, Wednesday, June 12

At 3:00 p.m. Robert arrived to take me to Germany for his wedding. After getting settled in the hotel I went with Robert to his house, where I met Susanne, his bride to be, and her sister Beate, who had just arrived from New York. Robert, Susanne, and Beate all have spent lots of time in the

United States, so their English is fluent. Still, we spoke mostly German. My German is quite poor, but I'd better get used to speaking it so that I can lead the marriage ceremony on Saturday.

At midnight I was back in the hotel, quite tired and a little depressed. The constant going from place to place somehow makes me lose my sense of belonging and gives me a feeling of alienation. I deeply crave times of prayer but never feel quiet enough to just sit down and pray. My mind is not very creative. The constant fatigue makes me always look for an opportunity to sleep. But I have the rosary, and letting the beads move through my hands with the Hail Mary on my lips offers me a little connection with my true home.

Thursday, June 13

Why can't I get rid of my fatigue? I keep looking at my bed as the only desirable place to be. Everything exhausts me, even putting on my clothes. And everything, even seeing wonderful people and sharing wonderful meals, seems a burden or an obligation. I just want to be alone, sleep, pray, and write. But I am always in the center of things. I can't just be a simple guest who is too tired to show up for an event. I am not sure what the problem is. It seems as if my body still lives in the United States — that is, six hours earlier — and my inner household is in chaos.

At 1:00 p.m. Robert picked me up for lunch with Susanne and Beate. After lunch Robert, Susanne, and I had our first "spiritual meeting." In our conversation Robert and Susanne placed much emphasis on the importance of admiring, respecting, and honoring each other as two independent, self-motivated people. This was understandable considering their successful medical careers. I also felt the need to share about how their love finally means daring to be vulnerable to each other and offering each other a sense of home and safety in a very competitive world. It was a good conversation.

After returning to the hotel, I slept a few hours, then met Franz and Reny, Robert's parents. We drove to Mettingen for dinner with Irene, Robert's sister, and her Portuguese boyfriend, Louis, and with Jim and Elise, Robert's American "parents."

As we all sat around the dinner table I marveled at the way we had come together. Jim and Elise have been close friends since my time at Yale Divinity School. When my parents came to visit me there in 1978, Jim diagnosed my mother's pancreatic cancer. A day after my parents arrived they returned to Holland. Shortly thereafter my mother underwent surgery. She died a few days later.

When, a few years later, I spent time writing in Germany in the home of Franz and Reny, I came to know Robert and heard about his desire to study medicine in the United States. I wrote Jim about Robert, and that was the beginning of Robert's three-year stay at Yale University. During these years Jim and Elise became very close to Robert and more or less adopted him as their German child. Although there had been a lot of contact by phone and letter between Robert's parents and Jim and Elise, tonight was the first time they ever saw each other.

Many things were coming together: tragedy and joy, death and new beginnings, old friends and new friends, stories and memories, writing and publishing. I continue to marvel at it all, even though I wasn't sure that my friends were as impressed with all these converging lives as I was!

I was back at my hotel at 11:00 p.m. totally exhausted. I watched CNN for a while and prayed a little. Then I fell into a deep sleep.

Friday, June 14

At 11:00 a.m. Susanne and Robert were legally married at the city hall. It was a simple, short ceremony with only the family present. In Germany as in Holland, the marriage for the state is separated from the marriage for the church. For people who marry in the church, the state marriage is usually more a formality than a celebration.

At 6:00 p.m. both Robert and Susanne came to my hotel for another "spiritual meeting." While we had coffee and tea in the hotel dining hall, we talked about marriage as a sacrament, and especially about the intimate connection between marriage and the Eucharist. In the Eucharist Jesus shows us his faithful love by giving us his Body and Blood as spiritual food and drink. When marriage is a visible witness to this divine love, participation in the Eucharist is a way to deepen and strengthen the marriage vows. Thus the Eucharist becomes a spiritual discipline for married people to constantly renew their commitment to each other, as living signs of God's love in this world.

After our conversation Susanne and Robert left for Münster to celebrate their wedding with their medical colleagues.

In my room, by myself, I celebrated the Eucharist. Today is the Feast of the Sacred Heart, and I have experienced much inner anxiety, fear, restlessness, and fatigue. I wanted to be alone, pray, and bring all these intense emotions and feelings into the presence of Jesus and ask for healing. Ever since I wrote a small book about the heart of Jesus, this feast has been very dear to me. I hope that my prayer for relief of my inner agonies will be heard. I trust that God hears me when I pray.

Saturday, June 15

Robert and Susanne's wedding took place in the little Alexander Church, which was built in 777. It was recently restored in all its beauty and made available for weddings and special ceremonies.

The little church was packed with family and friends. The atmosphere was joyful and informal. Robert and Susanne looked radiant and were fully present to every part of the celebration. In my homily I spoke about three truths: God has chosen you, you have been chosen to bring forth fruit, and you have a special call to care for your sick and dying neighbors. As the three disciplines to live according to these truths, I suggested prayer to God, ongoing conversation with each other, and care for the poor. I had a very attentive audience, and quite a few people responded warmly to my words during the reception and the dinner.

The party at the hotel in Mettingen was elegant, festive, tasteful, humorous, and quite abundant in food and drink. In a short time I met many cardiologists, internists, and neurologists, all colleagues of Robert and Susanne.

At 11:00 p.m. Franz offered to drive me back to my hotel. While I was saying good-bye to several people on the dance floor, I was able to ask Susanne for a dance. I never danced with a bride before. It was a wonderful, joyful way to close the evening.

Geysteren, Sunday, June 16

After many embraces, kisses, and handshakes, Franz, Reny, and I were on our way to Geysteren. Shortly after 3:00 p.m. we arrived at my father's home. He was very glad to have Franz and Reny as his guests, especially since they both had been so kind and generous to us during our trip to Freiburg at Christmastime.

At 6:00 p.m. my brother Paul, my brother Laurent and his wife, Heiltjen, and my sister, Laurien, with her partner, Henri, arrived, and all of us went out for dinner at my father's favorite restaurant. It was a beautiful evening — soft light, cool air, and a splendid view of the river Maas and the lush green meadows on each bank. Before and after dinner we all sat on the large terrace overlooking the peaceful landscape. Franz and Reny were very happy to meet the whole family. Franz kept saying, "How wonderful to feel so welcome in the intimate circle." I was especially glad to see my father so happy with his family and friends around him.

Tuesday, June 18

Today everything was soccer in Holland. Tonight many Dutchmen were glued to the "tube" to watch the match between Holland and England in London. There hardly is a quieter time on the roads than when Holland watches an important soccer game. People were watching this game with the hope that the Dutch might make it to the European finals.

Before the games the Dutch players were quite self-confident, even arrogant, when speaking about their English opponents, but it soon became clear that the English team was far superior. It became a soccer tragedy for Holland since England hadn't beaten the Dutch in the past. England celebrated their 4–1 victory as a true revenge.

Rotterdam, Wednesday, June 19

This afternoon I took the train to Rotterdam, where I was invited to animate the conversation of a theological club of Catholics which has been meeting monthly for the last twenty years. I felt a real spiritual interest. Good questions emerged such as, How should I pray? How can I keep focused on God? How can we live spiritual lives when we have very competitive jobs? What disciplines can be of help? People were kind, direct, open, loving, and very attentive. I was deeply moved by their interest in L'Arche. At the end of the evening, I had a sense of having met a unique group of Dutchmen, whom I would love to come to know more personally.

Geysteren, Thursday, June 20

Early in the morning I took the train to Utrecht, where I had been invited to speak at the biweekly meeting of the deans of the archdiocese.

After I had spoken for half an hour about prayer, community, and ministry in the context of my own life, there were many questions. There was a genuine interest in the topics I talked about.

After the deans' meeting I took the train to Venray and a cab to my father's home. Tomorrow my father and I start our vacation together.

Herbeumont, Belgium, Friday, June 21

After our successful trip to Germany over Christmas and New Year's, my father had asked me to accompany him on a ten-day summer vacation to Herbeumont. He had heard that there is a good, quiet hotel here, from which we will be able to make little day trips. I was happy to have another vacation with my father.

This morning we drove the three hundred kilometers to Herbeumont. A special attraction for me is that the large Trappist Abbey of Orval is nearby. The hotel, which once was a priory, is small and intimate, and we are treated very personally. I was exhausted from the trip, and I slept for three hours. At 8:00 p.m. we had an exquisite "French" supper.

I am glad to be here and look forward to a quiet week, with time to work on the several manuscripts I brought with me.

Saturday, June 22

After a late breakfast, we drove to the Trappist Abbey at Orval. I was quite overwhelmed by the huge complex. The monastery had been de-stroyed several times during the past centuries, but it was completely rebuilt during the 1950s. Large buses were parked in front of the en-trance, and hundreds of people were walking around. It was clearly a big tourist attraction.

Once we were there the great difficulty was to make it with my fa-ther to the entrance of the church. The distance from the gate to the church, and the many steps, seemed a huge obstacle for him. But he insisted on walking and climbing the steps without a wheelchair or as-sistance. Although he made it, he completely exhausted himself. Happily my two friends from Trosly, Marie Hélène and Paul, who presently live a few miles from the abbey, came to our assistance. After the Eucharist, Paul found a wheelchair and got my father to the car without so much walking. We quickly returned to the hotel, where my father fell on his bed totally spent from our little outing.

I have been thinking a lot today about the abbey. It is huge and was built when the church was strong, powerful, and self-confident, expecting many vocations to the monastic life. Today this attitude seems completely out of place. Very few young men are joining the community, and only about thirty-five monks are left, most of whom are middle-aged or older.

The liturgy, with about sixty guests, was sober and simple. Following the celebration from a great distance, I realized how much I miss the intimate home liturgies at Daybreak and in Peapack.

For some reason I became sad and melancholy realizing that this was *my* community, *my* church, *my* spirituality, and *my* liturgy. I felt like an outsider, a tourist, an observer. When we left I said to my father, "Tomor-row we'd better celebrate the Eucharist in my bedroom. That might save you a heart attack and me a depression."

Sunday, June 23

A very quiet day. At noon I celebrated the Eucharist with my father in my bedroom. No sermon! Most of the day we both worked on our manuscripts. My father is busy writing his memories of me from the time I was born in 1932 until my ordination to the priesthood in 1957. On some points he needs my memory to verify his, so he walks into my room from time to time. I am busy working on the Dutch translations of *Here and Now* and *Can You Drink the Cup?* As the author of these books, I have the freedom not only to rework the translations but also to change the contents here and there and thus make the text more accessible for Dutch readers.

Thursday, June 27

Our days have been very low key and quiet because my father has not been feeling too well. Today he was quite miserable. Several times he changed his plans, but he did decide to join me for dinner with Paul and Marie Hélène.

My father loves turbot, because it is a white fish and very light but the turbot truck hadn't arrived yet, so the waiter suggested something my father didn't much care for. At the last minute the truck arrived, and we got our turbot after all! Well, old age does focus our attention, and not always on heavenly things!

My father enjoyed the drive as well as the meal and the conversation, even though he looked completely exhausted by 9:00 p.m.

Saturday, June 29

Today is the Feast of Saints Peter and Paul. The church celebrates their perseverance, spiritual insights, strong commitment to bring the Gospel to the whole world, and most of all their deep personal relationship with Jesus. Celebrating this day with my father in my hotel room reminded me again of my vocation, maybe not to travel far and wide but to keep writing about Jesus in many ways and to work on the translations of my writing into different languages.

Today we didn't leave the hotel at all. The weather was poor, and we both had enough to do on our manuscripts. My project was the book by Jurjen Beumer about me. I certainly didn't do anything about Jurjen's language or vision, but I wanted to be sure that the concrete information he offers is correct.

Sunday, June 30

The big event tonight was the soccer match between Germany and the Czech Republic. My father and I had an early dinner so we could watch it on TV.

I will always remember the Czech goalkeeper. He played an astonishingly good game; many times he prevented the Germans from scoring. His agility, courage, foresight, and iron nerves made him in my eyes the great hero. But in overtime, when the match was 1–1, he couldn't hold on to the ball that the German player shot into his hands, so he was the reason why the Germans, not the Czechs, received the European Cup from Queen Elizabeth. He will be remembered not as a hero but as the man who failed to give the Czech Republic its victory. While the Germans were dancing on the field, embracing one another, crying with joy, and raising their arms victoriously, this talented goalkeeper sat against one of the goalposts, his head buried in his knees. Nobody was there with him. He was the loser.

I feel deeply moved by the image of the defeated goalkeeper. All his great performances will be forgotten, in light of the one mistake that cost the Czechs the greatly desired European Cup. I often wonder about this "final mistake." After a long and fruitful life, one unhappy event, one mistake, one sin, one failure can be enough to create a lasting memory of defeat. For what will we be remembered? For our many acts of kindness, generosity, courage, and love, or for the one mistake we made toward the end? "Yes, he was fabulous, but he failed." "Yes, she was a saintly person, but she sinned." "Yes, they were great, but at the end they disappointed us."

Sometimes I think about dying before the great mistake! What if the "saints" had lived longer and had not been able to keep the ball in their hands at the final moment? Would such a small mistake have brought their saintliness to nothing? It frightens me to think this way. I realize that finally human beings are very fickle in their judgments. God and only God knows us in our essence, loves us well, forgives us fully, and remembers us for who we truly are.

July 1996

Holland, Tuesday, July 2

It has been so good to have another pleasant and peaceful vacation with my father. Although he was suffering physically, he was interested in dialoguing about many things that interest him and interest me. Our trip today was pleasant and uneventful, and we got home about 3:00 p.m.

After supper my father went to bed and I watched a most interesting documentary about the life and work of Igor Sikorsky, the inventor and producer of the helicopter. His story is the story of a Russian boy obsessed with the idea of building a plane that could fly vertically as well as horizontally. Against all odds he kept working on his project. After the Bolshevik Revolution in 1917, seeing that many czarist pilots were being executed, Sikorsky fled Russia and eventually made it to the United States. There, with incredible tenacity and will power, he developed the helicopter and built one of the largest helicopter industries in the world.

More than anything it was the determined character of Igor Sikorsky that fascinated me. If I could be half as determined in realizing my vocation as Igor was in realizing his dream — as a young boy he actually had a dream in which he saw his helicopter — I would be able to help a lot of people to fly!

Thursday, July 4

Most of the day I have been busy getting ready for my trip to Germany. Getting train tickets, packing my suitcase, and telling Kathy in Toronto and several friends where I can be reached. Tomorrow I will go to Berlin to visit friends, and Monday to Oberursel, near Frankfurt, to spend a few days with the Rodleighs. On Thursday I plan to visit Hans, an artist who lives near Koblenz.

I am somewhat concerned about leaving my father, since Tilly, his housekeeper, is on vacation and he will be mostly alone. But happily my brother and sister will come to visit on the weekend and plan to come more often if necessary. My father himself insists that he is fine and doesn't need any special help.

Berlin, Germany, Friday, July 5

Today I had a very long train ride. My friend, Tom Day, was on the platform at the Berlin station. I had not seen him since 1971, even though we
had spoken a few times by phone and exchanged a few letters. His voice
hasn't changed, but his hair, like mine, was grayer after twenty-five years!

When I first met Tom he was a Holy Cross priest. At that time I was
teaching at Yale Divinity School and Tom was studying at Union Theological Seminary. I vividly remember how impressed I was by Tom's ability
to play jazz saxophone. Somehow he incarnated for me an ideal: being a
priest while also being an excellent jazz musician.

While he was studying at Union, Tom left Holy Cross. There too, he
met Helga, a German theological student working on her doctoral disser-
tation. They fell in love and decided to marry. After finishing their studies
and living for a while in Princeton, they moved to Berlin, where they both
have had theological and pastoral careers. And they had two children.

As Tom and I traveled by subway and car to Tom's home, he told me
about his son's sudden and tragic death at his university. What incredible
grief! A brilliant life cut short. When we got to the house, Helga was
there to welcome us.

I can hardly believe how they are surviving this enormous tragedy.
Their son, Lars, the pride and joy of their lives, had died suddenly and
totally unexpectedly.

Saturday, July 6

After breakfast and the Eucharist, Tom and Helga took me on a tour
of Berlin. Visiting Berlin is quite an emotional experience for me. There
are many familiar names and images: Brandenburger Tor, the Reichstag,
Unter den Linden, and so on. But seeing these things all at once in
their natural setting and hearing Tom and Helga speak about them was
like seeing my own life from a new perspective. The end of the Weimar
Republic, the burning of the Reichstag, Hitler's coming to power, the Second World War and the hatred of Jews; the Russian invasion of Berlin and
the destruction of the city; the Allied control of the city in three sectors;
the division into East and West Berlin; the building of the Berlin Wall in
1961, and John F. Kennedy's words "Ich bin ein Berliner" (I am a Berliner)
in 1963; the taking down of the wall and the end of Communism; the
decision in 1990 to make Berlin the center of the German government
again; and the total rebuilding of the city. All of these events I lived from

a distance, and many of them I remember as significant moments of my life. Now I could see it all in stone and live it all again within a few hours.

It was history coming alive. I deeply feel my own responsibility. It *does* make a difference how I live my life. It *does* make a difference where I go, with whom I speak, and what I write. Yes, my life is very short and seems so insignificant in the context of our immense universe. But seeing what I saw today and hearing what I heard today, I experience a great desire to live with as much integrity, as much clarity, and as much courage as I can.

All through the day we talked about Tom and Helga's son. He was very present and very absent. It feels as if I came just too late to meet an exceptionally beautiful young man, full of life, full of love, and full of hope. What enormous pain. I feel some of it in my own heart. I cannot even fathom what Tom and Helga were feeling as they showed me this city, and as we walked and talked together.

Sunday, July 7

At 10:00 a.m. Tom led the service for the Evangelical Reformed Bethle-hem Community in a suburb of Berlin. It was a very simple but moving service in a small building with four elderly women, two elderly men, a young organist, the sacristan, Tom, and me present. One of the women told me that usually there are quite a few young people at the service but that today they were all on holiday. Since the congregation was too small to have their own pastor, a different pastor of the Reformed tradition was asked to help out every Sunday.

I was moved by the service since I felt ministered to as well. The songs, the readings, and Tom's words reached me at the place of my inner anguish and offered me a sense of God's love and mercy that I hadn't ex-perienced for quite some time. The poverty of the service, the simplicity of the people, and the German language allowed me to hear something very healing.

On our way home we again talked about Tom and Helga's son. "Where is he? What happened to him after his death?" his mother asked. Ideas and thoughts are so powerless in the face of a deeply wounded heart.

When we came home we celebrated the Eucharist together around the table in the garden. There we read Paul's words "If the Spirit of God who raised Jesus from the dead dwells in you, he who raised Christ from the dead will give life to your mortal bodies also through his Spirit that dwells in you" (Rom 8:11). Paul's word and the simple Eucharist offered us some consolation and comfort.

Oberursel, Germany, Monday, July 8

Around 11:00 a.m. Tom, Helga, and I went to the cemetery. It was rain-
ing heavily, but we carried umbrellas and the distances were short. As we
stood in front of the grave I felt a great inner pain. During these two days
I had come, through Tom and Helga's stories, to know this young man
so well that it seems as if they had prepared me to meet him and speak
to him. In front of his grave I realized that I would never see his face
or hear his voice. It felt like losing a friend I had never met. I prayed in
front of his grave in gratitude for having come to know him through Tom
and Helga and in the hope that his memory would inspire me in my own
mission and ministry.

Shortly after our visit to the cemetery we drove into town, had lunch
together, and said our farewells. This has been a very special weekend.
Although I hadn't known Tom and Helga very intimately before coming
to Berlin, our time together has profoundly nurtured our relationship.

At 2:00 p.m. I had a fast and easy train ride to Oberursel, where Rodleigh
was waiting. This Monday is one of the few days during the season
that the circus has no show. It was good to see the Flying Rodleighs
again. They were in good spirits and happy with the new shape of their
trapeze act. Since I last saw them, Rodleigh and Karlene's oldest brother,
Quentin, had suddenly died at age fifty. That was very painful. But
Rodleigh and Jennie also had good news to share; they are expecting a
baby in December.

Last year Jennie had stopped flying because of increasing shoulder
pains but also because of her hope of having a baby before getting too
old. Except for the bad weather the season has been good so far. A good
show, a good trapeze act, and often a full tent.

Still, from all the stories it became clear that the Flying Rodleighs are
gradually coming to the end of their years as a trapeze troupe. They had
signed a contract for the 1997 March–November season, but that may
be their final year. Rodleigh, Karlene, and Jonathon are beginning to
feel more fatigue, more stress, more pains. Last year Jonathon had knee
surgery. "I am fine now," he said, "but I got a warning. It might be time
to start thinking about something else."

It has been more than five years since I met the Rodleighs in Freiburg.
At that time they had just started to work for this circus. They hadn't
expected to stay this long because the circus director seldom hires an

act for more than three seasons. Next year will be their eighth with this circus.

I never expected to become so close to this wonderful group of people. Every time I meet them again I feel excited and grateful. The book I want to write about them still has not been written, but I trust that it will be. Maybe our long friendship will allow me to write something quite different from an interesting story about the trapeze. The spectacular trapeze act has gradually moved out of the center of my attention and become little more than the background of the lives of eight people who struggle to work and love well in our contemporary society.

Jonathon and Karlene offered me hospitality in their caravan. I can sleep on their "living room sofa." I am very tired and happy to lay down after a long day.

Tuesday, July 9

After a long sleep and a relaxed breakfast with Jonathon and Karlene, I wrote for an hour in this journal and then walked with Jonathon to the tent where Rodleigh, John, Slava, and Jonathon were going to level the rigging. They had set it all up yesterday but still needed to do the fine tuning of the cables, poles, swings, and so on. Every new place requires a careful checking of distances, floor level, heights, and many other details. A trapeze act is such precision work that small irregularities in the rigging can be fatal.

I am suddenly aware of how intimate the circus tent is. Last year and the year before last I saw the Rodleighs performing in halls in Rotterdam and Zwolle that could seat sixty thousand people or more. There the trapeze act took place at a great distance and lost some of its warmth. Now I can see it in its normal surroundings.

The 3:30 p.m. show brought in hundreds of children. I hadn't expected that I would be so moved seeing the Rodleighs again, but I found myself crying as I watched them flying and catching under the big top. Their act was a lot better than when I saw them last year at the winter circus. The choreography was elegant; there were many wonderful surprises, and the whole performance felt very energetic. Even though I have seen the Flying Rodleighs for five years now and have attended dozens of their shows, they never bore me. There always seems to be something new, something original, something fresh. I can understand why they are continually offered new contracts.

As I watched them in the air, I felt some of the same profound emotion as when I saw them for the first time with my father in 1991. It is hard to describe, but it is the emotion coming from the experience of an enfleshed spirituality. Body and spirit are fully united. The body in its beauty and elegance expresses the spirit of love, friendship, family, and community, and the spirit never leaves the here and now of the body.

Tonight I saw the show again. I was fascinated by a pair of blood brothers who performed a quite amazing contortionist act. The way they folded their bodies and wrapped themselves around each other created a feeling that these brothers are the most intimate of friends. But I heard after the show that they do not like each other, they live in separate trailers, they talk to each other only about work; and they are in competition about who is the best. It is so sad that people who act out brotherhood, friendship, and intimacy live the opposite. What attracts me so much to the Rodleighs is that their act and their lives are telling the same story. But it is becoming increasingly clear to me that the Rodleighs are an exception.

Wednesday, July 10

This morning I visited Jennie in her trailer just to ask her about the baby. She is so beautiful as an expectant mother. We had quite a discussion and even spoke about what would happen if the baby had Down's syndrome or any other abnormalities. Jennie's main concern was that Rodleigh might have to leave the circus if there were problems with the baby. Hopefully these decisions won't be necessary.

At noon I went to the tent to see the practice session. Rodleigh was teaching Slava the triple somersault. He makes the triple into the net all right, but so far he has not been able to reach catchpoint with John. They have been touching hands, but that is all.

At the end of the practice session Rodleigh asked me if I would like to make a swing or two. I said, "Sure, I'd love to." First he helped me get into the net and showed me how to climb the long ladder to the pedestal. It is an intimidating place to be. The space below, above, and around me felt enormous and awesome. Kerri and Slava pulled me up onto the pedestal, put the safety belt around me, held me tight, and handed me the bar. As I held the bar I wondered if I would be able to hold my own weight, but when they pushed me off I felt at ease swinging above the net a few times. I tried to kick a little to get higher but simply didn't have much breath left, so Rodleigh told me how to drop into the net. I repeated the whole sequence once more with a tiny bit more grace. Then Rodleigh agreed to give me a sense of the catcher's grip. So I climbed the ladder on the catcher's side, and Jonathon, who was hanging head down on the catchbar, grabbed me by my wrists and held me hanging there for a while. I looked up into his upside-down face and could imagine how it would be to swing while being held by him. Altogether I was happy with the experience. It got me as close as I will ever come to being a trapeze artist!

When we returned to Rodleigh's trailer we watched the video Jennie had made of the practice session, of my "performance," and of the afternoon show. Seeing myself hanging on the trapeze bar made me feel very silly. It was a pathetic sight. But seeing the whole afternoon act in slow motion was a great treat. More than anything else a slow-motion presentation of the complicated trapeze tricks makes you appreciate the Rodleighs' highly skillful art.

During the evening show I realized how anxious I am when I watch the Rodleighs at work. The more I know about their act, the harder it is to watch it. Knowing the Rodleighs so well and being aware of how much can go wrong, I look at them as a parent who sees his or her child doing dangerous things. I felt great relief when everything came to a good end. The large audience was ecstatic, stamping their feet and clapping their hands with wild enthusiasm.

Geysteren, Thursday, July 11

At 8:30 a.m. Rodleigh and Jennie drove me to the Frankfurt rail station. It was a warm and heartfelt good-bye. The two days in Oberursel were very life giving for me because being with the Rodleighs is one of the best ways for me to experience relaxation and restoration. Karlene and Jonathon made me feel really at home in their trailer. Rodleigh and Jennie are wonderful friends, and they never tire of explaining the details of the act. Slava, John, and Kerri also treated me with much kindness and gentleness. I feel deeply grateful for having such kind and generous friends.

I arrived in Koblenz, and Ralf was waiting for me. After a short stop at his house we drove to the home of the sculptor-painter Hans and his family. After a lovely lunch we looked at Hans's work, and discussed our new Dayspring chapel and spiritual center. Finally we had a quick look at a nearby church where Hans had remodeled the sanctuary. It was a very instructive visit. I hope that Hans will be able to come to Toronto in the coming year to help us with the interior design of our new chapel.

Ralf drove me to Bonn, and on the way we talked about his eight months' stay at Daybreak, which will begin in September. He will work as an assistant to prepare himself for his ministry to handicapped people in the Trier diocese. We talked about him taking an active role in the ministry and especially the liturgical life of Daybreak, which would also allow me a little more free time to write. Ralf is an enthusiastic and committed priest with a great love for Daybreak and a wonderful open and free spirit. By 4:45 p.m. we reached the Bonn station, and I took the train to Cologne.

From Cologne I traveled to Venlo and on to Venray. At 7:00 p.m. I was at my father's home. He had left a note telling me to come to a nearby restaurant, where he was having dinner with friends. When I got there I saw that it was the old theological club having its yearly meeting and dinner. My father, being an emeritus professor and a former colleague of several of its members, is always invited when the club meets in Geysteren.

Around the table were Mr. and Mrs. Vollenberg; Martin, the emeritus dean of Nijmegen; Mr. and Mrs. van SuSanta; Mrs. van Laarhoven; Professor Schillebeeckx; and my father. It was an unexpected occasion for me to have a conversation with Professor Edward Schillebeeckx, whom I had met only a few times and only in passing.

I was struck by his kindness, openness, and great willingness to share his experiences. Although he is one of the most influential theologians of our time, he also is a very humble and gentle man. Schillebeeckx clearly belongs to that generation of theologians who want to be faithful servants of the church. It is the generation of Karl and Hugo Rahner, Caspar Metz and Schoonenberg. They all were in their prime during Vatican II and played an important role in the formulation of its documents.

Today Schillebeeckx is in his early eighties. "I am working on a book on the sacraments," he said. "I have already three hundred pages written and will probably have to cut it a little." He showed great excitement about using the computer.

One thing that struck me during the dinner was that the people seemed preoccupied with the "Dutch scene" and "Dutch issues." It was clear that nobody had read or seen any of my books. I was more puzzled than hurt, more surprised than offended. I didn't feel rejected, just ignored. There simply was no space for me there.

This unexpected experience rekindled some of the feelings that I had when I left Holland in 1971 to join the faculty of Yale Divinity School. I guess it was a good decision for me to leave the parental home for a new country.

Utrecht, Friday, July 12

At 11:00 a.m. three of my father's sisters, Truus, Ella, and Paula, came for coffee and lunch. All three are in their eighties and full of humor, stories, and memories. After they left I packed my suitcases, said farewell to my father, and took the train to Utrecht.

In Utrecht I went to the house of Louis and Maria. During and after dinner we had a good conversation about my presentation to the deans of the diocese last month. Ever since that event I had felt a certain disappointment. Although everyone had been kind and friendly, and although most of them had participated actively in the discussion, I had felt like a stranger. I went there with the somewhat romantic expectation of being welcomed back in my own diocese as a lost brother! I had also come with the hope that my fellow priests would show some interest in my books and my work at L'Arche. None of these expectations and hopes had been fulfilled, and I had left more lonely than when I came.

Maria, who was at the meeting, had a very different evaluation. She assured me that people *had* been moved and told me that several had expressed the hope that I would come back often. She helped me to see that the deans weren't used to expressing their feelings and emotions in the way Americans do, and she urged me to realize that they had experienced the meeting much more positively than I had.

She also said that I shouldn't expect these priests to read my books, not even those translated into Dutch. "They need direct personal contact, and you gave them that."

I was very happy to be with Maria and Louis.

Saturday, July 13

In the afternoon Jan and I went to see the film *Richard III*, based on Shakespeare's play. It is a story of resentment, jealousy, anger, ruthlessness, and unrestrained murders. After the movie, during dinner, Jan told me how his recent trip for Pax Christi to Colombia, where he spoke with "the three proprietors of the war" — the head of the military, the head of the paramilitary troops, and the leader of the guerrillas — had made Shakespeare's drama very real for him. He told me how those who kidnap enemies are often killed by their own people to wipe out all traces that can lead to the victim. That's exactly what Richard III did: he ultimately murdered those who had helped him most in the execution of his evil plans. "Many of the Colombians I met had a lot more blood on their hands than Richard," Jan said.

Jan told me many stories about his Richard III experiences in Colombia. What struck me most was his conviction that his own mission there was not to stop the war — that is presently impossible — but to save lives by minimizing the killing of civilians and innocent people. "Wars will continue," he said, "in Bosnia, Northern Ireland, the Middle East, Chechnya, Colombia, and so on, but we might be able to curb the massive killings." A very sobering vision.

One of the great surprises was that my brother Laurent and two of his lawyer friends showed up at the restaurant where Jan and I were having dinner. I had just said to Jan, "I had better call Laurent in Rotterdam to tell him that I am coming tomorrow," and there he was! Laurent told me that nobody would be home tomorrow. So I decided to stay in Utrecht until Monday morning and go directly from here to the airport. I am glad I can have a very quiet day tomorrow. It will give me a chance to collect myself a little on my last day before the long flight back to New York.

Sunday, July 14

A week from today I will celebrate the thirty-ninth anniversary of my ordination to the priesthood. On the twenty-first of July, 1957, together with twenty-seven other candidates, I was ordained by Bernard Cardinal Alfrink in the St. Catherine Cathedral here in Utrecht.

This morning I decided to attend the 9:00 a.m. Eucharist at the cathedral and pray to God in gratitude for my thirty-nine years of priesthood. To my surprise I saw that Bishop Hendriksen, Cardinal Alfrink's former auxiliary bishop and vicar-general, was celebrating the Eucharist. He is eighty-nine years old, but he looks healthy and speaks with a strong voice. In the first row I noticed Ms. Stienstra, who translated my books *With Burning Hearts* and *Here and Now* into Dutch.

It was a strange experience for me. An old, nearly forgotten world came back to life. I can't remember the last time I celebrated or attended a Latin Mass, but I still knew most of the Latin texts of the Eucharist by heart. They were deeply engraved within me. Seeing the old bishop, the young singers, and the graciously moving acolytes, I felt as if nothing had changed during the last thirty-nine years with one exception; the packed church of the fifties was now mostly empty.

After the Eucharist Ms. Stienstra and Bishop Hendriksen invited me for a cup of coffee at the bishop's home. I didn't stay very long. I still wanted to walk around the city a little and drop in at different churches.

It is clear that those who practice Christianity in this city are a tiny minority of the people. Near the cathedral a skinhead walked up to me and said, "I went into that church and gave them a guilder! You think they would let me stay in there with my head shaved like this?" I said, "Sure, you are very welcome to go there, and you don't have to give any more money!" I wonder if he did. The distance between this boy and the ceremonies in the cathedral seems huge, but is it really? Since the CD with Gregorian music became so popular among the rock youth, I am less sure about it all. Maybe many skinheads are waiting to be welcomed!

The rest of the day I spent in my hotel room, catching up on my sleep and my journal.

New York, Monday, July 15

At 7:30 a.m. Jan came to the hotel, and I felt deeply grateful to him for taking me and my heavy suitcases to the train station, and traveling on with me to Schiphol airport. I still remember my arriving on June 10 and falling with my five suitcases on the escalator.

The plane left exactly on time and arrived at noon at Kennedy Airport in New York. I took a cab from the airport to Wendy and Jay's home. It is good to be in New York safe and well!

We talked for a while about our "vacations," then I went to bed until 6:30. After a nice Chinese dinner with Jay and Wendy and sharing many stories, I went back to bed in the hope of getting over my jet lag quickly. I am very glad that my five-week European trip is over. Everything went well, but it was quite tiring, and I feel a deep desire to stay in one place for a while and work on my writing.

Peapack, Tuesday, July 16

What a great support Wendy is to me! From 9:00 a.m. to 2:00 p.m. we worked — with a few interruptions — on the edited and already corrected manuscript of *Bread for the Journey*. Wendy had already critically read more than half of the text. She made many suggestions for changes. We worked quickly and decisively. I could hardly believe that after so many revisions and so much editing there still were so many possibilities to make it better.

At 2:00 p.m. Wendy took me to Port Authority, and at 4:20 p.m. I arrived at Bernardsville, where Ginny was waiting for me. I was exhausted but too curious about what was in the mail to go to bed.

Wednesday, July 17

When I walked into the living room of my "little red barn," to celebrate the Eucharist this morning, there were about fifty people waiting. In my absence the story about the daily Eucharist "at Peggy's place" had made the rounds, and nearly everyone who came in the past had brought one or two friends.

After the Gospel I spoke a little about the suffering in Colombia, Bosnia, Northern Ireland, and Chechnya, and about the importance of being quiet witnesses of hope in the midst of this violent world. When Jesus speaks about the mystery of love he prays: "I thank you, Father, Lord of heaven and earth, because you have hidden these things from the wise and the intelligent and have revealed them to infants; yes, Father, for such was your gracious will" (Mt 11:25 26). How then can we prevent ourselves from being so "wise and intelligent" that we are not truly free to let the simple but difficult message of Jesus penetrate our hearts? How can we become "infants" who witness to God's love? I am so aware — especially after my trip — of how preoccupied we all are with our own little problems and not empty enough to let God speak through us. Before we realize it we are participating — with our words and concerns — in the violence we protest against.

Most of the day I worked on finishing the *Bread for the Journey* manuscript, answered letters, and called friends. It was a very busy day, hot, but happily not humid.

Thursday, July 18

There were many new people at the Eucharist this morning. We talked about connecting our burdens with the burden of Jesus, which is a "light" burden even though it is the burden of all humanity. A burden, even a small one, when carried alone and in isolation can destroy us, but a burden when carried as part of God's burden can lead us to new life. This is the great mystery of our faith.

I had a lot of telephone conversations with Nathan, Carl, and the architect Joe, because it looks as if the plans to build my own little apartment can be realized in the fall. They want me to come to Toronto on Friday to finalize the plans.

At 4:00 p.m. Neal came to take some more pictures of me (in color this time) to be used for future publications. He took thirty shots. I hope one of them will be publishable. It is not easy to get a relaxed, friendly, smiling picture of yourself, especially when you are so self-conscious. Nobody was around to help me forget the photographer and just chat a little. But I trust that Neal will come up with something "friendly."

Amidst all these little things there was a great tragedy when the TWA airplane exploded off the coast of Long Island. All the people onboard — 230 — lost their lives. I can hardly comprehend the enormous grief that comes from this tragedy. A group of high school students from Montoursville, Pennsylvania, a forty-seven-year old mother joining her family on vacation in France, a thirty-nine-year-old TV producer going to cover the finish of the Tour de France, a forty-seven-year-old interior designer going to buy antiques in Paris, and an eleven-year-old French boy returning to his family after a summer as an exchange student in the USA were all people with different hopes and expectations who were plucked out of life in a second. A large cloud of mourning hangs over this country. Where is God, where is love, where is justice, where is our hope? No answers. Only the silence of the huge ocean swallowing up all these people. What prayer can be said?

Friday, July 19

At 4:30 p.m. I drove in the midst of a huge rainstorm to Madison to visit Michael, Rebecca, and their two daughters, Rachel and Megan.

I had come to know Michael in Yale Divinity School, followed him as a minister working in a center for homeless people, and later working with people living with AIDS and with the victims of Chernobyl. Over the years Michael became an ordained minister in the Methodist Church. Rebecca, his wife, was an associate editor at a publishing house and is presently the editor of a bimonthly magazine on prayer.

Michael and Rebecca are contemplative activists! They are very interested in spirituality in its different forms. Michael regularly spends time in monastic communities to deepen his interior life. But he is also a very astute organizer, fund-raiser, and planner, and is always involved in some major project to help the poor, the sick, and the dying. It was a great joy to reconnect with Michael and Rebecca after so many years of going our separate ways. I hope that we will be able to stay in touch and work together a little on their several projects.

After returning home I watched the last hour of the opening ceremonies of the Olympic Games in Atlanta. Great show!

Saturday, July 20

Yesterday Diana from the Church of the Saviour in Washington sent me a remarkable letter with a small book. In the letter she told me about her recent trip to Bosnia. The small book was the Croatian translation of my book *Letters to Marc about Jesus*.

What is remarkable is that Diana found this book on the floor of a totally demolished church library in a tiny Bosnian town where she and a small group of Americans were visiting. The book was covered with sand and looked dirty. But it was still quite readable since it was wrapped in a plastic cover. Diana sent me pictures of the destroyed library with the book lying on the floor and of a young Franciscan priest holding the book.

I had no idea that *Letters to Marc about Jesus* existed in the Croatian language nor that this book had found its way to a small Bosnian town in the middle of the war zone. I was deeply moved to have this book, which I wrote in Dutch with the hope of bringing my nephew closer to Jesus and helping him to become a source of hope to people surrounded by violence and war. Somehow this little event seemed to me an encouragement to keep writing.

Monday, July 22

At 3.00 p.m. Don and Fran called me from "downtown" Peapack to tell me they had arrived. I immediately went to the deli, where they were waiting for me. It was good to see them both again. They were impressed by my set-up and loved the Pleasant Valley. We had a nice meal together in my house and shared many stories. Fran has suffered some bad falls and has to have knee surgery in August. She needs a crutch to get around. Don is unable to lift anything heavy as the aftereffect of a severe neurological muscular collapse he suffered more than ten years ago. So they both are quite limited in their physical movements. I unexpectedly felt like the strong one among the three of us.

At 8:00 p.m. Fran returned to Princeton. Don is staying for a few days. He and I watched a little of the gymnastics competition at the Olympics. Seeing the incredible feats on the rings, bar, and floor makes you feel quite handicapped. For Fran, Don, and me there won't be much tumbling. We will be happy to continue to be able to walk well on the floor and reach high enough to get our luggage from the overhead bins of a plane!

Tuesday, July 23

It is good to have Don here. He simply wanted to live the day with me. He participated in the Eucharist, joined me on my daily trip to the post office and the deli, and watched a little of the Olympics with me.

I still have not gotten back to the Adam book. There are so many little things to do — letters, phone calls, visits, and so on — that I can't find a few peaceful hours to get back into my writing.

Wednesday, July 24

I am not feeling very well. I am tired, distracted, and slightly depressed. My room looks sloppy — papers all over the place and all of them asking for attention. I wish I could throw them all in a big plastic bag and forget about them, but every time I look at one of them I realize that I should write a letter, an introduction, or a recommendation.

I decided to clean up as much as I could and get a sense of order. I am amazed how much I collect in a short time. At the end of the day I had filled at least two large bags with junk. My room looks a little better now.

After all of that Don and I sat together and talked about new directions in his life. It seems that the time for a new direction is coming. Don is dreaming about possibly working with the Hispanic people in Chicago. He has a great love for Latin America, speaks Spanish quite well and wants to dedicate himself to the poor. I promised to give him all the support I can. As always in situations like this, I wonder where we will be and what we will be talking about five years from now!

Thursday, July 25

During the celebration of this morning's Eucharist in honor of St. James, I spoke about Jesus' question to James and John, "Can you drink the cup?" and summarized the book I wrote about the question. Blair, who raises challenging questions, asked, "But what if I really do not want to drink my cup?" I responded by speaking a little about the tension between wanting and not wanting, being able and not being able, and about how that tension can best be lived in a loving community.

In the evening Peggy took me to the house of friends for dinner where several others had been invited and where we had a good discussion about politics and religion. A Democratic senator was pondering how to influence people the most — as a politician who is able to introduce laws that can help millions of people, or as a minister who continues to offer hope and consolation to people in their daily struggle? These seemed to be life issues for the people present.

For me it is not a question of how we can most influence others. What matters is our vocation. To what or whom are we called? When we make the effect of our work the criterion of our sense of self, we end up very vulnerable. Both the political and the ministerial life can be responses to a call. Both too can be ways to acquire power. The final issue is not the result of our work but the obedience to God's will, as long as we realize that God's will is the expression of God's love.

Richmond Hill, Friday, July 26

After the Eucharist this morning I took the car to Newark Airport and flew to Toronto. The purpose of this quick trip was to finalize the plans for my new house. It was a good meeting, and if all goes well, building can start by the end of September.

The last few hours of the day I spent with Kathy and little Sarah, who is such a beautiful baby.

Peapack, Saturday, July 27

Nathan came back with me to Peapack. He is going to stay here for the next ten days. I am very happy that we can have this time together.

As we flew to Newark and drove from there to Peapack, our minds were heavy because of the tragic bombing in Atlanta this morning. Two people died, and many were wounded as a knapsack containing a bomb with shrapnel exploded near an outdoor podium where a rock band was playing for a large audience of Olympic fans. What madness! What cruelty! What anger! There is something profoundly wrong with our society when people murder innocent spectators during a sports event simply to express their rage. Whether this was an act by foreign terrorists who hate Americans or by paramilitary Americans who hate their own government, the increasing events of violence — the Oklahoma bombing, church burnings in the South, and maybe the downing of TWA Flight 800 — create an overall sense of danger, anxiety, and even doom.

After a delicious dinner with corn that Peggy had cooked and wine that Clair had brought, we concluded the evening by praying compline together. I was struck by the words of Psalm 4: "You have put into my heart a greater joy than they have from abundance of corn and new wine." It was good to pray together and to thank God for giving us a peaceful day in the midst of a violent world.

Monday, July 29

Joanie and Jim invited Nathan and me for dinner with Therese, and Bill and Judith. Bill is known for his TV programs with Joseph Campbell, Huston Smith, and other American thinkers and writers. Therese is a harpist-singer who founded the Chalice of Repose Project, at a hospital in Montana.

Bill is a professional listener. That became evident tonight. He systematically asked Nathan and me about our lives, our community, our spiritual vision and future plans. When later Therese came, he gave her equal time. Bill was, long ago, ordained as a Baptist minister but has worked his whole life in communications: newspapers and television. He and his wife are deeply spiritual people with a great desire to offer vision to the American culture. In many ways Bill makes me think of Fred, even though his work for TV is very different from Fred's. But, like Fred, Bill is clearly committed to bringing "good news" to TV; he is independent, hardworking and produces programs that stand out by their relevance, educational value, and spiritual-social vision. Like Fred he is a humble man, truly interested in other people and more concerned with service than with fame.

We listened with great interest to Therese when she described her specialty: music thanatology. Certified graduates in music thanatology are called chalice workers because with voice and harp, in teams of two or more, they attend the dying at the actual bedside, in hospitals, geriatric homes, hospices, and homes.

A very rich evening for sure!

Tuesday, July 30

It is already two weeks since I returned from Europe, and I still haven't been able to find a good block of time to work on the Adam book. Very frustrating. Everything else seems to take priority: the morning Eucharist, the correspondence, the many calls about layouts and covers of other books, dinners, et cetera. But I want to go back to Adam. It is such an important story. I feel I am saying something fresh and original. The vision that the story of Jesus allows me to understand Adam while Adam's story makes me understand Jesus keeps fascinating me. Adam is a sacrament, a sacred place where God spoke to me. Remembering Adam is

more than thinking about him and praying for him. It is enabling me to
keep close to the Jesus I met in and through him. Adam became real to
me because Jesus was real to me, and Jesus became real to me became
Adam was real to me. Somewhere, somehow, Adam and Jesus are one.

Jan van den Bosch wants to delay the St. Petersburg trip to late
September instead of early September. I am happy with this delay.

Wednesday, July 31

Today at the Eucharist we talked about the Kingdom of God as a reality
among us. The Kingdom of God is at hand, at our fingertips. Jesus calls
us to repent, which means to have a contrite heart, a heart broken open
by the plow of suffering, a heart able to receive the seed of the Kingdom,
a heart able to see the treasure in the field, a heart capable of hearing
the soft voice of love. Even though we live in a violent world, full of
hatred and war, we can already enter the Kingdom now and belong to a
community of faith, hope, and love.

I pray that this little eucharistic community will discover that it is part
of God's Kingdom.

In the early evening Nathan and I had a nice dinner. At one point
we talked about the anxiety that had been plaguing me during the last
few months. I felt somewhat embarrassed and ashamed to put my inner
burden on my best friend, but, in the end, I am glad I did. Nathan told
me that he found it hard, not so much to listen to my pain, but to realize
that I had walked with it so long without sharing it. I explained that it
had not been possible for me to talk about such things on the telephone,
and he understood. That was a comfort for me. I sometimes wonder how
I am going to survive emotionally.

August 1996

Thursday, August 1

Well, Michael Johnson won the gold medal in the 200-meter run as well as in the 400-meter run. A "history-making event." In the 200 meter he also broke the world record. The commentators speak about the fastest man in history. To describe his spirit they said, "He doesn't take prisoners, he goes for the kill." But in an interview he expressed a less violent view, "The crowd was wonderful — I never felt so much support. The people are great!"

Donovan Bailey, the Canadian, ran the 100 meter in 9.84 seconds. Michael Johnson ran the 200 meter in 19.34. The greatest speed ever! And what about the pressure of millions watching you and expecting you to win? Michael said, "I can't even describe the pressure, but that's what makes it all happen!"

The unrelenting emphasis on winning the gold makes it hard to watch these Olympic games. They become an emotional roller coaster. It is hard for me to believe that all the pressure, all the intensity, all the winning and losing contributes to a peaceful and compassionate world. There is little if any "play" left in the games. Competition is the core word, and the tears of the losers as well as of the winners are not tears of a contrite or grateful heart. How possibly can they heal our world! Still ... I, with millions of other people, keep watching and admiring those who go beyond what we thought to be the limit of human possibilities.

Nathan and I had a peaceful day. We both spent a lot of time in our rooms working.

Friday, August 2

When Jesus came to his hometown and began to teach the people in the synagogue, they said: "Isn't this the carpenter's son? Is not his mother called Mary? And are not his brothers James and Joseph and Simon and Judas? And are not all his sisters with us? Where then did this man get all this? And they took offense at him" (Mt 13:54–58). It fascinates me that Jesus finally had to establish his authority outside the circle of his family and friends. All we know about his relationship with his parents is his taking distance from them: in the temple when he was twelve years old, in Cana when Mary wanted to intervene, during his preaching or when the family wanted to visit him.

Family is where we grow up into adult, mature people, but we have to leave our families to fulfill our deepest vocation. Family can give us a sense of belonging, but in order to claim our deepest belonging, our belonging to God, we have to move away from those who pretend to know us and discover the deepest source of our lives. Our parents, brothers, and sisters do not own us. Without leaving them it is hard to fully become free and listen to the One who called us even before we were born.

Jesus often had to say no to his family in order to be able to say a full yes to his Father in heaven.

Saturday, August 3

Today's Gospel reading about the death of John the Baptist made me think about servant leadership. John the Baptist certainly was one of the most important spiritual leaders of his time, but his whole mission was geared to put Jesus into the light. All he did and said finally served to create the space for Jesus' leadership.

Robert Greenleaf and many of his students have developed the concept of servant leadership in ways that it also could be a guiding concept in contemporary business and management. A good leader is able to "decrease" so that others can "increase." It certainly requires a great inner strength and confidence to "let go" of the dominant position and let others develop their leadership with your affirmation and support. It is no secret that in church and society many leaders cling to their positions as long as they can.

It was a great joy to spend the evening with Phil and Peggy. This morning, after the Eucharist, I offered them both a reflection on marriage as covenant. They want to prepare themselves for their marriage, which will take place on Sunday, October 13. During dinner Peggy and Phil told us how they first met and how their love for each other had grown during the past few months. It touched me deeply when Peggy said, "It was during the eucharistic celebration, when I was most at peace, that I saw most clearly that God wanted me to marry Phil." As Phil and Peggy sat across from each other at the round dinner table, they both were radiant with love for each other and didn't hesitate to let us know and see it. We felt very privileged to be such close witnesses of the deep love of two people, seventy and seventy-five years old, ready to commit themselves to each other and bring their very rich and varied lives together in a committed union.

Sunday, August 4

During the Eucharist we had a very lively discussion about the Gospel of the multiplication of bread. What we give away multiplies, and what we hoard becomes less. One of the participants was especially intrigued with the thought that the multiplication of bread might in fact have been the result of people's willingness to share the little they had with their neighbors. The true miracle might have been not that Jesus made many loaves out of a few but that he called people to not cling to their own food but trust that there was enough for everyone. If this generosity would be practiced universally in our world, there would not be so many starving people. But this is also the eucharistic vision: Jesus shares his Body and Blood so that we all can become a living Christ in the world. Jesus himself multiplies through giving himself away. We become the body of Christ, individually as well as communally.

A very quiet day. Nathan and I spent a good deal of time sitting near the swimming pool, reading and taking an occasional dip in the water. At 7:30 we drove to Gladstone and had a nice dinner there.

Tuesday, August 6

The Feast of the Transfiguration! When and where do we have an experience of God's Glorious Presence, an experience of unity, an experience of inner fulfillment, an experience of light in the darkness? Peter says: "You do well to be attentive to this as to a lamp shining in a dark place, until the day dawns and the morning star rises in your hearts" (2 Pt 1:19).

Maybe we do not always fully recognize our mountaintop experiences, we write them off as insignificant and trivial compared with all the important and urgent things we have to do. Still, Jesus wants us to see his glory, so that we can cling to that experience in moments of doubt, despair, or anguish. When we are attentive to the light within us and around us, we will gradually see more and more of that light and even become a light for others.

We have to trust that the transfiguration experience is closer to us than we might think. Trusting that, we may also be able to live our Gethsemane experience without losing our faith.

I am extremely tired today and experience little creative energy.

Wednesday, August 7

Today Nathan returned to Toronto. We had ten very good days together: quiet, peaceful, and homey. We didn't go to New York, we didn't even go to the movies! But the time was good, and I feel blessed in the friendship.

Thursday, August 8

My good old friend Dean drove from Middletown, Connecticut, to Peapack to spend the day with me. I have a deep admiration for Dean. He always challenges me. He calls me to a radical faith, a deep commitment to the poor, a prophetic ministry among the rich, and an always closer bond with Jesus. He is my conscience. He loves me but also criticizes me. He cares for me but also unsettles me. He supports me but also calls me to reach out beyond my limits.

Our discussions are always intense, serious, and probing. It is clear to me that this Jewish friend is my prophet. I have to listen to him. If *he* tells me to grow closer to Jesus, I better take that very seriously.

Friday, August 9

"Those who lose their life for my sake will find it," Jesus says. There is no day without many losses. If we are attentive to our inner life, we quickly realize how many times things are not happening in the way we hoped, people aren't saying what we expected, the day is not evolving as we wanted, et cetera, et cetera. All these little "losses" can make us bitter people who complain that life is not fair to us. But if we live these losses for the sake of Jesus — that is, in communion with his redemptive death — then our losses can gradually free us from our self-centeredness and open our hearts to the new life that comes from God. The real question is: "Do I live my losses for my sake or for Jesus' sake?" That choice is a choice for death or life.

At 8:00 a.m. before the Eucharist I drove to Peapack's post office to meet Werner, who had driven from his home in Rye, New York, to visit me. Werner is a longtime friend and the president of Continuum Publishing. We had a good hour to talk about business things as well as personal matters. It was a very good and hope-giving conversation. Werner's friendship is a great gift to me.

I was glad to have a quiet night alone. I prayed a little, read a little, and went early to bed.

Saturday, August 10

During the Eucharist we spoke about generosity. I was moved by Paul's words: "The one who sows sparingly will also reap sparingly, and the one who sows bountifully will also reap bountifully. Each of you must give as you have made up your mind, not reluctantly or under compulsion, for God loves a cheerful giver. And God is able to provide you with every blessing in abundance, so that by always having enough of everything, you may share abundantly in every good work" (2 Cor 9:6–8).

I think that generosity has many levels. We have to think generously, speak generously, and act generously. Thinking well of others and speaking well of others is the basis for generous giving. It means that we relate to others as part of our "gen" or "kin" and treat them as family. Generosity cannot come from guilt or pity. It has to come from hearts that are fearless and free and are willing to share abundantly all that is given to us.

At 5:00 p.m. I drove to Newark Airport to welcome my dear friend Borys. Borys has been teaching summer school at Harvard and is coming to spend some time with me before returning to Ukraine. It was wonderful to see him again. He looked well and was full of enthusiasm. The theological academy in L'viv, of which he is the vice-rector, now has close to six hundred students. Borys said, "It is a once-in-a-millennium opportunity, to affect the future of the Greek Catholic Church." Borys wants to attract the best possible teachers, to collect money to endow chairs, to send Ukrainian students to the West, to build up a theological library, and to find a large building in L'viv to house all his students.

I said, "Well, maybe you should invite me to teach spirituality at the academy. Send me a formal invitation!" Borys laughed. "You might get your letter before you want it!" I realized that if I ever would do some more teaching, Ukraine may be the place to do it. It is so exciting to teach students who are truly excited about their future and want to work hard to prepare themselves for leadership.

Elmsford, New York, Monday, August 12

After a very prayerful Eucharist, Borys and I drove to Elmsford, New York. When we arrived we were met by Doug and two Greek Catholic priests. Borys left with the two priests to discuss setting up a foundation in the United States to support the academy in L'viv, and I joined Doug to make an audiotape of *Life of the Beloved*. Borys's visit was a true grace.

The taping went well but was quite tiring. Sitting for four hours, with small breaks, in a little, hot cubicle, speaking in the microphone is not as simple as it seems. Often I stumbled over my own words and had to repeat the same paragraph several times. Bruce, who handled the control panel, was very patient and had a good sense of language. Sometimes I didn't know the pronunciation of words I wrote myself! But by 5:00 p.m. we had done more than three quarters of the book. Tomorrow morning we will finish the job.

Peapack, Tuesday, August 13

After a very pleasant breakfast with Doug and his wife, Betsy, I spent a few more hours in the little "box" to finish taping *Life of the Beloved*. With quite a few repeats, I made it through the text within two hours.

Although I wrote *Life of the Beloved*, I never read it. It is quite an experience to read a book that you yourself wrote more than four years ago. All through I wanted to make changes, rewrite, correct small mistakes, and adapt it to the circumstances of today. But I realized that the best thing would be simply to read it as it was and save my energy for new books. It is amazing how, within a few years, one's ideas and feelings shift. Today I would have written *Life of the Beloved* quite differently. And still, the book continues to be quite popular. That obviously is the reason for making this audiocassette.

Wednesday, August 14

A very busy, somewhat restless day.

During the Eucharist we spoke about dealing with conflict in the community. How to deal with people who sin against us. Jesus is very specific: "If your brother or sister sins against you, go and point out the fault when the two of you are alone." Only when that doesn't help should you call others in, and only when that doesn't help should you "tell it to the church" (Mt 18:15–17). Only when it is clear that the person doesn't want to listen to the church should you leave him or her alone.

It is clear that "confrontation" only is fruitful in love. We have to keep the well-being of the other in mind. But when the other finally does not respond and keeps doing harmful things, then the well-being of the community becomes a priority.

Thursday, August 15

Assumption Day. While my publisher's office in Belgium is closed today because of this special Catholic feast day, people here hardly know what the Assumption is all about. The Magnificat speaks about "lifting up the lowly." Mary was lifted up, and not only Mary but all of us who claim for ourselves our true spiritual identity. As people raised up by God's immense grace, all generations will call us blessed.

A full "social" day. I have to accept the fact that there is little time to write anymore and that these last weeks in Peapack will be mostly people centered.

Tomorrow I am off to San Diego to visit Joan for the weekend.

San Diego, Friday, August 16

By noon I was at Joan's home. She welcomed me warmly and took me right away to a restaurant where we met friends from New York. We had good discussions about art, religion, and spirituality.

At dinner tonight Joan and I talked quite seriously about many issues and questions, such as abortion and the right-to-life. It was a very open discussion about the sacredness of life and the importance of creating communities to welcome children who cannot be brought up in their own families. I talked quite a bit about Adam, who by "progressive" pro-choice standards might not have had a chance to live. Without him my own life and the lives of many others would not have been so richly blessed. I don't often speak about abortion and always fear the heated debates that people engage in.

Joan, who is very much a supporter of women's causes, spoke about her vision and how it was always being shaped and changed. I feel very grateful for Joan and for this time we are sharing together.

It has been a very long day and I am ready for a long rest.

Saturday, August 17

This morning Joan and I had a good discussion about God and God's covenant of love while sitting on the terrace. I did a lot of the talking about God's desire to share our human struggles, to protect us, and to be always closer to us in our hearts, because love does not tolerate distance. God wants to be bonded with us, and that is the covenant. God is not to be feared but to be loved.

At 1:00 p.m. Joan said, "Let's go to the races. After your lesson in spirituality I will give you a lesson in decadence!"

It was fun! We sat in a box where there was a lounge with a betting machine, a large balcony overlooking the racetrack, and a TV to give you closeups of the races. Joan gave me a voucher for fifty dollars to play with. Soon I wanted to win! I quickly experienced the power of gambling. "Maybe next time I will make a fortune, maybe next time, maybe next time."

I played two dollars on each of four different horses. When we left I had lost more than won. Joan said, "Why don't you cash your voucher, so you have the feeling you won something!" I cashed the voucher and got thirty-two dollars. It was a good afternoon for less than twenty dollars.

When we got home again, we celebrated the liturgy in the living room. Joan invited Angela, who comes from Mexico, to join us. It was so simple and so intimate to be together to pray and celebrate the mystery of God's covenant. I feel very blessed.

Peapack, Sunday, August 18

All today's travel went exactly as planned. At 5:15 p.m. I am back in my little barn house, looking at the mail and checking out phone messages. I felt good after the long flight because I slept most of the time!

The visit was a very good one. I feel that Joan and I are becoming friends, and our friendship allows us to speak openly and directly about our real concerns.

En Route to Cork, Ireland, Monday and Tuesday, August 19 and 20

At 7:40 p.m. my plane left for London. I arrived at 7.30 a.m., and at 10:00 a.m. I was on my way to Cork.

Cork, Wednesday, August 21

Every time I am in Ireland, I am struck with the different rhythm of life. Because of my jet lag, I decided to "sleep in" until 9:00 a.m. But when I arrived at the breakfast table at 9:30, I was one of the first! No hurry, no urgencies. As they say in Ireland: "God created time, and He created plenty of it."

My visit to Ireland has a long history. In 1961 I presided over the wedding of Sophie and Seamus and in 1966 over the wedding of Leonie and Paddy. Their weddings took place in Holland, but both couples moved to Cork, Ireland, where Seamus is a businessman and Paddy a surgeon.

Last year I came to Ireland to preside over the marriage of David, the oldest child of Sophie and Seamus, to Mary, and now I am here again to celebrate the marriage of Leonietje, the oldest daughter of Leonie and

Paddy, to Morgan. Meanwhile Mary and David have their first son, Cian, and I promised to baptize him on Sunday. I wonder if I still will be alive to marry him!

Leonie took me to Oisterhaven, where her family has a summer house overlooking the beautiful bay. When we arrived there I met Leonietje and Morgan for the first time. Wonderful, bright, adventurous people — full of love for their families and, at the same time, quite independent and critical. We had a good long talk about their journeys, their vision of life, and their spiritual attitudes.

After our talk I celebrated the Eucharist for the whole family in the living room. The view is spectacular: a lovely blue bay, green rolling hills surrounding it, a distant view of two rock islands behind which the ocean stretches far and wide, romantic cloud formations letting the bright sun come through here and there, and the trees gently moving in the evening wind. Thanking God in this landscape is easy. Everything speaks of grace and beauty.

We reflected on the story of the workers of the eleventh hour, especially on the words "Are you jealous because I am generous?" (Mt 20:15). When we trust in God's immense love, shouldn't we rejoice when God offers the latecomers as much as those who have worked the whole day? When we experience it as a privilege to work in God's vineyard, why should we be angry that those who came late are treated as equals to those who came long ago? Jealousy is such a divisive emotion. Isn't it possible to truly rejoice when we see someone other than ourselves being given an unexpected gift? The truth, however, is that we can only fully enjoy God's generosity toward others when we truly know how much God loves us.

Much of what we talked about was quite visible in the family that sat around the altar table. I sensed no jealousy, just an immense gratitude that two of them, Leonietje and Morgan, were going to be showered with special love, extra attention, and many, many gifts.

Oisterhaven, Ireland, Thursday, August 22

When I got up this morning, Paddy said, "Well, are you ready for a swim?" It was very cold, but when I got out of the water the warm air created a pleasant sensation and my blood was running fast.

Later in the morning I had another session with Morgan and Leonietje, talking about the details of the marriage ceremony. The rest of the day was full of people, coming in and out with gifts and running left and right

to get everything ready for the wedding. I found a quiet corner to read
and write a little.

Kenmare, Ireland, Friday, August 23

As Morgan, Leonietje, her sister Rosemary, and I were driving over the
small Irish road toward Kenmare, we came across a very serious accident.
An American couple with two children had crashed with a young Irish
man. Both cars were completely demolished. When we saw the accident
we realized that it had just happened. It seemed that the Americans were
okay, but the Irish man, David, had hit the front window of his car with
his head and was still sitting behind the wheel in a state of shock.

Morgan had a cellular phone and immediately called for an ambulance
and for the police. Then both Leonietje and Morgan tried to determine
how seriously David was hurt. Morgan made sure that he didn't move to
prevent any possible nerve damage, and Leonietje and Morgan both kept
talking to him to prevent him from going into deep shock. Meanwhile I
talked to the Americans.

What impressed me most was the competent, self-confident, and caring way in which both Morgan and Leonietje responded to the sudden
interruption of their journey. They were completely present to the situation and did all the right things. They kept the injured man quiet and
still, thus preventing a spinal injury. They also spoke to the police, the
American family, the ambulance people, and the local doctor, who came
just after the ambulance had arrived. They gave them helpful information, spoke reassuring words, and did everything to prevent confusion
or panic.

At 3:00 p.m. we arrived at Kenmare, where the wedding will take
place. When evening came all the wedding guests gathered for a bar-
becue. I was amazed by the people from many parts of the world who had
traveled here for this wedding. There was a group of friends from New
Zealand and a large group of family from Holland. People had also come
from Hong Kong, China, Zimbabwe, South Africa, Denmark, the USA,
and England. All together there were about 170 guests, all living together
for a weekend.

Talking to so many people from so many parts of the world, I couldn't
but marvel at the ways people get connected and grieve for the fact that
there still are so many mental, psychological, and religious distances on
our small planet. If it is possible to come from the ends of the earth to
celebrate the commitment of a man and a woman to each other, why

does it remain impossible to stop people from killing each other because of religious, social, and economic differences?

Restless thoughts in the most restful surroundings.

Saturday, August 24

Even though I have been the celebrant at many weddings, every time again I feel quite nervous and anxious. There seem to be so many details that I am seldom very peaceful inside until it is over.

The celebration took place at 2:00 p.m. It was a very beautiful and festive liturgy. The Gospel from John about the great commandment to love one another prompted my words about care: care for your own heart, care for each other, and care for others.

At communion time I asked everyone to come to the front to receive the consecrated bread or a word of blessing and encouragement. Many came for a blessing, and quite a few of those who had come to receive the host came up to me later and asked for a blessing. So I have been speaking words of blessing to many people during the afternoon. I realize how deeply people are touched by simple words of reassurance, encouragement, and empowerment spoken in the Name of God.

The wedding dinner was splendid. By midnight I was exhausted and left the — by then — dancing crowd, glad to be able to have a good long rest.

Cork, Sunday, August 25

At 11:00 a.m. I celebrated the Eucharist in one of the smaller hotel rooms looking out on the bay. At the last moment so many people came that we opened the window so that many could follow the service while sitting outside. Then at communion time the rain came pouring down, and everyone came into the small room.

After a nice lunch I said good-bye to the bride and groom and as many others as I could, and drove to Cork.

In Cork, David and Mary were waiting for me to baptize Cian, their four-month-old boy. Before the baptism I spoke a little with David and Mary about the significance of baptism. I tried to explain that it is a proclamation that the child is not the property of the parents but a gift of God to be welcomed into the human community and led to the freedom of the children of God. Mary said, "It is often hard to realize that I do not own my little Cian, but as I see him growing so fast I realize that he has been leaving me from the moment he was born. Yes, I feel a certain sadness when I see him growing up so soon."

A little later a small circle of family gathered around Cian. He was crying, so we needed time to let him fall asleep and receive all the baptismal blessings. The oils, the water, the white cloth, and the burning candle became real signs of transformation and hope in this small circle of family and friends. David commented that it was "unbelievably special." In such a simple context baptism is not a ritual or a ceremony but an event that directly touches us and affects our lives.

After a very homey, cozy dinner, I made it to bed hoping for a long, deep sleep that would allow me to make the long flight back to Newark without getting miserable.

Peapack, Monday, August 26

An endless day! From Cork to London, to Newark, to Peapack. It was a very tiring trip, where I experienced long lines, packed planes, poor food, and bad movies!

I am very tired from my Irish week, but it was a very good week. I know that Leonietje, Morgan, and their parents were happy with the wedding and that David and Mary were glad that I could baptize Cian.

But I come back again to the question that is more and more with me: Is this my vocation or is it better to stay home and write more? Is it good to be constantly surrounded by so many people and involved with their lives? Yes, it is pastoral care and true ministry, and I have a gift for it and love it. But it is very hard to do it and at the same time to be able to develop new, nurturing ideas, and to write them. When I saw all the young people in Ireland who probably will marry within the next few years, I realized that I could have lots of invitations ahead of me. But I am feeling that I must begin to say no, and that is very hard. I love my many young friends and so much want them to have joyful and meaningful beginnings to their marriages. I realize that I should trust more that they will find the pastor they need when I remain faithful to my primary vocation.

Tuesday, August 27

This morning at the Eucharist we spoke about hypocrisy, an attitude that Jesus criticizes. I realize that institutional life leads to hypocrisy, because we who offer spiritual leadership often find ourselves not living what we are preaching or teaching. It is not easy to avoid hypocrisy completely because, wanting to speak in the Name of God, the church, or the larger community, we find ourselves saying things larger than ourselves. I often call people to a life that I am not fully able to live myself.

I am learning that the best cure for hypocrisy is community. When as a spiritual leader I live close to those I care for, and when I can be criticized in a loving way by my own people and be forgiven for my own shortcomings, then I won't be considered a hypocrite.

Hypocrisy is not so much the result of not living what I preach but much more of not confessing my inability to fully live up to my own words. I need to become a priest who asks forgiveness of my people for my mistakes.

Most of the day, I was busy with small errands, spending lots of time on the telephone and with visitors.

My sabbatical year is coming to its end. Two more days! Tomorrow Nathan is flying from Toronto to help me move. Thursday morning we will have the last Eucharist in the barn and Thursday night a farewell dinner at Peggy's house. Jay and Wendy will be coming from New York to be part of the farewell from Peapack. Early Friday morning Nathan and I will drive back to Toronto. I am glad, very glad, to be returning to Daybreak, but I also feel that what I have started during this year cannot simply stop. Lots to think about.

Wednesday, August 28

During the Eucharist we spoke about courage. The word *courage* comes from *coeur*, which means "heart." To have courage is to listen to our heart, to speak from our heart, and to act from our heart. Our heart, which is the center of our being, is the seat of courage.

Often we debate current issues and express our opinions about them. But courage is taking a stance, even an unpopular stance, not because we think differently from others but because from the center of our being we realize how to respond to the situation we are in. Courage does not require spectacular gestures. Courage often starts in small corners: it is courageous not to participate in gossip, not to talk behind someone's back, not to ridicule another. It is courageous to think well of other people and be grateful to them even when we live different lives than they do. It is courageous to reach out to a poor person, to spend time with a troubled child, to participate in action to prevent war and violence, abuse and manipulation.

Often we praise prophets after they are dead. Are we willing to be prophets while we are alive?

Thursday, August 29

At 9:00 a.m. we celebrated the last Eucharist in the barn — at least for the near future. It was a special celebration with Wendy and Jay from New York, and Nathan from Toronto. After the Gospel some of those present expressed how much this little eucharistic community has come to mean to them during the past six months. Peggy said that it was during the Eucharist in the barn that she had come to the clarity to marry Phil; Ginny spoke about the friendship between us that had developed during these months; Fred expressed how much this community has meant for his priesthood, and quite a few others were simply grateful for the experience.

After the Eucharist there was a wonderful coffee hour with many good cakes to eat, and many warm words of farewell.

The first part of the afternoon was packing. Jay, Wendy, and Ginny all gave a hand to put all my things in boxes and suitcases, and load up my little Honda. The second part I spent with Wendy going through the printed pages of *Bread for the Journey*, which Harper sent us for a final check. Wendy still found many little errors and suggested a few minor changes. I am so grateful to Wendy for doing all this minute work. I wouldn't have the patience or the perseverance to keep reading the same texts again and again and focus on punctuation, correct quotations, cap italization, utilization, and so on. But with Wendy's help we got through the whole manuscript within an hour and a half.

The farewell dinner was at 6:30 p.m. Ginny offered me a beautiful album with photographs of my stay at Peapack. Clair had written very funny titles under the pictures. It was a true work of love. There were even photographs of this morning's liturgy. I was very moved by this beautiful gift and all that Ginny and Clair had done to put it together.

The dinner was delightful and delicious. We all sat outside. It was a nice cool evening and there was much laughter. I thanked everyone for their love and friendship, and expressed how much these months in Peapack had meant to me. Maybe I wrote less than I planned, but I made many new friends, and the development of the eucharistic community had been a unique gift from God. I especially thanked Peggy for being such a beautiful friend. She gave me all the space and freedom I wanted and opened her house and guesthouse to me, my friends, and all the people who came for the daily Eucharist. I also said a special word of thanks to Ginny for all she had done and been for me during the last few months.

It was a beautiful conclusion of my sabbatical year.

Richmond Hill, Friday, August 30

At 7:00 a.m. Nathan and I said good-bye to Peggy and went on our way to Toronto. It was an easy drive. By 6:00 p.m. we were at Daybreak. The last part of the trip — from Buffalo to Toronto — was the hardest because of bumper-to-bumper traffic. It is the beginning of the long weekend, and everyone is on the road.

Kathy, with little Sarah in her arms, and Timmy, welcomed us as we drove in. Also Keith and Jeffi with their little baby, Devon, were there. Timmy was playing basketball, having just gotten a beautiful net for his birthday.

I spent a hour unpacking my things and creating a little order in my little room. And at 8:00 p.m. I went to Kathy's home and had a nice welcome-home meal with Timmy and Sarah.

A little later I was back in my own room again. It was full of flowers — Shiobhan had sent a beautiful basket with lilies, Lorenzo a lovely plant, and Jutta a red bouquet of long-stem carnations and other flowers. There were many balloons and large welcome-home cards with the names and drawings of many community members. What a night! What a warm welcome! Indeed, the sabbatical year is over, and it is good to be back.

Afterword

I have just returned from the official opening of the Father Henri Nouwen School, a new Catholic grade school about five minutes drive from our L'Arche Daybreak community. "Welcome to Father Henri Nouwen!" the young greeters say to us as we enter the building. In the main auditorium, filled to capacity with the children and their parents, I am aware of Henri's presence. He would have loved the multicultural flavor of this budding school community. Henri, who could be so delightfully childlike at times, would have cheerfully plunked himself down on the floor in order to be with the children.

When it was time for the Daybreak community to participate in the program, Joe and Bill stood up to speak. Joe is Daybreak's lay pastor and Bill the founding Core Member (person with a disability) of our community. As they began to speak Bill unexpectedly bursts into tears. Bill's grief, like that of many others of us, lays just below the surface and is easily and often awakened. Grief's intensity will diminish over time, but there will always be a Henri-sized hole in Bill's heart, in mine, and in the heart of our community.

The two weeks between the time Henri and I returned to Daybreak and Henri's departure for Saint Petersburg were difficult. The transition from a year of enormous freedom back into intense community life with its many demands was not easy. As well, the community had made a much anticipated decision to call Henri into a new role as senior pastor. Joe, our new lay pastor, would engage the many pastoral needs of our day-to-day life. Henri would continue to exercise overall pastoral leadership and do much more writing. Though Henri wanted this very much, it was at the same time unsettling for him to move away from a role that he had shaped over the past ten years.

Sunday, September 1, was a memorable day for me. Early in the morning Henri, Sue, and I went to the hospital to celebrate the Eucharist with Susanne, our close friend and member of the Daybreak community. It was a bright sunny day, and I was excited to be with this little group of close friends. Susanne was so grateful, as were we, for the visit and the opportunity to pray together. Henri, Sue, and I left and enjoyed much of the day together. We had a long lunch and walked by the lake, talking on many topics. We were also eager to be together because we knew we would not be together often in the coming year. Although Henri had just returned, Sue was leaving to be the Acting Community Leader of the L'Arche Community in Stratford. In fact this was to be our last time together, we three whose lives had been bound together over the past twelve years. On September 10, Henri asked me to join him for dinner with Dean Levitt, a senior member of Daybreak's board of directors. Henri wanted to talk through some issues relating to his will.

Henri left Daybreak on Sunday afternoon, September 15. He was going to Saint Petersburg to make a documentary film on his book *The Return of the Prodigal Son.* He would stop over in Holland for a night's rest and to connect with the Dutch film crew before continuing on. Early Monday morning, September 16, I returned to Toronto from a brief trip to Calgary. About 8:00 a.m. (2:00 p.m. in Holland) the first frantic phone call was received by Kathy, Henri's secretary. Henri had had a heart attack and was in intensive care. It was serious, but information was sketchy.

I immediately knew that I would go to Holland. I also "knew" that Henri would survive; this trip was about being with a friend in a time of crisis. I had a quick meeting with Paula and Carl who assured me that I should leave. Six hours later I was flying over the Atlantic ocean.

Henri had arrived in Holland and gone directly to a small hotel in Hilversum to rest. After sleeping for a couple of hours, he called the hotel manger and asked to see a doctor. The manger called the doctor and went to Henri's room. Upon seeing Henri he immediately called an ambulance. Due to the narrow stairwells the ambulance attendants were unable to transport Henri horizontally and called upon the fire department to evacuate him through an upstairs window.

By the time we in Canada had been contacted, Henri's father and siblings Laurien, Paul, and Laurent were with Henri in the Hilversum hospital. Jan van den Bosch, director of the film company with whom Henri was working, was also present. Henri experienced enormous pain throughout the day. Laurent stayed with Henri throughout the night.

I arrived at the hospital about 2:00 p.m. on Tuesday. Although the medical staff had indicated that Henri's condition was no longer critical, his suffering was evident and he scarcely had energy to speak. I was deeply moved. Thanks be to God for preserving Henri and for all the arrangements that had been made to allow me to be with him. Later in the evening, during one of the few times that Henri spoke, he took my hand and said: "If I die, do whatever is easiest. I can be buried in Holland if that is best. And tell everyone that I am grateful. I am so very grateful."

Wednesday was yet another difficult day. Although the pain was severe, the doctors assured him that it would subside. Henri was anxious and felt fearful because he was not able to think clearly. And he was tired, very tired. But by early Thursday morning a radical change had taken place. He was sitting up in bed for the first time and was obviously feeling much better. The change was remarkable. Henri was truly alive. My initial intuition that Henri would survive this crisis was confirmed. I felt deeply grateful.

I will always cherish my memories of the next two days. Henri's recovery was so speedy that his heart attack quickly felt like a distant event. He was moved out of intensive care, and by Thursday afternoon he had even managed to hook up a private telephone! Life was rapidly returning to normal. Henri had visits with his family and several close friends. On Friday Henri began the hospital discharge process by meeting with a nurse who, plastic model in hand, showed him what had happened to him. Henri would stay in the hospital over the weekend and be discharged on Monday or Tuesday. I would return to Toronto on Monday, and after visiting his family for a few days, Henri would follow.

Henri experienced this heart attack as a gift to be received, as all gifts, with gratitude. It was a "wake-up" call. Henri needed to slow down, to change his lifestyle in significant ways. It strongly corresponded with his desire to make a passage to a new phase of life. He would travel much less, write more, and explore new forms of writing. He was excited by the impelling construction of Daybreak's new Dayspring retreat center, which would allow him to lead more retreats at Daybreak with various community members. Henri's questions were not: "Why has this happened and how will I cope in the future"? Rather, he was saying: "I am grateful for this unexpected event that will help me to be faithful to the new work to which I am called."

On Friday morning we pulled the curtain around his bed, and amid the hustle and bustle of hospital life Henri and I celebrated the Eucharist together. It was simple, prayerful, and truly a moment of giving thanks. Less than twenty-four hours before he died, Henri yet again entered into the mystery of what had been for him the most central act of his life. Around nine in the evening Henri, Jan, and I ended the day by saying night prayer together. Henri walked down the stairs to the front doors with us, and as we left I turned to wave good-bye.

Some have suggested that being close to Henri during those last days had somehow better prepared me for his death. Nothing could be further from the truth. Those of us who were with Henri were preparing for his new life, not his death. His death was painful beyond telling. Henri died of a massive cardiac arrest early Saturday morning. The nurses state that he died quickly. There was no time for anyone to get to the hospital to be with him.

In his life Henri lived close to those who suffered and he accompanied many people as they prepared to die. What then can be said of the death of our friend and teacher? Though not the one he was expecting, Henri's heart attack was indeed a gift that helped him to make a passage. It is amazing grace that Henri died in his homeland close to family and a couple of close friends. The presence of these people, many faxes, and several phone calls reminded him of how deeply he was loved. Although he was fully expecting to live for many more years, Henri was not afraid to die. He had many struggles and had shared them openly with his friends and through his numerous writings. But this I know: Henri died at peace with himself, his family, his own faith community of L'Arche, his friends, his vocation as a priest, and the God whose everlasting love had been Henri's beacon for sixty-four years.

NATHAN BALL
L'Arche Daybreak
April 29, 1998

Sabbatical Journey is the last book that Henri Nouwen wrote. His legacy, however, lives on. For information about Henry's legacy please see the Henri Nouwen web page at http://webhome.idirect.com/~nouwenhj/index.html. For information about becoming a "Friend" of the Henri Nouwen Society, please write to P.O. Box 523, Ansonia Station, New York, NY 10023.

ALSO BY

Henri J. M. Nouwen

Here and Now
0-8245-1409; $14.95 hardcover

In the Name of Jesus
Reflections on Christian Leadership
0-8245-1259-6; $8.95 paperback

Life of the Beloved
0-8245-1184-0; $14.95 hardcover

Life of the Beloved
Audiocassette, read by the author
0-8245-3014-4; $18.00
Two audiocassettes, 171 minutes

Show Me the Way
Readings for Each Day of Lent
0-8245-1353-3; $9.95 paperback

THE PATH SERIES
The Path of Waiting
0-8245-2000-9; $3.95 paperback

The Path of Freedom
0-8245-2001-7; $3.95 paperback

The Path of Peace
0-8245-2002-5; $3.95 paperback

The Path of Power
0-8245-2003-3; $3.95 paperback

Please support your local bookstore, or call 1-800-395-0690.
For a free catalog, please write us at
The Crossroad Publishing Company
370 Lexington Avenue, New York, NY 10017

crossroad